The Gender Face
of Asian Politics

The Gender Face
of Asian Politics

EDITED BY

Aazar Ayaz
and
Andrea Fleschenberg

OXFORD
UNIVERSITY PRESS

OXFORD
UNIVERSITY PRESS

Great Clarendon Street, Oxford OX2 6DP

Oxford University Press is a department of the University of Oxford.
It furthers the University's objective of excellence in research, scholarship,
and education by publishing worldwide in

Oxford New York

Auckland Cape Town Dar es Salaam Hong Kong Karachi
Kuala Lumpur Madrid Melbourne Mexico City Nairobi
New Delhi Shanghai Taipei Toronto

with offices in

Argentina Austria Brazil Chile Czech Republic France Greece
Guatemala Hungary Italy Japan Poland Portugal Singapore
South Korea Switzerland Turkey Ukraine Vietnam

Oxford is a registered trade mark of Oxford University Press
in the UK and in certain other countries

ISBN 978-0-19-547516-6

Typeset in Minion Pro
Printed in Pakistan by
Namaa Lica Printers, Karachi.
Published by
Ameena Saiyid, Oxford University Press
No. 38, Sector 15, Korangi Industrial Area, PO Box 8214
Karachi-74900, Pakistan.

Contents

Preface

The political journey of women dates back to more than a hundred years when the first women were enfranchised—nowadays, their political empowerment is visible on the national, regional international level. This journey has been arduous, tiring and frustrating yet productive in its own dynamics. We stand at crossroads enquiring where we are, if it is where we wanted to be and where to go from here. Today this is our paradigm, which perplexes, yet motivates all those who have dedicated themselves, by commitment or conviction, to improve, strengthen, consolidate and further the cause of women in the political arena for a progressive impact.

Despite the relentless struggle for equity and equality of opportunities, women still constitute 70 per cent of the world's poor and almost two-thirds of them are illiterate. Their efforts constitute a large portion of undocumented, unreported and unappreciated socio-political economy. This exclusion ignores their role as catalytic agents of socio-political and economic change, which is a living indictment to modern day's claims to progress. The fact remains that gender equality is not a technocratic goal but a socio-political and socio-cultural commitment.

Women represent almost 50 per cent of the population of Asian countries. The political space available to them to be counted, participate, and influence political bodies constitutes an important parameter of political development and democratization in the Asian context. Mainstreaming women in politics and their subsequent representation in positions of power remains a crucial step towards obtaining a gender balance in politics. The Asian region has its own unique dynamics when it comes to mapping women in politics. Asian women have created, supported and furthered the political legacies and development to become charismatic leaders and role models.

In 2005, The Researchers (a research-based development organization of Pakistan) followed in the steps of three previously held conferences on *Women and Politics in Asia*, i.e. in 2003 at Halmstad University, Sweden; in 2004 in Colombo, Sri Lanka and in 2005 in Islamabad, Pakistan. The level of academic research and interest of activists and practitioners generated was such that these conferences became a catalyst of commitment to launch the *Women and Politics in Asia Forum* (*WPAF*, www.wpaf.org) as a platform and network to consolidate further research, exchange, cooperation and conferences.

The aim of WPAF is to observe, research, document and disseminate knowledge about experiences and best practices gathered related to different dimensions of Asian women in politics. Through an international approach and concerted effort, WPAF attempts to examine the gender face of politics in its dynamics and implications for Asian polities. WPAF's future path is aligned to institutionalize mechanisms, which substantially enhance the political mainstreaming of women in the region and which create synergetic effects through (a) a kind of 'knowledge warehouse' focusing on problems, challenges and recommendations to advance the cause; and (b) providing a platform to women politicians to exchange experiences and best practices in order to create a much needed regional women politicians' caucus.

As a first step, this book compiles a selected range of papers from international and Pakistani specialists in the field of Women in Politics in Asia, which were presented during the 2005 WPA conference and which focus on women's diverse political roles and gendered political processes. The topics presented in the book are varied and range from women's impact on public policy, electoral gender quotas. Women in war and peace, to women and politics in Pakistan.

We would like to thank all the contributors for their valued contributions and time and the publisher for their commitment and cooperation to realize this project in record time. Finally, we would like to thank the staff of 'The Researchers' for extending all their help in making the book possible.

Aazar Ayaz
Dr Andrea Fleschenberg

Some Introductory Reflections

Andrea Fleschenberg

The chapters of this book originate from the conference proceedings presented at the Third International Conference on Women and Politics in Asia held in Islamabad, Pakistan, in late November 2005.[1] 'Discovering the Gender Face of Politics' was the overall topic of this two-day conference which dealt with experiences from different South and Southeast Asian countries, such as Bangladesh, Burma, India, Japan, Malaysia, Nepal, the Philippines, Pakistan, Sri Lanka, Thailand and Vietnam. The aim was to study different dimensions of Asian women in politics and to examine the implications of gender in political life throughout Asian countries.

So far so good?—A tentative assessment of women's political participation

Asian countries have been in the lead when it comes to women entering the top echelons of political power, with Sirimavo Bandaranaike, Indira Gandhi, Benazir Bhutto, Corazon Aquino, Gloria Macapagal-Arroyo, Megawati Sukarnoputri and Khaleda Zia being just some examples of female political leadership throughout the region. In contrast, the history of active and passive voting rights for women in general, particularly their political representation on different legislative levels and thus their political citizenship status is characterized by exclusion and marginalization. The United Nations organization UNIFEM highlights the gendered nature of politics and polities, not only in Asia:

> Citizenship is inextricably linked to the political rights to vote and to stand for political office. On account of socially constructed gender roles, women face a greater number of obstacles in participating in political decision making activity than men. These obstacles need to be acknowledged by policymakers, lawmakers and electoral authorities when they determine the conditions of free and fair elections. Overlooking them will result in the conclusion that women and men are equally placed to participate in political life. This conclusion can lead to unfair discrimination on the grounds of gender...and an oversight of the unfair and deeply entrenched, systemic attitudes and stereotypes that assign women to the private, and men to the public domain.[2]

Patterns of Female Political Participation in Asia

Waylen points out that 'it is now very well documented that men and women participate differently in all forms of formal politics in both the First and Third World, whether getting issues on the political agendas, or in policy making and implementation,'[3] despite different political and socio-cultural systems. At the same time, inter-regional differences between European and (East) Asian political participation derive from a still strong public-private-dichotomy in socio-cultural organization with the consequence of (East) Asian women being selectively integrated as *women* into politics (i.e. the extension of semi-official gender roles into the public realm of politics), while men are integrated as politicians. As a result, women politicians are even more constrained by problematic gender stereotypes limiting their agency to subordinate positions.[4]

In conventional politics, Asia's women participate rather equally in elections, attend public meetings and rallies, are members of elective bodies and political mass organizations and engage in political struggles and movements (e.g. independence and/or pro-democracy movements like in India, Pakistan, Burma, Malaysia and Indonesia).[5] Although they show an equal rate of participation, this does not tell us anything about the significance, effectiveness (i.e. interest articulation) and character of their political activity and their representation share in organs of decision and policy-making.[6] Often, women act in supportive roles, as 'unrecognised foot-soldiers than as leaders'[7] or less in formal than informal structures such as social reform movements, community organizations and NGOs.[8] Their increased number as women legislators started in the late 1990s when several Asian countries implemented quota provisions; in South Asia repeatedly in the form of reserved seats.

To mobilize women 'on an ad hoc basis to support specific cases and issues', and letting them loose as soon as the routine political game of power distribution starts, is quite a worldwide phenomenon.[9] Nevertheless, examples like Benazir Bhutto, Corazon Aquino, Khaleda Zia, Sheikh Hasina and Megawati Sukarnoputri seem to prove the contrary, as all of these women led pro-democracy movements/opposition parties in transition times and gained a normally elected top political office after the phase of power distribution. Furthermore, women politicians like Aung San Suu Kyi and Wan Azizah Ismail are recognized opposition leaders in a political transition context, which lasts, as in the case of the two, for several years and with male alternatives having been available. Currently, three out of fourteen elected women head of state or government come from Asia: Gloria Macapagal-Arroyo (President of the Philippines since 2004), Hang Myung-sook (Prime Minister of South Korea since 2006) and Khaleda Zia (Prime Minister of

Bangladesh 1991–6, 2001–7). One out of five women vice presidents, Annette Lu from Taiwan (since 2000), operates in East Asia while, in contrast, Brunei Darussalam still does not grant voting rights to its female citizens.[10] Since 1945, one-fourth of women head of states or government worldwide took their office in Asia or the Pacific in very diverse socio-political systems and with very diverse political mandates. The latter ranged from interim head of state or government for some weeks to re-elected executive presidents or prime ministers, e.g. in the Philippines, India and Sri Lanka. The overall majority (59 per cent) served as prime ministers, some of them in various terms in Bangladesh, India, Sri Lanka, Pakistan or New Zealand.

**Table 1: Female Heads of State or Government since 1945
(number/per cent of total)**

	Asia	World
Acting & Interim Head of State (President)	3/13.6	12/13.8
Acting & Interim Head of Government (Prime Minister)	2/9.0	6/6.9
Others (e.g. Joint Council of State)	–	10/11.5
President	4/18.2	19/21.8
Prime Minister	13/59.0	40/45.9
Total	22	87

(www.guide2womenleaders.com/Female_Leaders.htm, 20.10.2006)

The paucity of women in Asian politics prevails across the heterogeneous region of South and Southeast Asia, and even beyond. At the same time, the discrepancy is striking between successful female political top leadership vis-à-vis the systematic under representation of women politicians at lower legislative and executive levels.

In gender- and Asia-related literature, a specific socio-cultural and political context is perceived to engender severe constraints for female political agency and leadership. First, due to widespread, dominant male-related honour concepts, women and the 'integrity' of their bodies are essential bearers of cultural identity and socio-cultural boundary markers.[11] Subsequently, women are restricted from establishing protégé–patron relationships other than within the family cycle or kinship related networks. Potential political sacrifices such as imprisonment, possible abuse[12] and other threats to a woman's physical integrity lead to the notion that political agency is an inappropriate public field of female activity. As Rounaq emphasises, 'the norms of *purdah*—gender separation and limiting women's physical mobility—are widely prevalent amongst all communities and classes in South Asia, making it difficult for women to seek [the] critical routes to leadership.'[13] Consequently, politics is perceived as a male domain due to its public nature, narrowing culturally acceptable female agency and participation options (e.g. mobility, social interaction, acceptance as leader or representative of a community). Political parties may be reluctant to choose a female candidate due to the perceived or alleged gender bias of the electorate (and political gate-keepers themselves), impairing a woman's potential as 'winning candidate' and complicating necessary financial (party) support for running an election.[14]

> Often using customs and traditions as a tool, women have been sidelined from most decision-making processes. While the past few decades have witnessed an improvement in the status of women, especially for the urban middle class women who have a degree of freedom in making decisions, for the majority of South Asian women such freedom remains an elusive dream. This lack of liberty is a tradition that is rooted in the home and the community, where male members maintain strict control over decision-making and it follows through the highest levels of national legislatures and parliaments.[15]

The United Nations' *Gender-related Development Index* and *Gender Empowerment Measure* calibrate women's societal status compared to men with regard to their socioeconomic life standards, access to social infrastructure, decision-making and leadership positions as well as income.[16] Earning on average half the income compared to men with the same job positions represents a striking strategic disadvantage with regard to their access to societal leadership positions where higher education, income and professional leadership experience are highly indispensable passage openers.

Throughout Asia, women's political citizenship rights are linked to their country's independence and full citizenship rights in the wake of post-colonial nation-building. In many countries, women entered the political floor as elected or appointed parliamentarians, ministers or councillors within the first five years after gaining the right to vote and to stand for election. In countries such as Singapore, Thailand, Sri Lanka and Pakistan, women had to wait an average of one and a half decades before gaining access to power politics. But in both scenarios, their numbers remained negligible until recently, as Table 2 shows.

**Table 2: Women's socioeconomic and political empowerment
(as of 2006, % of total)***

	GEM Rank—Value	Year women received voting rights	Women in Leadership Positions	Ratio of female to male income (est.)
High Human Development				
Japan	43–0.534	1945	10	0.46
Singapore	22–0.654	1947	26	0.51
South Korea	59–0.479	1948	6	0.48
Medium Human Development				
Malaysia	51–0.502	1957	23	0.47
Thailand	63–0.452	1932	26	0.61
Philippines	46–0.526	1937	58	0.59
Sri Lanka	72–0.370	1931	21	0.51
Cambodia	73–0.364	1955	14	0.76
Pakistan	71–0.379	1947	2	0.34
Bangladesh	79–0.218	1972	8	0.54

* Countries such as China, India, Indonesia, Laos or Vietnam had to be excluded since data was missing.
(*Source*: http://hdr.undp.org/statistics/data/, 20.10.2006)

At the turn of the millennium a significant change in the gender ratio of Asian parliaments was witnessed, as Tables no. 3 and 4 indicate.

Table 3: Parliamentary Gender Ratio in 1975 and 1998 (% of women)

Country	Lower/Single House 1975	Lower/Single House 1998	Upper House/Senate 1975	Upper House/Senate 1998	Rank in 1975	Rank in 1998
Bangladesh	4.8	9.1	–	–	10	7
India	4.1	8.1	7.0	8.6	11	8
Indonesia	7.2	11.4	–	–	7	6
Japan	1.4	4.6	7.1	13.9	16	18
Malaysia	3.2	7.8	3.3	17.4	13	10
Pakistan	4.1	2.3	2.2	1.1	11	21
Philippines	2.8	12.4	12.5	17.4	14	5
Sri Lanka	3.8	5.3	–	–	12	15
South Korea	5.5	3.7	–	–	9	19
Total	4.1	7.2	6.4	11.7	–	–

(*Source*: Inter-Parliamentary Union)[17]

SOME INTRODUCTORY REFLECTIONS

Yet until today, 75 to 90 per cent of legislators remain men; the gender ratio worsens with regard to executive positions in government and parliament. In response to this slow, incremental track of women's advancement into political positions, quota provisions have been introduced in many Asian countries within the last ten to fifteen years at the local, provincial and/or national levels. While some countries, in particular in South Asia, chose reserved seat provisions in order to ensure a certain electoral outcome, others opted for compulsory or voluntary gender quotas at the candidacy lists of political parties. The outcome is mixed, as shown by Tremblay & Steele and Dahlerup in their respective chapters.

Table 4: Parliamentary Gender Ratio after National Parliamentary Elections held 2001-2006

Country	Parliament				Senate			
	Election	Seats	Women	%	Election	Seats	Women	%
Afghanistan	09/2005	249	68	27.3	09/2005	102	23	22.5
Bangladesh*	10/2001	345	51	14.8	–	–	–	–
Cambodia	07/2003	123	12	9.8	01/2006	61	9	14.8
China	02/2003	2980	604	20.3	–	–	–	–
India	04/2004	545	45	8.3	06/2004	250	28	11.2
Indonesia	04/2004	550	62	11.3	–	–	–	–
Japan	09/2005	480	43	9.0	07/2004	242	34	14.0
Laos	04/2006	115	29	25.2	–	–	–	–
Malaysia	03/2004	219	20	9.1	03/2004	70	18	25.7
Pakistan	10/2002	342	73	21.3	03/2006	100	17	17.0
Philippines	05/2004	236	37	15.7	05/2004	24	4	16.7
Singapore**	05/2006	85	18	21.2	–	–	–	–
South Korea	04/2004	299	40	13.4	–	–	–	–
Sri Lanka	04/2004	225	11	4.9	–	–	–	–
Thailand***	01/2001	500	46	9.2	03/2000	200	21	10.5
Vietnam	05/2002	498	136	27.3	–	–	–	–
Total Asia				15.5				16.5

* In 2004 parliamentary seats were raised from 300 to 345 to accommodate 45 reserved seats for women. These quota seats were allocated in proportion to political parties vote share in the 2001 elections.

** According to the Inter-Parliamentary Union (IPU) ten additional seats will be appointed when parliament convenes for its first session in late 2006 (last assembly: 15 out of 94 seats were held by women, equal to 15.95 per cent).

*** Last available data. Parliament dissolved by military junta in autumn 2006 (last elections held in April 2006).

(Source: www.ipu.org/wmn-e/world.htm, 20.10.2006)

In summary, on a regional level, socio-political structures and institutions severely obstruct women's engagement in politics. Hence decision-making in politics, economics and other social functions survives as men's business throughout Asia. 'Guns, goons, gold and patriarchy' are common characteristics, combined with a parochial political culture, the lack of substantial devolution in contrast to powerful male-dominated elites and institutions which manipulate democracy without allowing greater participation to the people in day to day democracy and governance. Marriage of crime and politics and the use of unfair means in invariably all countries of the region have lowered the esteem of public representatives, politics and political parties and often lead to violently reinforced authoritarian tendencies.[18] Furthermore, no trickle-down-effect has been generated by female political top leadership and decision-making from the upper party and government level down to the lower levels of political life and decision-making. This partly needs to be blamed on the female politicians themselves, who often came to power with the support of women organizations and lobby groups, but failed to initiate women-friendly policies and to build their own second line of female leadership in the respective executives and legislatures. But although the political patriarchy is still quite firmly in place, some significant rifts will be seen in the case studies of this book. The crucial question remains; what steps can be taken to break up this widespread phenomenon in order to build genuinely inclusive, gender-sensitive democracies with women occupying their equal share in the mainstream of politics and polities.

Transforming the Gender Face of Asian Politics—some Propositions

Conference recommendations called for more interactive and participatory research to be conducted on a comparative level linking academics with women politicians and activists to understand the parameters of women's political participation and to develop best practices. For this purpose, more gender-segregated data of women's development, empowerment and political agency parameters is said to be required to fully evaluate and understand the gendered nature of Asian politics and to develop mechanisms for improvement. Several speakers called for a fast-track policy to women's political advancement, i.e. institutional provisions to achieve a *critical mass* at various decision-making levels in times of peace, in transition contexts after a regime change or in post-conflict situations. To achieve this purpose, many speakers, academics, activists and women politicians, stressed that *institutions matter*: the composition of the political gatekeepers needs to be changed while at the same time democratic settings are required to ensure that women are empowered and their interests are represented and addressed at the various levels and dimensions of political life. *Femocrats* from both sexes have to enter the echelons of power and decision-making to change the traditional face of androcentric politics.

Numerous participating South and Southeast Asian scholars, politicians and activists emphasized the necessity for women parliamentarians, especially those entering male-dominated spaces via quota provisions, to enlarge and to be innovative about their means of political agency. They need to enter the political mainstream rather than remaining sidelined on reserved seats and in women's wings of political parties. To avoid gaps in representativeness and accountability, women politicians' policy-making options lie inside as well as outside of political institutions, e.g. parliamentary caucuses, grass roots alliances with civil society, and as a contextual measure in the field of rule of law to ensure effective, institutionalized and universally implemented citizenship rights. Any kind of discriminatory legislation, such as the Hudood Ordinances in Pakistan, which downgrade women to second-class citizens, have to be abolished as a precondition for gender equality and genuine female political participation.

While quotas and other affirmative actions are important to enhance women's political participation, they do not necessarily guarantee substantial representation of women or accountability to women voters, their interests and needs. To maximize their effectiveness, quotas should ensure that elected women have their independent power base to advance their own political agenda, i.e. an improved socioeconomic status, sufficient funding allocation and capacity building as prerequisites of electoral politics; apart from gender sensitization trainings for all kinds of relevant decision-makers and opinion leaders. This applies especially to the media which should not present women politicians as models, but as role models, covering their success stories and not only their outfits and failures.

In many of the still highly stratified, fragmented or segmented Asian countries, quota provisions even need a 'quota within the quota' to encourage and allow women from marginalized backgrounds to successfully enter politics. The paucity of social diversity is echoed by a certain gender-blindness of Asia's female top politicians, on the one hand, and the serious elite bias and ascendancy among female legislators at different levels of the polity, on the other hand. Both should not be apprehended per se as victims of androcentric power politics, since their significant representation share reflects the desire of societal elites to hold on to power and privileges. In such a socio-political mind-set, gendered structures are seldom taken into account to advance genuine democratization towards gender-inclusive democracy.

Studying the Gendered Dimensions of Asian Politics and Polities

Do women matter in overcoming the democracy deficit became *the* question prevailing in all sorts of discussions on the topic.[19] The aim of this book is to study different dimensions of Southeast and South Asian women in politics and to examine the gendered nature of political life in various countries of this heterogeneous region. Consequently, the authors of the different chapters try to evaluate which inroads to the political mainstream women parliamentarians achieved so far, focusing on their socio-political impact, their ability and efforts to transform the political set-up, agenda-setting and policy-making.

A Cartography of Women in Asian Politics

Kazuki Iwanaga and Patricia Loreskär follow the question whether women politicians matter in public policy-making as suggested by feminists and gender scholars. The central aim of their study is to explore the generalizability of findings regarding whether women legislate differently than men in Asian settings, in particular if women who have only token representation in several national legislatures are able to pursue a legislative agenda related to 'women's issues'. Four case studies serve as examples for their analysis: Taiwan, Thailand, the Philippines, and Sweden (the latter is often classified as *the* role model for gender-inclusive democracy and women's empowerment). The Asian case studies show tendencies both to enhance 'women's issues' as well as tendencies not to enhance it to any significant degree despite different gender ratios in political representation. In contrast, the example of Sweden seems to prove that the greater the number of women legislators, the more considerable and faster legislative and policy changes take place and women's specific policy agenda and interest is taken into consideration.

Claudia Derichs criticizes traditional transition theories as gender-blind although women have proved to be important agents of social and political change in several Asian countries. She analyses the Bertelsmann Transformation Index (BTI) as an example of a consolidated attempt to measure transformation and change with regard to the gender sensitivity of its normative framework and indicators. Indonesia and Malaysia serve as case studies for analysing the importance of elites and civil society for political change and a gender perspective on transition and change which is still neglected in respective indices such as the BTI.

Drude Dahlerup reviews the widespread use of electoral gender quotas, implemented in order to enhance women's political participation in various countries worldwide. A particular focus of her analysis lies on the question of 'tokenism' or 'proxy women', which is very central to the discussion of women's empowerment, especially in South Asia. She discusses the specific effects for female legislators of being elected on the basis of gender quotas. She contradicts the one-sided perception that only 'quota women' will be tokens and points to the fact that male politicians are also highly dependent on party leaderships and family connections. For quota systems to serve as a window of opportunity for women, they need to match the electoral systems in the individual countries.

Manon Tremblay and Jackie Steele develop in their chapter a comprehensive categorization of electoral gender quotas and evaluate the Asian experiences with such quotas, using similar experiences from elsewhere around the world. In their comparative analysis they find that despite the early introduction of gender quotas in Asia, such measures have not served as an efficient path for feminizing parliaments. Moreover, write Tremblay and Steele, electoral gender quotas in Asia are primarily a symbolic or rhetorical (rather than a practical) measure to promote gender equality through the feminization of legislatures to levels enjoyed by male citizens.

In contrast, the chapter of *Khalida Ghous* focuses on the grassroots level, investigating displacement and the status of Afghan refugee women in Pakistan and its implications for humanitarian assistance, women's status and gendered conceptions of peace and security. In her opinion, soft or failed states and their weak and fractured state capability further exacerbate governance and development responses to political crises as well as its failure to protect its people as in the case of Afghanistan.

Dynasties' Daughters or Asia's Roaring Tigresses?

Moving in focus up the political ladder, the following chapters scrutinize the career paths, leadership skills and political agendas of female heads of state/government as well as opposition leaders in the Philippines, India and Burma.

For Lourdes Veneracion-Rallonza, the current crisis in political leadership of Gloria Macapagal-Arroyo, President of the Philippines, has brought into question (once again) the integrity of the country's political institutions and its leaders. Through the lens of Guy Debord's concept of the *Spectacle*, she studies three women politicians—President Gloria Macapagal-Arroyo, former President Corazon Cojuangco-Aquino, and Susan Roces, a veteran actress who happens to be the widow of a defeated presidential candidate, Fernando Poe, Jr.—in their quest for political legitimacy within the framework of the country's wider democracy project and its gender dimension. According to Veneracion-Rallonza's findings, the reproduction of feminine images of the three women politicians is a mere reiteration of the masculinized character of Philippine politics which does not contribute toward an authentic societal transformation.

In India, the Nehrus and Gandhis have been dominating politics at least since the late nineteenth century. Lately, however, it has been the women of the dynasty who have drawn the attention, with Indira and Sonia Gandhi being the two most important ones. Dagmar Hellmann-Rajanayagam compares both these female politicians and addresses the question what 'female rule' has meant for India and India's women in general. With regard to the already second generation of female leaders in India (and Sri Lanka), her analysis emphasizes, among others, two points: first, gender and (even more) dynastic descent play a significant role; secondly, once in power, different women are endorsed or rejected for different and individual character traits and policies—features that are difficult to predict. Even if those women politicians have been picked as symbols, writes Dagmar Hellmann-Rajanayagam, they become political players in their own right who can succeed and fail.

In contrast, Aung San Suu Kyi is the unchallenged leader-in-waiting of Burma's democracy movement, remaining popular throughout her decade-long house arrest. Andrea Fleschenberg looks into the challenges of a female democratization agent operating in one of the last remaining praetorian regimes in Asia with moral capital and symbolic politics as one, if not the only available, leadership tools. Given the continuous firm grip of the ruling military regime under General Than Shwe, the author concludes, it seems unlikely for Aung San Suu Kyi to be able to determine her political fate by herself in the near future unless an unpredictable window of opportunity opens like it does quite often in the history of democratization.

Beyond Numbers: From the Grassroots towards Top Political Power?

Marion R. Müller applies the framework of the 'voice-to-representation-to-accountability' relationship, developed by Goetz. In her case study on Pakistan, Marion Müller questions whether the devolution of power process promoted female participation or opened up space for the translation of women's representation into political influence. A hostile institutional environment limits the support available to women's political effectiveness due to the highly patriarchal structures and conservative nature of the state and its political system. Rhetorical gender equality and affirmative action policies need to be accompanied by measures that support women in demanding these rights and overcoming traditional power relations which also requires a joint strategy and strong links with civil society.

Shahnaz Wazar Ali, herself a former politician in Pakistan, gives a brief overview of the progress made in female political representation at different

tiers of executives and legislatures in Pakistani politics since the introduction
of the reserved seats provision. In her assessment, advances have been made
with regard to women's political representation, but, due to their personal
background as novel entrants into politics, a male-dominated party system
and lacking interaction mechanisms between women parliamentarians at
different legislative and executive levels as well as within parties, 'women
continue to face challenges that hinder the full realization of their potential
as active interlocutors of policy-making and implementation processes'.

An account of women parliamentarians' inroads at the local government
systems in Pakistan is presented by *Riffat Munawar*. She argues that despite
the institutionalisation and legitimisation of reserved seats for women as well
as their significant quantitative number, a more conducive, a violence-free
environment is paramount. She suggests several changes to the current
election and quota set up: Local government elections should be party-based
with each political party fixing its own women quota for candidacy lists.
Furthermore, quotas should also be introduced for administrative positions
at the local government system (such as mayors) to ensure effective female
role models and a continuous change of traditional gender role perceptions.

Social change generally occurs at a slow, incremental pace and unfortunately
not, as desired by most activists, in 'historical jumps', write Fleschenberg and
Ayaz in their introduction to the last chapter of this volume which presents
voices from female Pakistani politicians themselves. Coming from different
political parties and social backgrounds, women legislators (and their
experiences portrayed through five of their representatives in this chapter)
certainly differ on issues and agenda-setting strategies, but generally agree on
what problems women parliamentarians face. In this chapter, transcriptions
are given of manuscripts of speeches delivered by Pakistani female legislators
and politicians Tehmina Daultana, Kashmala Tariq, Begum Jan, Fauzia Wahab
and Samia Raheel Qazi during the WPA conference in 2005 in Islamabad.

NOTES

1. All conference proceedings can be downloaded from the website of the *Women and Politics in Asia Forum*, available at http://www.wpaf.org/wpafhome.aspx.
2. Quoted in: Milena Pires, Enhancing Women's Participation in Electoral Processes in Post-Conflict Countries. Experiences from East Timor, EGM/ELEC/2004/EP6, Rev. 7. Online. Available: http://www.un.org/womenwatch/osagi/meetings/2004/EGMelectoral/EP6-Pires.PDF.
3. Georgina Waylen, *Gender in Third World Politics* (Boulder: Lynne Rienner Publishers, 1996), 10.
4. Ilse Lenz, 'Modernisierung der Ungleichheit? Zur selektiven politischen Integration von Frauen in Ostasien,' in *Frauen-Los? Politische Partizipation von*

Frauen in Ostasien, ed. Thomas Heberer and Kerstin K. Vogel (Hamburg: Lit Verlag, 1997), 78-96, 93-94.

5. As Rounaq confirms, they 'participate in great numbers and often assume leadership during crisis periods but the rate and the level of participation often falls during normal times' (Jahan, Rounaq, 'Women in South Asian Politics,' *Third World Quarterly* 9/3/1987): 848-71, 862).
6. See Rounaq, Women in South Asian Politics, p. 858.
7. Rounaq, Women in South Asian Politics, p. 863.
8. Rounaq, Women in South Asian Politics, p. 864.
9. Rounaq, Women in South Asian Politics, p. 862; Rita Mae Kelly et al., *Gender, Globalization, & Democratization* (Lanham et al.: Rowman & Littlefield Publishers, 2001), p. 12.
10. www.learningpartnership.org/resources/facts/leadership.htm, 20.10.2006.
11. See Waylen, *Gender in Third World Politics*, p. 15.
12. Nevertheless 'for a woman, a well-known family background works as a relative safeguard against sexual harassment during imprisonment.' Therefore, it 'is worth remembering that the vast majority of women political activists who achieved national fame (...) came from rich, established families' (Rounaq, 'Women in South Asian Politics', p. 854).
13. Ibid., p. 854.
14. Mahbub ul Haq Human Development Centre, *Human Development in South Asia 2000* (Karachi: Oxford University Press, 2000), 147-8.
15. Mahbub ul Haq, Human Development, pp. 136, 140; for East Asia see: Lenz, Modernisierung, pp. 79-80.
16. 1.0 means gender equality in a given society with regard to life expectancy and standards as well as possibilities to access leadership positions.
17. Inter-Parliamentary Union (IPU), *Women in Politics 1945-2000*, Series 'Reports and Documents', no. 37 (Geneva: IPU), p. 34.
18. Imtiaz Alam, 'Electoral Politics in South Asia.' [Online] in *Journal South Asian*, July-September 2004. Available: http://www.southasianmedia.net/Magazine/Journal/previousissues5.htm. [20 October 2006]; Shirin Rai, 'Class, Caste and Gender—Women in Parliament in India,' [Online] in Women in Parliament, ed. International IDEA, Stockholm: IDEA, 2002). Available: http://www.idea.int. [20 October 2006];
19. *Gender* is understood and defined as a multi-layered social construct modified by context-specific factors such as religion, ethnicity, class/social status. Gender represents a basic principle of societal organization which structures opportunities and forms of political participation with the latter being primarily oriented towards a male model and image of politics.

References

Alam, Imtiaz. 'Electoral politics in South Asia.' *Journal South Asian* (July–September 2004) Online. Available: www.southasianmedia.net/Magazine/Journal/previousissues5.htm.

Inter-Parliamentary Union (IPU). *Women in Politics 1945-2000*. Series 'Reports and Documents', no. 37. Geneva: IPU.

Lenz, Ilse. 'Modernisierung der Ungleichheit? Zur selektiven politischen Integration von Frauen in Ostasien.' *In Frauen-Los? Politische Partizipation von Frauen in Ostasien*, eds. Thomas Heberer and Kerstin K. Vogel, 78-96. Hamburg: Lit Verlag, 1997.

Mahbub ul Haq Human Development Centre. *Human Development in South Asia 2000*. Oxford/New York: Oxford University Press, 2000.

Pires, Milena. *Enhancing Women's Participation in Electoral Processes in Post-Conflict Countries. Experiences from East Timor*, EGM/ELEC/2004/EP6, Rev. 1 January 2004: 7. Online. Available: www.un.org/womenwatch/osagi/meetings/2004/EGMelectoral/EP6-Pires.PDF.

Rai, Shirin. 'Class, Caste and Gender—Women in Parliament in India.' *In Women in Parliament*, ed. International IDEA. Stockholm: IDEA, 2002. Online. Available: http://www.idea.int.

Rounaq, Jahan. 'Women in South Asian Politics.' *Third World Quarterly* 9 (3/1987): 848-871.

Waylen, Georgina. *Gender in Third World Politics*. Boulder: Lynne Rienner Publishers, 1996.

Part I

A Cartography of Women in Asian Politics

1

Women Legislators and their Impact on Public Policy: A Comparative Perspective

Kazuki Iwanaga and Patricia Loreskär

The starting point of this chapter is the democratic assumption that societies are best governed by the people of the societies themselves. As society consists of separate individuals who *per se* cannot account for one another, they must all be included in the self-governing process for democracy to be realized. In establishing the necessary criteria for a democratic process, the democracy-theorist Robert Dahl names *effective participation* of *all adults*—implying equal and effective participation in the self-governmental process and granting all adult citizens this participation equally.[1]

While effective participation might seem self-evident, the equal inclusion of all adults is not. The democratic ideal has always been rivalled by the *plutocratic* ideal, leaving decision-making to an enlightened elite, better intellectually equipped for the task. Interestingly men have been seen as stronger, more rational and more sensible than women, and therefore more fit to rule the public sphere of life, including that of government,[2] thus resulting in a virocracy, instead of a democracy. Regardless of individual conceptions of desirable intellect, if a state has adopted a democratic form of government, it must also ensure the equal opportunity of all those affected by its policies to partake in the political process.

The political representation and participation of women has been slow and in great parts of the world even today remains well below equal to that of men. The inclusion of women is thought by many as allowing a widened political scope, where 'the missing half' of politics—women's experiences, needs and distinct political perception—is finally incorporated. It is important to note that women must be included in politics whether they bring a specifically female flavour to politics or not, as they first are citizens of a society before they are a gender, but it is also important to discuss *if* women in fact bring a distinct approach to politics in comparison to men, in order to incorporate these as yet missing pieces, as well as to achieve a society where both men and women are aware of and can promote those values which are of importance to the society in general.

Research on women's political participation and representation has for the most part been conducted in Europe and North America. The deficit of studies in other socio-economic, cultural or otherwise differing contexts makes it hard to observe if the same dynamics of female participation can be found also in other parts of the world. This chapter aims therefore at examining (a) the relationship between female representation and participation in politics and the contents of politics, (b) the lessons drawn from female political participation and representation in the post-industrialized countries and the developing countries, as well as comparing overlaps and differences in conclusions.

The political impact of female legislators

Until the 1980s most of the research about gender and politics centred on explaining why women were significantly under-represented at various levels of government. Since then, however, much of the research in Europe and the United States has examined the relationship between the 'who' and 'what' of political representation—*descriptive* representation deals with the question of 'who' is representing whom, while *substantive* representation deals with 'what' is represented. The existing literature seems to indicate that as more women become elected, there will be more evidence of gender-based differences in policy priorities in legislative bodies, as an increase of women would include other life experiences with alternative lenses through which to view issues. Great weight has been placed on whether women can make a difference in setting and implementing political agendas inside the assembly, whatever their numbers may be, since an increased number of women may raise the accountability of the government (descriptivity) as well as improve its legitimacy by way of including issues relevant to all members of society (substantivity).

Since women traditionally have not been considered to differ from men as far as political interests go, it has not been of interest for political science research to study specifically the way that women affect policy-making.[3] However, a survey of nearly 200 female parliamentarians in sixty-five countries conducted by the Inter-Parliamentary Union (IPU) showed that women have different priorities and interests compared to those of men. Nearly 82 per cent of the respondents believed that women hold conceptually different ideas about society and politics. A very high proportion of respondents to this survey agreed that women's involvement in politics makes a difference. Eighty-six per cent of respondents believed that women's participation in the political process changed the nature of politics by bringing about positive changes in form, political behaviour, and traditional attitudes, substance, processes and outcomes. Moreover, an overwhelming majority, nearly 90 per cent, felt that they had a responsibility to represent the interests and views of women.[4] This leads us to believe that women themselves have made a conscious decision to bring new issues and new form to the political process.

Even when the attention given to the matter increased, the studies of any issue preferences were significantly obstructed by the fact that women members of parliament (MPs) until recent years were so few that it seemed premature to ask what difference their presence made. Researchers have argued that it is when women move from being a small to being a large minority in legislative assemblies that women can make a difference.[5] As long as they make up a small minority, certain researchers argue that women in a lawmaking body often adapt to the existing conditions and act more like their male colleagues than their female kinswomen. Some scholars claim that a 'critical mass' of women legislators will be needed in order to pursue a women's agenda in the legislative body[6]—an argument based on the assumption that large numbers of women in the parliament will increase their ability to work for women's issues, and that there exists a threshold ('critical mass') at which there are enough women to not only try to conform to the male-dominated framework but also begin to address issues specific to their group. Norris and Lovenduski argue:

> When a group remains a distinct minority within a larger society, its members will seek to adapt to their surroundings, conforming to the predominant rules of the game…But once the group reaches a certain size, critical mass theory suggests that there will be a qualitative change in the nature of group interactions, as the minority starts to assert itself and thereby transform the institutional culture, norms and values.[7]

It has been argued that 'critical mass' numbers of women are crucial in transforming policies and politics. Few women do not represent a broad base for change, nor can they represent women of diverse backgrounds. Dolan and Ford, for example, argue that '[t]here is a variety of evidence to support the "critical mass" thesis'.[8] Many others also claim that it is difficult to keep women's substantive concerns on the agenda in the absence of a strong presence of women within parliament.

The female political representation and participation in Thailand is well below a critical mass level (10 per cent in 2005), and in a recent study of female policy priorities the MPs stated that they felt a 'concern about being pigeonholed as exponents of women's issues. There was a feeling that if they devoted themselves to women's issues, they could experience this as an obstacle in their political careers, by becoming associated with "soft" issues with a low status.[9] The women felt no particular anxiousness to prioritize issues traditionally associated with women just because they themselves were women. However, they did state that if gender solidarity could be developed, it would be much better.[10]

One of the most convincing arguments for the 'critical mass' thesis comes from Sue Thomas's study of female and male politicians in twelve state legislatures in the United States.[11] In states where the proportion of women in the legislature was below 15 per cent, women were reluctant to take a high profile on women's issues. However, in states where the proportion of women was 20 per cent or more, female legislators gave priority to legislation that addressed traditional women's interest areas as well as increased their legislative activity and success at obtaining enactment for their proposal in such areas.

The previous findings that have been made on the policy priorities of women in respect to men have been mixed. The belief that there does not exist gender differences regarding priorities and interest areas among politicians has to an increasing degree been questioned in more recent political science research. Now many researchers assume that women approach their legislative activities from a distinctive perspective, one shaped by their life experience. Studies of female politicians, especially from state legislatures in the United States and Europe, show that they have distinctive priorities and interests, especially when the numbers of women legislators increase beyond token levels. These studies indicate that female politicians are more attentive to issues of special interest to women such as families, children, health, education, and social issues.[12]

> It is claimed that women or ethnic minority politicians will articulate different concerns, and will bring different issues, into the public arena. Systematic evidence supporting the claim that women will make a difference is starting to emerge in the United States, Europe, and Scandinavia.[13]

In a study of the Arizona (United States) state legislature, Saint-Germain concluded that women do make a difference in state legislatures.[14] She found that when women were present in small numbers in the legislature, the proportion of bills proposed by women and men with regard to areas of traditional interests to women was not noticeably different. However, once women captured more than 15 per cent of the seats in the legislature, women changed their legislative behaviour—they were more likely than men to propose such bills.[15] It has been said that, with the proportion of women below 15 per cent of a legislative assembly, women members may be relegated to token status. As Taylor-Robinson and Heath argued, 'the problem for token women is that they may not feel that they have enough support to rock the boat and bring up topics of interest to women, because such topics may be criticized or ignored by the male majority.'[16]

Previous research regarding gender differences in legislator policy priorities has been confined to a small number of industrialized democracies in the West, where women have achieved high levels of representation. In contrast to the proliferation of studies examining whether women pursue a different legislative agenda compared to men in advanced industrialized democracies, there has been relatively little research specifically addressing the issue of women's political representation in less developed countries in substantive terms. Although the number of women holding office at various levels of government has increased incrementally since the 1960s, Asia has experienced among the slowest rates of growth in women's parliamentary representation of all the world regions. The overall percentage in Asia of female members of parliament in 2005 is just slightly above that in 1995. Between 1995 and 2005, the proportion of female members of parliament in the world has increased from 13.8 to 15.7 per cent.

With the small numbers of women serving in legislative assemblies in Asia, it seems unlikely that they would 'act for' women. It is difficult to test the 'critical mass' proposition—that women act more distinctively once their numbers reach a certain threshold, since the proportion of women in parliament in Asia is far from being a sufficient critical mass to enable them to pursue a legislative agenda different from that of men. For women politicians in many parliaments in Asia, the idea of a critical mass ranging from 15 to 35 per cent women is of little relevance. The percentage of women in these bodies remains well below 15 per cent. In any case, one can ask the question: do women politicians in Asia legislate differently than men, even if they are in key positions? As mentioned previously, research on gender differences in policy priorities have focused on the US and Nordic legislatures. These studies have in many cases shown that women do pursue a different legislative agenda to men. Although the presence of even small numbers of women can make a difference in certain cases, significant systemic change will take place when there is a sufficient number of women or significant minority of women in parliament to affect political change.

Taylor-Robinson and Heath have extended the research on gender difference in policy priority beyond the US and Nordic countries to the Honduras.[17] Their research does not support the generalization that women legislators tend to place a higher priority than men on legislation relating to issues of traditional interest to women such as children and family issues. They found no gender-based differences in policy priorities on these themes, yet they saw that the results of their study support the contention that, as with women legislators in advanced democracies in the West, women politicians in the Honduran Congress put a higher priority on women's rights than their male colleagues, even when they have only token representation:

> (…) even in an inauspicious setting, where women have only token representation in the legislature, and economic and social forces make the task of women in politics difficult, women still legislate differently than men. Particularly when it comes to women's rights issues, even token women's representatives play an important role in bringing legislative attention to women's concerns.[18]

Yoon and Bunwaree examined how the extreme minority status of female parliamentarians in the Mauritian parliament makes a difference in the lives of women and whether the recent increase of women's representation (from 5.7 to 17.1 per cent) has brought any positive change, even though the numbers of women in the parliament is still far short of 30 per cent, a proportion suggested by some scholars as the requirement for being a 'critical mass'.[19] Their preliminary findings suggest that even a low proportion of women in parliament can improve the lives of women by putting women's issues on the legislative agenda and by bringing about successful outcomes of several acts of legislation.

Beyond numbers

The extent to which women legislators can make a difference depends not only on the number of women in parliament but also on other factors. Five other dimensions of the problem are examined: *motivation, women caucus, ties to women organizations, party loyalty* and *media/public attention.*

Motivation—deals with the type of women who are motivated to represent women's interests and concerns. The idea of women legislators representing women's interests is part of the argument for the increased presence of women in the legislature. It raises the issue of whether women legislators have a gendered, or even feminist, awareness that leads them to espouse issues that are marginalized in male-dominated legislative body. Research indicates that identification with feminism also affect the extent, and the ways in which women legislators have an impact on public policy.[20] Women who identify themselves as feminists are more likely than non-feminist women to represent women's concerns and issues. In the absence of a critical mass, a feminist orientation among women legislators seems to have an impact on legislation dealing with issues of women, children, and the family.[21] Studies in Europe show that where there exist women legislators who are sufficiently motivated to bring about change, even small numbers can make a difference.

Caucus—in addition to the number and type of women who are in parliament, the extent to which women parliamentarians work together through a caucus may affect the impact of women politicians on public policy. Existing research tends to suggest that the presence or absence of an organized women's caucus can influence the extent to which women legislators actively discuss and work on legislation that affects women and have a positive influence on the passage of such bills.[22] Where women legislators constitute a critical mass and are organized into a caucus, women may be more likely to make a difference. In their study of state legislatures in the United States, Thomas and Welch found that legislatures where women are present in great numbers, and especially where they work together collectively through a caucus, are more likely to focus legislative attention on, and pass legislation benefiting, women, children, and families.[23] However, a study conducted in a non-western country revealed reservations about the argument that the presence of a formal women's caucus has a gendered impact on policies. In Thailand, a study of female impact on public policy concluded that efforts had been made to provide a focal point for women legislators of all parties—the Women's Parliamentarian Club—consisting of women members of the lower house and senators. It was established in 1992, and was intended as a forum for women legislators in both houses of the national legislature to sit together and provide encouragement and support for efforts that they make on behalf of women. Although it is the only formal space for women legislators, the Club has not been very successful in forging unity as a majority of women legislators are infrequently involved in its activities. It seems that women legislators in the parliament do not have a strong collective sense of group membership since women are not a homogenous group. Its core membership consists of only about twenty members and, in the absence of a feminist identity or orientation among Thai parliamentarians, it meets quite infrequently.

Women groups—in any shape and form—presuppose the ability for women to unite around an issue. It is, however, important to note that women as a group are not monolithic. They differ not only from men but also among themselves in their backgrounds, their party affiliations, their political ideologies, and their perceptions of their roles as public officeholders and members of society in large.

Ties to women's organizations—some researchers suggest that the extent to which female legislators can act for women's concerns and interests seem to be related to their connections to women's organizations and networks that could provide support for actions on behalf of women.[24] Women legislators who are members of women's organizations were found to be considerably more likely to have acted for women's rights than those who are non-members.[25] Joint efforts of female legislators and women's NGOs have been instrumental in formulating and passing laws important for women in many Asian countries.

Party loyalty—It is important to keep in mind that the ability of female politicians to act on issues having an impact on the lives of women and on areas of traditional concern to them, such as children, welfare, and education, is constrained by factors such as their party loyalty and their position within legislature. In many cases, women's political loyalties rest with their political parties and constituents rather than with women *per se*. The impact of party loyalty is often stronger than the impact of gender. Party loyalty has prevented women legislators from establishing cross-party collaborations and women MPs of a party often find it difficult to get support from their female colleagues of other parties, making it difficult to form a united front on women's issues. Even among women of the same party, it seems that their solidarity and loyalty rest primarily with the party and their constituents—not with the other women in the party. Moreover, women who hold elective and appointive office are not monolithic. They differ not only from men but also among themselves in their backgrounds, interests, preferences, and political ideologies.

Media and public attention—In addition, factors such as the level of media and public attention to the issue in question may have an impact on the willingness of parliamentarians to promote women's issues.[26] The effect of media or public attention on bringing issues to the agenda is well-researched and concludes that an actor may want to gain political influence by bringing forth a popular issue, or he/she might find the courage to address an issue that otherwise has been taboo.

Comparing women's substantial impact on the legislative process in Asia

It is through research that an understanding can be achieved of what the increased presence of women in politics means for both the political system and for women's lives. The knowledge and understanding of gender differences in policy priorities and interests among legislators is based mainly on studies of US State and Nordic national legislatures. The extent to which the findings of these studies' can be applicable to societies where the level of socioeconomic development, culture, and status of women are different from those of the United States and Nordic countries is not well researched. The available evidence seems to suggest that the impact of gender differences may be less evident and inconclusive in parliaments in Asia than in Europe and the United States, partly because of the small numbers of women in the legislators. Small numbers may lead female legislators to be more like their male colleagues. However, women's impact varies from country to country in Asia. Very few gender differences are found in some contexts while in others gender differences are clearly apparent. Three examples—Taiwan, the Philippines and Thailand—will be looked at more closely.

Taiwan

Lichun Chiang provides evidence regarding the nature of differences between female and male legislators in Taiwan.[27] Her study, in keeping with previous research in the West, shows that female legislators clearly show their policy preferences differently from male colleagues and the presence of women in Congress in turn has an impact on the legislative agenda. She has found that in comparison to men, female legislators exhibit a greater commitment to incorporating issues of traditional concern to women, including welfare, health, and education.

In Taiwan, all speeches by legislators are recorded in the Congressional bulletin, which includes contents and time of speeches. Chiang categorized the 235 speeches made by female MPs in the 4th Taiwan Legislative Yuan (from 1998 to 2000) as follows: children/healthcare, education, crime protection, foreign/military and economic.[28] Out of these five categories, children/health and economic were quite over-represented, amounting to almost 30 per cent each. The 1921 earthquake, hospital equipment, medical treatment, special diseases, welfare of soldiers and family problems were issues that were addressed. As Taiwanese farmers are vulnerable in the political system, being frequently less educated than other groups, they have been shown unusual concern by the female legislators and addressed in more than half of all economic issues. Education and protection from crime constituted the majority of the remaining speeches, with 19 per cent each, covering such issues as the educational budget, school textbooks, pre-school children, the situation of financially unstable couples, human rights, civil law and the safety of students and women, especially teenagers. Finally, it is easy to see how the typically male-dominated field of military and foreign policies is only addressed on some 6 per cent of all occasions.

Regardless of their different partisan backgrounds, women legislators will speak similarly on women's issues. Chiang argues that since women and men politicians in general have different attitudes and perspectives on many issues, it is important to elect more women who are likely to support women's demands in Congress. She found that their common life experiences do not transcend partisan differences for issues related to economics, defence policies, or foreign relations. The study also indicates that the presence of even small numbers of women can make a difference. However, long-term significant transformation of politics will only be realized when there are a sufficient number of women in parliament who are motivated to represent women's concerns. Lichun Chiang argues that women may constitute the biggest potential agents of change in Taiwan in the future.

The Philippines

Lourdes Veneracion-Rallonza has also examined the impact of female legislators on legislative priorities, this time in the Philippines. She argues that women legislators have not been able to act as agents of change in the bicameral legislature.[29]

Veneracion-Rallonza looked at a number of 'women's issues' to see how many had been addressed by women. The areas included education/training, girl-children, health, human rights, violence against women, media, women in poverty/economy/work, women in power and decision-making, violence against women, and institutional mechanisms. Out of the 9,333 bills filed in the eleventh Congress (1998–2001), only 209—that is 2.2 per cent—pertained to women's concerns. In the twelfth Congress (2001–2004), the number of bills filed by women on these issues amounted to 3.5 per cent.[30] Her study thereby indicates that women legislators did not have different priorities than their male counterparts and party affiliation was more determining than gender regarding the legislative priorities of legislators.

During this same period the number of women in parliament increased from 13 to 17 per cent. She maintains that an increased presence of women would not automatically lead to enhanced substantive representation.[31] She finds that in spite of the relative increased presence of women in the legislature, there has not been a substantive increase in the number of women-related laws. There is even a decline in enacting women-friendly laws where there was a relative increase in women legislators.

Therefore, it would seem that women have worked hard to enter the political sphere playing by the same rules as the men, i.e. following the party line. She notes: 'Women legislators themselves are not keenly sensitive to women and gender issues and thus, women being in power does not necessarily mean the empowerment of women.'[32] The driving force behind the proposal and passage into law of women-related bills have instead been various women's groups and organizations in the Philippines. These groups negotiated with women and male legislators sensitive to their cause, thereby ensuring pro-women legislation within the Congress. Veneracion-Rallonza points out that most of the bills that were filed in the 11th and 12th Congress were a response to the Beijing Platform for Action, following the 1995 Women's Conference. However, the real effort to ensure the implementation of the Beijing Platform directives came from the lobbying, monitoring and strategizing of women's groups.

Thailand

A third study examines the impact of women on legislation in the Thai parliament to find out the extent to which female legislators work in areas traditionally considered of interest to women.[33] The legislative agendas of both female and male legislators in the House of Representative were examined during Prime Minister Thaksins government. The bills were grouped into six categories by subject area (children, education, environment, health care/public health, welfare-social security, and other). The data was obtained from the offices of the House of Representatives, which keep records of all bills proposed and the bill's fate. It was difficult to assess whether the token presence of women in the male-dominated parliament had a gender-related impact on legislation due to the small number of women MPs, as well as the prevailing strong party discipline.

Very little is known about the various factors inhibiting women's advancement in electoral office at the national level in Thailand and almost nothing regarding whether policy outputs differ due to women's participation in policymaking. A number of in-depth interviews with female members of both houses of the Parliament, including one former cabinet member, were conducted in December 2002. The interviews covered a wide range of issues and provided first-hand insight into how women in national politics actually function. Since an analysis based on a single session was found to be unlikely to give a complete picture, additional data was gathered on the legislative agendas of female and male members of the House of Representatives in the Thai parliament for several legislative sessions beginning from the advent of the government led by Thaksin Shinawatra, the leader of the Thai Rak Thai Party, in 2001 to September 2003. Given the small proportion of women in the House of Representatives and the small number of bills initiated by the MPs, all types of bills were included in the analysis.

The presence of women legislators has made a difference in the number of bills introduced and passed dealing specifically with children and welfare-social security, the areas where women have traditionally shared a disproportionate responsibility. Proportionally speaking, the single subject of children has received an unusually large amount of legislative attention. However, there is no significant gender-based difference in the numbers of proposed bills relating to children. It is possible that male legislators in Thailand have become more diverse and knowledgeable about the issue of children than their forefathers. Contrary to expectations and patterns of the long-established democracies in Europe and the United States, where women legislators tend more often than men to prioritize issues such as the environment, public health and health care, women legislators in Thailand did not introduce and work on legislation specifically relating to these areas.

In sum, with respect to the issues of children and welfare/social security, even token female legislators play an important role in introducing and pushing those issues through the legislative process. Perhaps the increased presence of women legislators will make a significant difference in the types of bills introduced.

Special attention was also paid to the influence of committee positions, particularly how a member's committee assignment and access to leadership positions impact the ability to pursue women's issues. Not surprisingly, nearly 65 per cent of the members of the House Committee on Children, Youth, Women and the Aged consisted of women (as of 20 April 2003), areas where women have traditionally borne disproportionate responsibility. Further, women constitute 24–29 per cent of committees such as Tourism, Public Health, and Social Welfare. Yet, as compared with the situation in the past, women were no longer exclusively confined to a narrow set of committee assignments since women have recently made their way to the more traditional 'male' committees, at least to a certain extent. Almost 24 per cent of the committee members on Science and Technology and nearly 18 per cent of the Foreign Affairs Committee in the Lower House are women. Despite their small numbers, women who did succeed in getting elected were no longer dominantly swayed along sex-stereotyped lines into 'women's committees'. With this said, women are much less likely than men to sit on business committees. In committees such as Communications and Telecommunications, Armed Forces, Economic Development, Monetary Affairs, Finance and Banking, either there was only one or no woman at all sitting on the committee. The picture is also quite similar in the Senate. The data on committee assignments appear to indicate that these women parliamentarians pay considerable attention to issues of traditional concern to women. It would be misleading, however, to conclude that Thai women parliamentarians as a group are exclusively concerned with issues having an impact on the needs and lives of women to the neglect of other issues.

Why have women's membership and their leadership been concentrated on certain types of committees? There are several plausible explanations. One is that women legislators may have been steered towards areas of interest to women because of stereotypical views about their expertise. Another plausible explanation is that women may have chosen 'female-oriented' committees because of their interest in these issue areas. Interviews with female legislators suggest that it is out of their own choice rather than outright discrimination that this gender disparity in committee assignments occurred. In short, appointments to committees tended to be based on the expertise and interests of the legislator.

Comparing lessons drawn in different parts of the world

Our conclusion thus far is that research from post-industrialized western democracies does in fact show a difference in policy priorities between the sexes. The research works on developing countries are few and far apart, leaving us with inconclusive and uncertain inferences. The cases of Mauritius and Honduras showed that even a small number of female legislators made an impact on public policies, giving emphasis to those issues traditionally associated with women. The conclusions of the Asian studies were more hesitant; while Taiwan proved that even a small number of women were effective to the case of the Philippines showed the opposite—women had no distinct policy preferences compared to men and could not be expected to act as agents of change. Thai women were not a clean-cut case of agents of change, and were found to be well below an expected 'critical mass', as was the case in all three countries. Further research on developing countries— below and above 'critical mass'—are therefore found to be very important. Is gender-specific legislation a world-wide phenomenon or confined exclusively to the post-industrialized western democracies? Under which circumstances do women tend to emphasize 'women's issues'? Are these circumstances alike in the western democracies and different parts of the developing world? Some argue that increased women's presence in national assemblies may not necessarily lead to improved representation of women's interests and issues. 'Changing the gender composition of elected assemblies', Ann Phillips argues, 'is largely an enabling condition...but it cannot present itself as a guarantee.'[34] In a similar way, Sawyer points out: 'to increase the number of women in parliament, or even to increase the number of feminists in parliament, is insufficient to ensure that "women" are better represented.'[35] Which may these other enabling factors be, and are they alike around the globe? The remainder of the chapter will therefore examine the idea of drawing lessons by comparing research findings in western democracies and the developing world.

Using Sweden as an example

Sweden serves as an example of a western post-industrial democracy where women have reached high numbers of legislative representation and simultaneously highlighted women's issues in parliament. Women currently hold 47 per cent of the seats in parliament, only surpassed internationally by Rwanda (48 per cent). While Rwanda's success rates come from gender quotas, Sweden has achieved its high numbers by way of voluntary introduction of gender quotas, and these were introduced only after Sweden had already surpassed a critical level of 30 per cent female legislators. Today not only women address the so-called women's issues, men are equally interested—in

2002, 49 per cent of all female MPs and 48 per cent of all male MPs addressed such issues as social policy, family policy, care of the elderly and health care.[36] 'Gender mainstreaming' has also been introduced to Swedish politics, implying that every decision taken by the parliament must be considered from a gender perspective. How has this been possible? Can it be attributed to an ever increasing number of women in parliament? What other factors may have affected this?

Lenita Freidenvall presents in her PhD dissertation, 'Vägen till Varannan damernas' [Every other second seat for a woman] a number of contributive factors to the Swedish success story.[37] Since the end of the Second World War, Swedish parliamentarian politics have been dominated by the Social Democratic Party, who have been a key factor in promoting female politicians, by implementing a long-perspective work of creating a well structured public welfare sector, women-friendly welfare politics, high frequencies of gainfully employed women and an institutionalization of equality by way of equality laws, public boards and councils etc.[38] In the 1970s, when female representation had already reached about 30 per cent, it was found democratically illegitimate that political organizations had so few female members. A discursive idea of the equal right to power in order to reflect the societal constitution at large which had begun modestly in the 1920s, now came into full bloom, and the female network, *The Support Stockings,* was created with the specific aim of augmenting the political parties representation of women in parliament.[39] Other factors, such as the recruitment process and particularly the rules governing candidate selection and the demands of the gatekeepers who choose from the pool of aspirants are mentioned as crucial; however, these need further research.[40]

Can Sweden be used as an example of how a successful increase in women's representation can be undertaken? Our suggestion is that Sweden may be seen as a *goal* for women's political participation and representation, but it may not be used as a *model*. Figures 1 and 2 show that many of the Asian countries are to be found at the levels Sweden was at in the 1970s. Sri Lanka, with a mere 4.9 per cent is at the same level of female legislators as Sweden was during the 1930s. Following a Swedish model to enhance women's issues on the legislative agenda, most Asian countries can hope for a Swedish level of 47 per cent female legislators by 2036, and Sri Lanka in 2080. These are obviously quite unacceptable prospects.

Reaching the Swedish descriptivity and substantivity also presumes that the countries might need several other factors than an increased number of women. An actual change in the discursive understanding of gender roles in society might be necessary. The Social Democratic Party enhanced the social welfare sector in a way that largely decreased women's disproportionate responsibility for care of the home, children, old, and disabled etc. As women entered the working force as gainful employees, it was also largely discovered how workplaces had been specifically formed and adjusted to a male norm (e.g. without flexibility for care of sick children or pregnancy), and as this was changed, men also were given the opportunity partake of areas previously enjoyed exclusively by women, such as parental leave. These changes to the welfare system were in part facilitated by a long prosperity boom following the Second World War.

What are the lessons that can be drawn from the experiences in Sweden and other western post-industrialized democracies? Studies suggest that it would be extremely difficult if not impossible, to move from a low proportion of women parliamentarians to a high proportion without going through a phase in which gendered patterns in the content of politics appear. It is also clear that a significant increase in women's representation and participation in all sectors, not only in politics but also in society at large is necessary, not to say crucial, in advancing the substantivity of women's issues in politics. If the inclusion of women's issues in politics has no real anchorage in society at large, it has no hope of actually changing the gendered understanding of politics. An example of this may be seen in the election of a number of top Asian political leaders, such as Khaleda Zia in Bangladesh, Gloria Macapagal-Arroyo in the Philippines, and Chandrika Kumaratunga in Sri Lanka or Indira Gandhi in India, whom certain scholars have perceived as acting just like their male colleagues. No substantial feminized 'trickle-down' effect was perceptible. The conclusion might therefore be that milestones in female issues being brought up on the political agenda, such as female leaders, has no real effect unless this is matched by equal achievements in society at large.

Fig. 1: Female legislators in the Swedish parliament 1921–2006 (%)

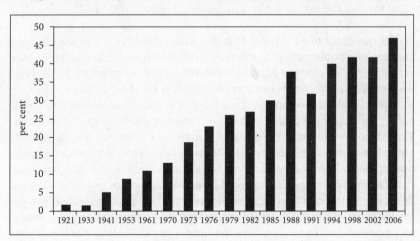

Source: The official website of the Swedish parliament Riksdagen, www.riksdagen.se

Fig. 2: Female legislators in a number of Asian countries (%)

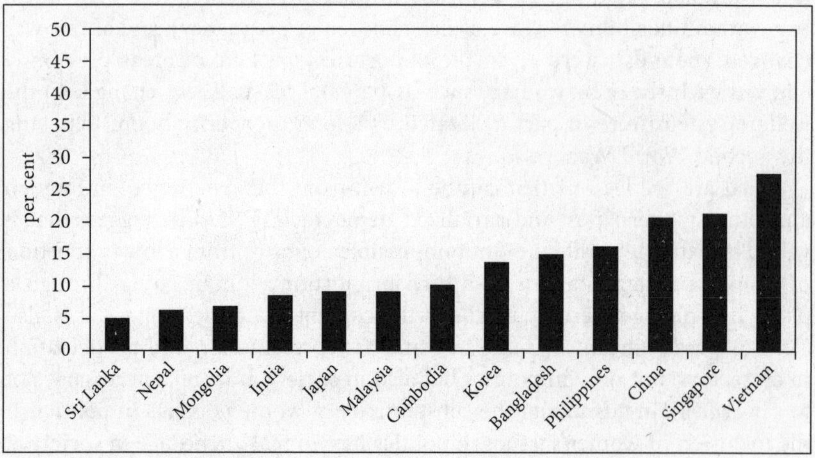

Source: The official website of The Inter-parliamentary Union, www.ipu.org

Comparing lessons drawn from various in-depth case studies brings some empirical and theoretical considerations to the fore. At least two points become clear. There is:

i) a need to develop and carry out more empirical research which will provide concrete evidence regarding the impact of gender on public policy in the developing world;

ii) a need to develop a model or conceptual framework that can be applied to various contexts in which this gendered impact is studied.

The questions to be asked are: under which conditions will women have an impact on public policy? Under which conditions would women politicians act as agents of change, pushing legislative action to improve the lives of women? This chapter provides some initial ideas for constructing a model, or at least a skeletal conceptual framework specifically about the impact of gender on public policy and thus offers a starting point for further research. The extent to which women legislators can make a difference may depend on a number of variables: *number of women in parliament, motivation, women caucus, ties to women organizations, party loyalty* and *media/public attention.* From the Swedish experiences could be added changes to gender discourses in society at large, facilitating conditions in society (such as state ideology, level of socio-economic development, egalitarian political culture) and finally, an understanding of men's role to the impact of gender issues in legislation.

Further research will be needed to assess the relative importance of these factors.

This final point is quite underdeveloped, but is here argued to have great importance. It has thus far been assumed that the increased presence of women in legislature would augment the recognition of women's issues, as they would bring hitherto missing experiences to the political agenda. It is, however, largely misleading to believe that 'women's issues' are only pertinent to women. Still, research has concluded that women are *affected* differently from men and therefore would have more incentives to bring 'women's issues' to the political agenda. What is thought provoking about this reasoning, besides the fact that men otherwise are able to represent the needs of groups to which they may not belong (such as businessmen, low-income workers etc), is that men too are negatively affected by socialized gender stereotyping, and that they do not legislate particularly in regard to this. Sex role socialization of men can thereby be seen as a particularly important factor in whether gender issues are legislated upon. Men play a crucial part in *excluding* topics from the agenda, as well as including them. It is obvious that women will handle 'women's issues' to a larger extent if these are the only issues they are assigned. Lourdes Veneracion-Rallonza cites Farah Kabir with respect to the Philippine legislative process: 'Even when women do become a part of the formal political process as members of elite political groups, they are usually assigned to soft portfolios 'appropriate' for women's concerns.'[41]

Researching the process of men excluding not only women but also themselves from bringing forth certain issues of relevance to themselves and others is therefore seen as important. One of the basic assumptions of gender studies is that gender stereotypes are constructions, created and sustained through socialization. This also implies that they may be deconstructed, which for example can be seen in attitude differences in Sweden.

Conclusion

Many studies in gender and politics have examined whether the presence or an increase in the number of women in parliament makes a difference in the lives of women in Europe and the United States. Their findings have shown that, in many cases, women do pursue a different legislative agenda than men. Research that goes beyond highly advanced industrial democracies of the West is rare, and their findings have been mixed. The Asian case studies (Taiwan, Philippines and Thailand) were all conducted in environments of female legislators well below 'critical mass', and showed both tendencies to highlight 'women's issues' as well as tendencies not to do so to any significant degree.

The experience from the Nordic countries tends to suggest that it would be extremely difficult, if not impossible, to move from a low proportion of women parliamentarians to a high proportion without going through a phase in which gendered patterns appear in the content of politics. The increased presence of women in politics has altered the legislative environment and created a generally supportive cultural atmosphere conducive to the achievement of gender equality. An increased number of female MPs are thereby seen as one of the most decisive factors in favour of enhanced substantivity of 'women's issues' in legislative politics. While the presence of even an extreme minority status of female parliamentarians can make a difference, long-term significant change will largely be realized when there exists a sufficient number of women in parliament who are motivated to represent women's concerns. A critical minimum of women seems to be a prerequisite to create the necessary political will. It will be difficult to obtain the political will for gender equality if women are not fully involved in decision-making. The Nordic experience shows that once women enter the arena of parliament in much greater numbers, changes are more considerable and take place at a quicker pace. The increased presence of women ensures that the various values, interests and life experiences of women are taken into account when decisions are made.

There exists extensive research on women's descriptive and substantive presence in the legislative process, but few studies on the necessary conditions for developing countries. It is suggested here that certain features of European or American gender accomplishments may be regarded as goals; they may not be regarded as models, as the changes have taken place during several decades. The lesson to be drawn may instead be a conceptual framework, a theory, or points of reference, which could help unite the research in all countries. One suggestion is to look at such factors as *number of women in parliament, motivation, women caucus, ties to women organizations, party loyalty* and *media/public attention*, as well as *changes to gender discourses* in society at large, *facilitating conditions* in society and finally, an understanding of *men's role* to the impact of gender issues in legislation.

NOTES

1. Robert Dahl, *On Democracy* (New Haven, NJ: Yale University Press, 2000), pp. 37–38.
2. Ann J. Tickner, *Gender in International Relations: Feminist Perspectives on Achieving Global Security* (New York: Columbia University Press, 1993), p. 7.
3. Susan J. Carroll, *Women as Candidates in American Politics* (Bloomington: Indiana University Press, 1994).

4. Inter-Parliamentary Union Politics: Women's Insight, IPU Reports and Documents No. 36, Geneva: IPU, 2000.

5. Drude Dahlerup, 'From a small to a large minority: Women and the substantive representation of women,' Scandinavian Political Studies 11/14/1988: 275-98; Sue Thomas, 'The Impact of Women on State Legislative Policies,' Journal of Politics 53 November/1991): pp. 958-76.

6. Arturo Vega and Juanita M. Firestone, 'The Effects of Gender on Congressional Behavior and the Substantive Representation of Women,' Legislative Studies Quarterly 20 No. 2/1995): pp. 213-22; Thomas, 'The Impact of Women on State Legislative Policies'.

7. Pippa Norris and Joni Lovenduski. 'Blair's Babes': Critical Mass Theory, Gender and Legislative Life,' Paper presented for the Women and Public Policy Program Weekly Seminar, Kennedy School of Government, Harvard University, Cambridge, MA, 28 September 2001, pp. 2–3.

8. Kathleen Dolan and Lynne E. Ford, 'Are All Women State Legislators Alike?' in Women and Elective Office, eds. Sue Thomas and Clyde Wilcox (New York: Oxford University Press, 1998), p. 77.

9. Kazuki Iwanaga, 'Women in Thai Politics.' Women's Political Participation and Representation in Asia: Obstacles and Challenges, ed. Kazuki Iwanaga (Copenhagen: NIAS Press, forthcoming in 2008), p. 186.

10. Iwanaga, 'Women in Thai Politics'.

11. Thomas, 'The Impact of Women on State Legislative Policies'.

12. Ruth Mandel and Debra Dodson, 'Do Women Officeholders Make a Difference?' The American Woman, ed. Sara E. Rix (New York: W. W. Norton, 1992), Sue Thomas and Susan Welch, 'The Impact of Gender on Activities and Priorities of State Legislators' Western Political Quarterly 44 No. 2/1991): pp. 445-56; Clark 1998.

13. Pippa Norris, 'Legislative Recruitment,' in Comparing Democracies. Elections and Voting in Global Perspective, eds. Lawrence LeDuc, Richard G. Niemi and Pippa Norris (London: Sage, 1996), p. 185.

14. Michelle A. Saint-Germain, 'Does Their Difference Make a Difference? The Impact of Women on Public Policy in the Arizona Legislature,' Social Science Quarterly 70 No. 4/1989): pp. 956-68.

15. Saint-Germain, 'Does Their Difference Make a Difference,' p. 965.

16. Michelle M. Taylor-Robinson and Roseanna M. Heath, 'Do women legislators have different policy priorities than their male colleagues? A critical case test,' Women and Politics (24/4/2003): pp. 77-101, 81.

17. Taylor-Robinson and Heath, 'Do women legislators', pp. 78-79.

18. Taylor-Robinson and Heath, 'Do women legislators', p. 94.

19. Mi Yung Yoon and Sheila Bunwaree, 'Is a Minority Truly Powerless? Female legislators in Mauritius,' Paper for the 20th IPSA World Congress, Fukuoka, Japan, 9-13 July 2006.

20. Susan J. Carroll, 'Representing Women: Women State Legislators as Agents of Policy-Related Change,' in The Impact of Women in Public Office, ed. Susan J. Carroll (Bloomington and Indianapolis: Indiana University Press, 2001), p. xxi; Debra L. Dobson, 'Acting for Women: Is What Legislators Say, What They do?'

In *The Impact of Women in Public Office*, ed. Susan J. Carroll (Bloomington and Indianapolis: Indiana University Press, 2001), pp. 225-242.

21. Dolan and Ford, '*Are all Women State Legislators Alike.*'
22. Thomas, 'The Impact of Women on State Legislative Policies'.
23. Sue Thomas and Susan Welch, 'The Impact of Gender on Activities and Priorities of State Legislators,' Western Political Quarterly 44 No. 2/1991): pp. 445-56.
24. Carroll, 'Representing Women'.
25. Ibid.
26. Michele L. Swers, *The Difference Women Make: The Policy Impact of Women in Congress* (Chicago and London: The University of Chicago Press, 2002).
27. Lichun Chiang, 'Women as Agents of Change in Legislation in Taiwan,' in *Women's Political Participation and Representation in Asia: Obstacles and Challenges*, ed. Kazuki Iwanaga (Copenhagen: NIAS Press, forthcoming in 2008).
28. Ibid.
29. Lourdes Veneracion-Rallonza, 'Women and the Democracy Project: A Feminist Take on Women's Political Participation in the Philippines,' in Women's Political Participation and Representation in Asia: Obstacles and Challenges, ed. Kazuki Iwanaga (Copenhagen: NIAS Press, *forthcoming in 2008*).
30. Ibid.
31. Ibid.
32. Ibid.
33. Iwanaga, 'Women in Thai Politics'.
34. Anne Phillips, *The Politics of Presence* (Oxford: Oxford University Press, 1995), p. 83.
35. Marianne Sawyer, 'The Representation of women in Australia: Meaning and Makebelieve' Parliamentary Affairs (55 1/2002): pp. 5-18, 17.
36. Kazuki Iwanaga, *Gender and Political Representation in Sweden,* Paper for the conference 'A Study on the Gender Gap in Legislative Activity and Measures for Raising Gender Sensitivity of Legislative Men and Women' at the Korean Women's Development Institute, Seoul, South Korea, 18 October 2006.
37. Lenita Freidenvall, 'Vägen till Varannan damernas. Om kvinnorepresentation, kvotering och kandidaturval i svensk politik 1970–2002,' (Ph.D. diss., Stockholm University, 2006).
38. Lenita Freidenvall, 'Vägen till Varannan damernas,' p. 5.
39. Lenita Freidenvall, 'Vägen till Varannan damernas,' p. 6.
40. Lenita Freidenvall, 'Vägen till Varannan damernas,' p. 268.
41. Lourdes Veneracion-Rallonza, 'Women and the Democracy Project: A Feminist Take on Women's Political Participation in the Philippines,' p. 251.

References

Bystydzienski, Jill M. *Women Transforming Politics: Worldwide Strategies for Empowerment*, Indianapolis: Indiana University Press, 1992.

Carroll, Susan J. 'Representing Women: Women State Legislators as Agents of Policy-Related Change.' In *The Impact of Women in Public Office*, ed. Susan J. Carroll, Bloomington and Indianapolis: Indiana University Press, 2001.

Carroll, Susan J. *Women as Candidates in American Politics*, Second ed. Bloomington: Indiana University Press, 1994.

Chiang, Lichun. 'Women as Agents of Change in Legislation in Taiwan.' In *Women's Political Participation and Representation in Asia: Obstacles and Challenges*, ed. Kazuki Iwanaga, Copenhagen: NIAS Press, forthcoming in 2008.

Clark, Janet (1998), 'Women at the National Level: An Update on Roll Call Voting Behavior,' in Sue Thomas and Clyde Wilcox (eds.), Women and Elective Offices Past, Present, and Future. (New York: Oxford University Press).

Dahl, Robert. *On Democracy,* New Haven, NJ: Yale University Press, 2000.

Dahlerup, Drude. 'From a small to a large minority: Women and the substantive representation of women.' *Scandinavian Political Studies 11* (4/1988): 275–98.

Dobson, Debra L. 'Acting for Women: Is What Legislators Say, What They do?' In *The Impact of Women in Public Office*, ed. Susan J. Carroll, Bloomington and Indianapolis: Indiana University Press, 2001.

Dolan, Kathleen and Ford, Lynne E. 'Are All Women State Legislators Alike?' In *Women and Elective Office*, eds. Sue Thomas and Clyde Wilcox, New York: Oxford University Press, 1998.

Freidenvall, Lenita. 'Vägen till Varannan damernas. Om kvinnorepresentation, kvotering och kandidaturval i svensk politik 1970–2002,' Ph.D. diss., Stockholm University, 2006.

Holmberg, Sören and Esaiasson, Peter. *De folkvalda. En bok om riksdagsledamöterna och den representative demokratin i Sverige*, Stockholm: Bonniers, 1988.

Iwanaga, Kazuki. 'Women in Thai Politics,' In *Women's Political Participation and Representation in Asia: Obstacles and Challenges*, ed. Kazuki Iwanaga, Copenhagen: NIAS Press, forthcoming in 2008.

Iwanaga, Kazuki. *Gender and Political Representation in Sweden,* Paper for the conference 'A Study on the Gender Gap in Legislative Activity and Measures for Raising Gender Sensitivity of Legislative Men and Women', at the Korean Women's Development Institute, Seoul, South Korea, 18 October 2006.

Lovenduski, Joni. 'Gender Politics: A Breakthrough for Women' *Parliamentary Affairs 50* (1997): 708–719.

Lovenduski, Joni and Karam, Azza. 'Women in Parliament: Making a Difference,' In *Women in Parliament*, ed. International IDEA, Stockholm: International IDEA, 2002.

Mandel, Ruth and Debra Dodson. 'Do Women Officeholders Make a Difference?' In *The American Woman*, ed. Sara E. Rix. New York: W. W. Norton, 1992.

Norris, Pippa. 'Legislative Recruitment,' In *Comparing Democracies. Elections and Voting in Global Perspective*, eds. Lawrence LeDuc, Richard G. Niemi and Pippa Norris. London: Sage, 1996.

Norris, Pippa and Joni Lovenduski. 'Blair's Babes': Critical Mass Theory, Gender and Legislative Life,' Paper presented for the Women and Public Policy Program Weekly Seminar, Kennedy School of Government, Harvard University, Cambridge, MA, 28 September 2001.

Norris, Pippa and Joni Lovenduski. 'Women Candidates for Parliament: Transforming the Agenda?' *British Journal of Political Science 19* (1/1989): pp. 106–15.

Phillips, Anne. *The Politics of Presence*, Oxford: Oxford University Press, 1995.

Saint-Germain, Michelle A. 'Does Their Difference Make a Difference? The Impact of Women on Public Policy in the Arizona Legislature,' *Social Science Quarterly 70* (1989): 956–68.

Sawyer, Marianne. 'The Representation of women in Australia: Meaning and Makebelieve,' *Parliamentary Affairs 55* (1/2002): 5–18.

Swers, Michele L. *The Difference Women Make: The Policy Impact of Women in Congress*, Chicago and London: The University of Chicago Press, 2002.

Taylor-Robinson, Michelle M. and Heath, Roseanna M. 'Do women legislators have different policy priorities than their male colleagues? A critical case test.' *Women & Politics 24* (4/2003): pp. 77–101.

Thomas, Sue. *How Women Legislate*, New York: Oxford University Press, 1994.

Thomas, Sue. 'The Impact of Women on State Legislative Policies,' *Journal of Politics 53* (November/1991): 958–76.

Thomas, Sue and Welch, Susan. 'The Impact of Gender on Activities and Priorities of State Legislators,' *Western Political Quarterly 44* (1991): pp. 445–56.

Tickner, Ann J. *Gender in International Relations: Feminist Perspectives on Achieving Global Security*, New York: Columbia University Press, 1993.

Vega, Arturo and Firestone, Juanita M. 'The Effects of Gender on Congressional Behaviour and the Substantive Representation of Women,' *Legislative Studies Quarterly 20* (1995): 213–22.

Veneracion-Rallonza, Lourdes. 'Women and the Democracy Project: A Feminist Take on Women's Political Participation in the Philippines.' In *Women's Political Participation and Representation in Asia: Obstacles and Challenges*, ed. Kazuki Iwanaga. Copenhagen: NIAS Press, forthcoming in 2008.

Wängnerud, Lena. *Politikens andra sida. Om kvinnorepresentation i Sveriges Riksdag*. Göteborg: Göteborg Studies in Politics, No. 53, 1999.

Yoon, Mi Yung and Bunwaree, Sheila. 'Is a Minority Truly Powerless? Female legislators in Mauritius,' Paper for the 20th IPSA World Congress, Fukuoka, Japan, 9–13 July 2006.

2

Strategy, Action, Transition: Women as Agents of Change

Claudia Derichs

Introduction

Theories of transition and transformation[1] became remarkably popular during the 1990s. Whereas most of the hitherto compiled indices held democratization as the ideal political path to follow and liberal democracy as the final goal of transition, recent research has approached the topic from different angles, namely the question of transformation management and governance. This quite new tendency has no doubt been spurred by development studies in the North and South. In this respect, the push effect of development studies has succeeded in detracting the discussion from biased theoretical terms such as 'defective' or 'illiberal' democracy, which have gained some (sad) prominence in the community of Western political scientists. Instead of pointing out failures in the process of democratization, the Bertelsmann Transformation Index and the World Governance Survey—just to pick up two recent approaches that deserve attention—have directed their view at actual performance of countries in politics and economics. The focus lies on what kind of change state and society have actually *been able* to bring about in a certain period of time and under certain political, economic, and societal conditions. The question of which kind of developmental and transformative performance has been achieved under what conditions is a highly welcome approach. It is particularly useful with regard to women's political performance, because this is all too often judged by what is seen at the surface and not by asking what might have simply been impossible to achieve under the given national conditions.

In the following section, the Bertelsmann Transformation Index (BTI) is picked as an example of a consolidated attempt to measure transformation and change. Its normative framework and its indicators will be introduced—and scrutinized for their gender sensitivity in the final section. From the BTI, a gender-sensitive perspective to transformation and change will be applied to two case studies. These studies are the Southeast Asian countries of Indonesia and Malaysia. In the second section, women's activism and their performance as agents of change are elaborated, comparing Malaysia and Indonesia. While reflecting on these issues from a more or less theoretical level, arguments in the third section are underpinned by questioning the indicators of the BTI from a gendered perspective. The core argument is that this index has failed to apply a gender sensitive view in its attempt to examine and measure political change and the quality of governance during transition period of the late 1990s and early 2000s in Malaysia and Indonesia. A gender-sensitive alteration of the BTI's indicators by way of a rewording is suggested, which may serve to increase awareness for women's contributions to transformation and change. The chaper concludes by pleading the case for the integration of a gender perspective in any measurement of transition and change.

A fresh approach to measuring transition and change

In 2004, the German Bertelsmann Foundation published the first results of an assessment of the 'transition management' of 116 countries around the world. What came to be known as the Bertelsmann Transformation Index was a set of data on these countries which had been obtained in a period between autumn 1998 and spring 2003.[2] Directed at the assessment of political transformation, data were collected concerning the following criteria:

- stateness
- political participation
- rule of law
- institutional stability
- political and societal integration.

With the help of these criteria, a picture of the political transformation that had taken place between 1998 and 2003 was drawn. In addition to these criteria, data was obtained in order to evaluate the countries' progress towards becoming a market economy.

The data referring to political transformation and that referring to market economic performance form the so-called Status Index—or put simply: The Status Index displays the state of affairs concerning political and market-based economic transformation.[3] In each of the 116 countries, data were not simply compiled according to what had changed between 1998 and 2003, but also according to the difficulty of achieving a certain target of change. It was therefore important to look at the level of political development and the structure of economic development. Also important was the national education index—literacy rate, illiteracy rate, and gross enrolment ratio for schools and institutions of higher education, as was ethnic, religious or social conflict, potential civil society traditions and an examination of whether rule of law is working properly or not and whether the state bureaucracy worked efficiently. All in all, the list of criteria was quite demanding so that each country report provided a solid profile of the political and economic performance of the sample states. However, it is clear from the design of the project that a consolidated market-based democracy is the *normative* framework of the BTI. This fact is emphasized by the BTI board as well.

While generally appreciating the fresh theoretical and methodological approach of this index, it is now inspected with regard to its gender-orientation.

Women's role

How can women's role in the process of transformation and change be assessed? Is the existence of an organized women's movement a conducive ingredient to the process of developing stateness, political participation, rule of law, institutional stability, and political and social integration? It definitely is. Where do women become visible in the arenas of civil society, political society, economic society, bureaucracy, government, and judiciary? If we take the criteria and indicators of the BTI seriously, the experts' sense of gender difference in evaluating the situation and in formulating their country reports will have to be looked at critically.

The BTI research design concerning country experts does not refer to the requirement of a gender balanced expert team anywhere.[4] It should, however, be taken into account that the results from research on gender and development as well as feminist political science suggest that women have a different view of social, political and economic reality because they are affected differently by policies in these respective fields. For example: How do we judge the introduction of market-based economic policies that may attract a great number of big multinational corporate players? A male observer in the BTI team may see it as a positive step, whereas a female observer may have in mind that (a) it will be mostly women who will have to work long hours for very little money, often under sweatshop conditions, and (b) these women will have to bear a double burden because they nevertheless have to attend to children and housekeeping after these working hours. Change is not one-dimensional, and what appears to be a positive change to one person may not give the same impression to the eyes of another. That is why social science should at least make an effort to look at women's role in society and at their—more often than not invisible—contributions to transformation and change. Further evidence to this argument is provided by highlighting the cases of women and women's movements in the transition states of Indonesia and Malaysia during the period under examination.

The case of Indonesia

Indonesia has probably gone through one of the fiercest periods of rapid change during the late 1990s. The fall of then-president Suharto in 1998, the subsequent carousel of presidents, and a decentralization policy with many potholes have not yet brought about the desired political stability. Yet the women's movement there has pushed forward some fresh ideas. Women come to the fore and express themselves in art and literature, which is a sign for a more open discursive space in comparison to the New Order regime (i.e. the authoritarian rule of Suharto). Well-known cases in point are the *Dangdut* dancer Inul Daratista and the female writers of the so-called *Sastra Wangi* or 'fragrant literature' novels.[5] Inul Daratista has become a transnational star, giving performances in neighbouring countries and attracting huge crowds with her style of *Dangdut* dancing. The new female self-assertion is not appreciated in all sections of society; some women have already experienced clashes with the conservative politico-religious establishment. The female president Megawati Sukarnoputri (2001–04) supported neither 'camp' in this regard; she behaved gender blind, as one informant put it, on conditions of anonymity. Diane Mulligan wrote that in the post-Suharto era of a democratically elected government and ironically in an era of an elected female president, 'the Ministry for the Empowerment of Women is still struggling to make significant gains for women due to religious and cultural barriers.'[6]

Indonesian women contributed greatly to the reform movement of the late 1990s. They played a vital role in the *Reformasi* movement, as it was called. In fact, 'it was women who began the popular uprisings.'[7] Their activities were numerous, but not regarded 'political' because women were not expected to act politically under the ideological framework of the New Order regime. [comment to Kommentar: already introduced, see above] One activist of *Suara Ibu Peduli* (The Voice of Concerned Mothers) is quoted as saying that they could not articulate their political demands in public, but had to cover them under 'feminine' concerns such as food supply for the family. This was because the patriarchal domination did not allow them to openly raise their voices for burning political issues such as corruption, nepotism, or collusion. These practices, known as 'KKN' (*korupsi, kolusi, nepotisme*), soon became the symbols of the condemned Suharto regime when the students took over the leadership of the reform movement. The (male) students' voices were picked up by the media as political demands, while in the background the women of *Suara Ibu Peduli* 'coordinated the dispatch of food packages to the students occupying the parliament building.'[8]

The National Coalition Against Violence to Women, or *Komnas Perempuan*, was also founded during the riots of 1998. The independent coalition was set up 'in response to Indonesian women's outcry against the sexual assault and violence during the May 1998 riots.'[9]

> In the face of significant gaps and inability of other government human rights institutions, *Komnas Perempuan* endeavours to increase public understanding through publications and strategic dialogues, create a conducive environment for the elimination of all forms of violence against women by advocating legal and policy reform and to strengthen capacities for the prevention of violence against women and for dealing with its consequences.[10]

Women were active on various fronts and were frequently the pioneers in raising awareness for issues that deserve attention by politicians on the national and sub-national level. Ironically, their new democratic space for fostering activities in favour of their sisters becomes increasingly narrowed down through the strength developed by influential Islamic institutions—which make use of the democratic space as well.[11] Under the New Order regime it was the hegemonic development ideology that assigned women to serve as wives and mothers. In addition to this patriarchy-inspired placement, a strong militarism defined the state as protector of women—and women as those being protected. A very similar assignment of the female sex is on the rise in post-Suharto Indonesia, but this time inspired by an Islamically inclined view of woman as the protected being.[12] Hence the question is: Is this facing new wine in old bottles or what kind of transformation is actually taking place?

According to the BTI, Indonesia's political transformation since 1998 has proceeded at a slow but steady pace, though still showing deficiencies in terms of a market-based democracy. In more detail, the score for the development of stateness, political participation, rule of law, institutional stability, and political and social integration is 3 (1 = lowest progress score; 5 = best progress score), thus indicating some hope for a positive development in the future. There is reason to presume that this hope for the future has been shattered in the view of many women's organizations. Successes of civil society initiatives for the encouragement of women's political participation are few, among them the enactment of a National Action Plan for the Elimination of Trafficking in Women and Children in December 2002.[13] A Domestic Violence Act passed parliament in 2003 and was enacted in 2004. However, one of the core problems in Indonesia during the *Reformasi* period was state-sponsored violence against women. This has been highlighted by many women's organizations, but since the military is still an extremely important stakeholder

·in Indonesian politics and since strong women's organizations are not present
in every affected region of the country, fighting this problem is a resource-
gorging task.[14]

An initiative to introduce a quota for women in political party lists in
elections was promoted by several women's NGOs and was endorsed as
Election Law No. 12, in February 2003. It stipulates that every party should
consider a women's representation of at least 30 per cent among its candidates
in national, provincial and municipal elections. 'Although the clause is not
compulsory,' says the executive director of the Indonesian Center for Women
in Politics, Titi Sumbung, 'the legal clause should be seen as a foundation to
increase women's political participation and representation.'[15] Elections for
the national parliament in 2004 were the first strong test for commitment of
the parties to the clause. According to the Bertelsmann country report, no
party achieved the goal of sending 30 per cent female candidates into the
electoral contest.[16] Since some of the parties complained they did not have
enough women power in their ranks to fill the quota, the women of the Center
for Electoral Reform (CETRO) went out on a fact finding mission and
eventually presented a hundred women willing to choose a party and run as
candidate. 'You need female candidates? Well, here they are!' was the signal
sent out to the complaining parties.[17] It remained a signal, because most
parties had already fixed their candidate lists and did not want to alter them
when elections were around the corner. Consequently, the female candidates
received positions only at the bottom of the lists.[18] The deeper implications
of this 100-candidates initiative, however, are remarkable. It demonstrated
that Indonesia's women were willing and able to participate actively in the
newly established democratic political system. By finding female candidates
outside the formal party ranks, CETRO referred to the pattern of systematic
exclusion of women from political careers, and showed a way to overcome
such structural impediments. Moreover, the women who climb the ladder in
political parties usually have to show qualifications which are hard to achieve
for them, given the neglected promotion of female party careers. One such
quality requirement, says Smita Notosuasanto from CETRO, is a minimum
of five years service on the district level of a political party. Very few women
can provide such experience.[19] Nonetheless, it is the district and village level
where more women in decision-making positions would make a difference,
for instance in debating the budget allocation. Simple issues such as whether
to build either a bridge or a hospital become vital questions that bear a
gendered aspect, but when women's agency is lacking, male-friendly decisions
are more likely to be made.

In this context, one policy area that has come under remarkable attack by
progressive women's groups (Muslim and non-Muslim women alike) is
decentralization, and particularly a number of local regulations that are

commonly known as *Peraturan Daerah* or *Perda*. By way of *Perda*, local governments are expected to meet the need 'to develop and create their own sources of funding.'[20] The post-Suharto central government associates a consistently positive development with its policy of decentralization, which it put into practice in 2001:

> In Indonesia, as elsewhere, decentralization was accepted as a reaction to inefficient and corrupt central government bureaucrats and was regarded as integral to democratization. Many politicians remain convinced that decentralization is needed to save money and ensure better delivery of public services.[21]

However, the flaws of the attempt to implement the policy accordingly, i.e. in a way that allows for the emergence of the intended results, are striking. Meanwhile, the central government has lost control over things happening at the local level.[22] The anti-hierarchical relationship between central and local governments has led to a situation that has 'minimized the vertical accountability mechanisms' and thus served to weaken the monitoring and legislative functions of elected local bodies.[23] Under the guise of *Perda*, executive bodies in the provinces and districts conduct their budget allocation according to their own preferences and limit the disclosure of the local budget. Apart from weakening the accountability of political authorities and legislative bodies, this 'new habit' has also led to an alarming malperformance of male-dominated executives in terms of gender budgeting. Initially, ministries or departments for women's empowerment were introduced and recommended for the national and the local levels alike. But the decentralization laws no longer require the maintenance of such institutions. Aside from the fact that the abolishment of institutions for the promotion of women's empowerment and policy interests has been extremely facilitated, even in those provinces and districts where they are still working, the budget allocated for them has been reduced to an almost ridiculously low amount.[24] Regulations on the province and district level are discouraging in many regards. Women 'caught' without a veil or a headgear are stopped by self-proclaimed defenders of law and order who forcefully shave their heads. Women get attacked and stigmatized even though they sometimes have no choice but to travel at night when without a *muhrim* (a close male relative) by their side. The enforcement of laws protecting women from such treatment by local police units is extremely weak. Some districts have established a women's police desk in order to encourage women to report cases of rape and domestic violence. But they do not yet cover the whole country. Women's NGOs who have specialized in assisting victims of violence against women and providing them with shelter and legal assistance have established branches in several provinces, but covering a country that consists of thousands of islands is truly a Herculean task. Yet women are organizing to change the status quo and raise awareness via media and community work.

In conclusion, the outline of the case of Indonesia shows that there remains much to be done concerning transformation and change—at least from the women's perspective. During the period under examination, Indonesian women were willing to perform as change agents, but within the realm of civil society they needed at least some kind of support from the political powers that be. Institution-building, the strengthening of civil society and women's empowerment to achieve gender equity are nowadays on their way, but other forces have gathered strength as well, particularly among the conservative religious circles. Moreover, the military continues to play a vital role in politics and economy. A coalition of civil society women and members of the political elite seems to be an urgent requirement in the pursuit of gender-balanced transformation.

The case of Malaysia

Malaysia is an interesting case in point because it has in some regards overcome the status of a developing country and is marching towards reaching the status of a fully developed one. This is at least envisioned by the Malaysian government which in the early 1990s propagated the so-called *Vision 2020*, introduced with the following statement (The Vision 2020 Statement):

> The ultimate objective that we should aim for is a Malaysia that is a fully developed country by the year 2020. We shall be a developed country in our own mould. We must be fully developed in terms of our economy, in terms of social justice, political stability, system of government, quality of life, social and spiritual values, national pride and confidence. There can be no fully developed Malaysia until we have finally overcome the nine central strategic challenges that have confronted us from the moment of our birth as an independent nation.[25]

The 'nine strategic challenges' that are mentioned circle around the establishment of a united nation, resilience, a democratic society, moral and ethics, inter-communal tolerance, scientific innovation and progress, familial welfare (preferable to individual welfare), equitable distribution of wealth, and prosperity.[26] All these challenges are considered the 'soft targets' of the vision, i.e. those that do not suggest any elaborate economic goal. The progress the country has made since 1998, when the goals of the Vision 2020 were pursued despite the regional financial crisis, has been assessed by the experts' team of the Bertelsmann Transformation Index, albeit in terms of transformation management and not with respect to the national vision.[27] According to this assessment, Malaysia ranks 3.9 in terms of its management to transform the country to a market-based democracy, but only 2.6 with regard to its political transformation. The scale for both ranks reaches from 1 to 5 (1 = lowest progress score; 5 = best progress score). Malaysia thus scores 0.4 digits lower than Indonesia, which ranked 3.0 in political transformation. The scores indicate management deficits in both the economic and the political realm. The deficits in political transformation are seen as severe, as the summary of the country report shows:

> During the period under review [1998-2003; C.D.], Malaysia made no progress toward political development. The trial of Anwar Ibrahim,[28] which was largely politically motivated, aroused the ire of many citizens, but the wave of protests was not enough to threaten the ruling coalition's majority in the 1999 elections. From a positive point of view, one could note that political stability remained intact.[29]

The BTI evaluation does not sound very encouraging for Malaysia's political reform movement. However, for our purpose it is legitimate to ask whether women's organizations in Malaysia have played a major role within the reform movement and to what extent women's rights and gender equity have been promoted during this transitional period. Malaysia's reform movement of the late 1990s was very much inspired by the neighbouring *Reformasi* movement in Indonesia. It had less success though, because the government under then-Prime Minister Mahathir Mohamad cracked down on it when the masses took to the streets. Nonetheless the mood of change was there and, among others, several women's organizations gathered in 1998 to formulate a Women's Agenda for Change (WAC).[30] Initially, four organizations joined the gathering, followed by another thirty-six NGOs and women's groups in a national consultation. Finally, seventy-six groups signed the thirty-page long document, which states in its introduction:

> The recent political developments in Malaysia have added the impetus and urgency to strengthen women's participation in the cultural, economic and political life of the nation. We deplore the manipulation of ethnicity and religion, as well as the use of fear and oppressive forces to divide us. We want to contribute towards the building of a just, democratic and peaceful society for ourselves and future generations.[31]

All sorts of issues which were thought important for women's life and well-being were covered by the document; it did not refer exclusively to 'women's issues' in a narrow sense. The WAC tackled a broad range of issues, covering the following topics: women and development; women and participatory democracy; women, religion and culture; violence against women; women and land; women and health services; women and the law; women and work; women and aids; women and environment; and women and sexuality. The declared aims of the women's groups were to draw attention to specific problems, issues and needs of women which were to be recognized and addressed; to raise awareness of women and men on the position of women in Malaysia; to strengthen the political participation and voices of women in Malaysia so as to promote and achieve gender equality and to work for a just and democratic society; and to strengthen a network of women's organizations and NGOs to work towards the advancement of the status of women in Malaysia.[32]

For this purpose and in order to spread the spirit of the WAC, in 1999 the women sent the document to 192 members of parliament and asked them to endorse it and raise the issues therein as part of their election platforms. Although Malaysia's major political parties have a female membership of around 50 per cent, the response from the members of parliament was feeble. Only seven out of 192 replied to the WAC. This painful experience led to the women's groups searching for another strategy to raise awareness for their demands. Shortly before the 1999 general elections, they started a Women's Candidacy Initiative (WCI). The strategy of this initiative was to run a female candidate in one of the urban constituencies near the capital of Kuala Lumpur. If this candidate was successful, she would raise her voice in parliament and bring in women's issues to the table.[33] This strategy was thought to have much more effect than continuing to lobby bureaucrats and parliamentarians. Unfortunately, this candidate was defeated by a male competitor in her constituency, albeit by a small margin. The initiative itself deserves merit, though, as does the Women's Agenda for Change, because both activities have demonstrated that Malaysian women are no longer willing to wait for a reaction from the political authorities but be pro-active and take things in their own hands. As Patricia Martinez, who has analysed the WAC and the WCI extensively, puts it:

> The [WAC] document represents a watershed in the way women's issues have been conceptualised and presented. Prior to the WAC [...], the women's NGOs were primarily reactive. They most often raised issues with a gender particularity (for example, rape, domestic violence or sexual harassment) or in relation to specific events first published in the media. The WAC is instead a proactive project and a deliberate attempt to bring together outstanding issues, problems and needs; it was not in reaction to any event, policy or programme.[34]

A similar reasoning stood in the background of the Women's Candidacy Initiative: 'The WCI grew out of the recognition that the political participation of women at every level of decision making is vital to advance and maintain the rights of women and to represent their concerns.'[35] The fact that half of the party membership is female does not help the country's women much, as many of them experienced, because the women in the party play supporting roles in furthering the agenda of their party and not necessarily that of their fellow women in the society at large. Against this backdrop, it appeared a natural consequence not to approach the women's wings of the parties but to turn to the members of parliament right away—regardless of their being a ruling or an opposition party member.

Although the women's initiatives did not bear immediate fruit, they were recognized by the political authorities and had a lasting impact on Malaysian politics. The political parties learnt that women are voters and that their needs are to be recognized to a certain extent when they seek their votes. The Ministry of Women and Family Development, which was established in 2001 as one consequence of the women's movement's activities, has begun to lend an ear to women's NGOs, hence to actors from the civil society. Of course the government capitalizes on this. In the election campaigns preceding the general elections of 2004, the ruling parties made the treatment of women in the opposition party PAS (Islamic Party of Malaysia) a talking point in the media. PAS was blamed for inhibiting its female members from running as candidates. It appears that the public discourse on gender equity affected the Islamic party's leadership to a certain extent, for the 2004 elections saw some PAS women contesting.

In conclusion, the Malaysian women's movement has proved its capability of acting as an agent of change with several unique initiatives. This is all the more remarkable because the ethnic and religious cleavages within Malaysian society still form an impediment to a fully-integrated movement. The political environment in Malaysia has been much more authoritarian than in Indonesia during the period of the late 1990s until 2003/2004. Yet Malaysia's women have not given up and, to the contrary, they have continued to raise their voices and to seek alliances within the political establishment and leadership. Some of the prominent women's activists such as Zainah Anwar from the Sisters in Islam or Cecilia Ng from the Women's Development Collective are well known in the region of East and Southeast Asia and even internationally. The success of Malaysian women and their efforts are, however, not reflected in the external assessment of political change by the BTI. Again, it may be assumed that women might have reported differently on political progress and backlash in their respective countries if they had been better represented in the expert teams of the BTI survey team.

Women as agents of change

Advanced gender studies of recent years have revealed that a whole range of conditions is responsible for women's effectiveness in politics. These conditions are 'civil society strength, institutional reforms which facilitate women's access to politics without stripping women politicians of legitimacy or of connections to the women's movement, a supportive and powerful party—all these combined with, indispensably, political skills in identifying allies, getting the timing right for pressing demands, and asserting electoral strength.'[36] This set of conditions suggests that if women want to be effective as change agents, it is not enough to be (numerically) represented in political institutions, and that it is not sufficient to be a strong segment of civil society. Rather, the connection between women in the higher echelons of politics and those in the women's movement is of great importance. Theories on social movements have discussed the importance of connection and alliance in the framework of political opportunity structures.[37] What counts for social movements in general, can be applied to the women's movement in particular. Can these findings be subscribed to say, women in transitional states? And if yes, what to in regard of transformation and change?

When Indonesia and Malaysia are compared, as two transitional states, the women's movements in these countries share some historical similarities. Both were incorporated in the struggle for independence and later on in the politics of nation-building. The bulk of the movement was (and is) formed by urban middle-class women. The political turmoil in the wake of the regional financial crisis in 1998 gave them fresh motivation. Their interest articulation pays tribute to the role of Islam in both societies. A striking difference lies in the fact that the regional disparity, or better, the Java-centricity of most progressive women's organizations in Indonesia, has a significant impact on the mobilization of a national movement. Malaysia is much smaller and the regional identifications are not that strong; this facilitates mobilization efforts to a certain extent. Concerted decentralization efforts in Indonesia may widen the existing regional cleavages. Another difference is the focus of action. In Malaysia, rape and domestic violence are prominent issues on the agenda, whereas Indonesian women's organizations appear to be more concerned with the trafficking of women and children and state-sponsored violence against women. Regarding the access to the political elite by women's groups, there is strong empirical evidence that Malaysian women have engaged in clear-cut strategic action in order to attract attention. The Indonesian women may have tried this as well, but the state's responsiveness in general and that of the various presidents in particular have hitherto not been very encouraging.[38] There are laws and regulations declaring the same rights of men and women in family and society since Indonesia's independence, and in 2000 a Presidential Instruction on gender mainstreaming was enacted, leading to a gender mainstreaming unit in the National Planning Board. But the laws and regulations lack effective implementation, monitoring and evaluation.[39]

In Malaysia, the Women's Ministry has not attended to all the demands of women NGOs and organizations, and, on the contrary, it picks and chooses the issues it wants to raise. The results are, for instance, state-sponsored national campaigns against rape, promoted throughout the mainstream media. The ministry organizes consultative forums where NGO representatives present their opinion, recommendation and policy proposals. There is no doubt that the state's responsiveness to women's demands is very much inspired by its aspiration for female votes. Nonetheless, the women's groups took advantage of this as well and displayed what has been pointed out above: political skills in identifying allies, getting the timing right for pressing demands, and asserting electoral strength. It may be assumed that this combination of factors has at least intensified the connection between elite men or women in political professions and activists in the women's movement. Progressive women's NGOs like the *Sisters in Islam* in Malaysia clash with the *Ulama* of the Islamic Party PAS quite frequently, but since the ruling parties do not defend PAS' attitudes anyway, the latter's chances to *Silence* the sisters' voices are rare.

In Indonesia, the government seems more reluctant to proceed against retrograde Islamic tendencies, most probably because this could cause social instability. Moreover, the 'cultural environment' in Indonesia is not (yet) ready for 'feminist ideas,' says Saparinah Sadli.[40] The debate about feminism, the liberation of women and unequal power relationships between the sexes 'is polarized between two camps: those who claim to be defenders of women's rights, without necessarily calling themselves feminists, and those who claim to be defenders of religious values and so-called traditional practices.'[41] Such polarization, although existing in Malaysian society as well, was purposely avoided by the women of the WAC and WCI initiatives.

All this adds up to the impression that the women's movement in Malaysia gained much more mileage than the women's movement in Indonesia. The interesting aspect is that from a systemic perspective, the 'democratic space' has been much more liberalized in Indonesia since 1998 than in neighbouring Malaysia—and not surprisingly, Indonesia was rewarded for this with higher scores in the BTI. Nonetheless in Malaysia, due to strategic action, the women's movement became more visible within the circles of policymaking. Its connection to the political elite could draw on established and in some cases formally institutionalized channels of communication. Indonesia's women's movement became more visible on the level of civil society, but its activities and achievements (e.g. for its role in the reform movement) still need proper recognition. It has fewer allies within the political elite—let alone the politically influential military elite—and has hitherto not been discovered as a voters' force. Hence the powers that be were less enthusiastic in their attention to women's demands.

These findings can be interpreted as a clear sign of women's capacity to act as agents of change *in both countries*. The problem, however, lies in the assessment of this fact. This is why the final section of the paper questions the criteria and principles of the Bertelsmann index mentioned above.

Women's situation and change measurement

The role of women in transitional societies rarely receives the merit it deserves. Drawing conclusions from what the case studies of Indonesia and Malaysia have revealed, and at the criteria for the assessment of a state's transformation management presented by the Bertelsmann Foundation, the relative neglect of gender aspects becomes evident. The indicators of the BTI could gain value if they included a gender sensitive view. The re-wording below suggests how a gender perspective may be integrated into the survey design (the underlined terms added to the original wording; C.D.).[42]

   BTI criteria for political transformation with an added gender perspective:

Stateness: Is there clarity regarding the nation's existence as a state with adequately established, 'gender balanced' and differentiated power structures?
Political participation: Does the population determine who governs and exercise other political liberties 'on a gender equal basis?'
Rule of law: Are state powers controlled through checks and balances and are civil rights guaranteed 'regardless of gender and sex?'
Institutional stability: Are democratic institutions capable of performing and are they sufficiently accepted 'by men and women alike?'
Political and social integration: Do stable and 'gender sensitive patterns' of representation exist for mediating between society and the state and is there a consolidated civic culture?

   What this exercise shows is that a gender perspective can easily be integrated into the design of the indicators. Recalling the fact once again that women make up half of the population in most states of the globe, it is more than legitimate to look at the world through their lens, too.

Conclusion

The issues addressed in this paper are based on two assumptions. One is that even the more progressive and recent indices which try to evaluate a state's transitional performance lack a gender perspective in their research design. Moreover, while their findings and data collections are based on external or even local expertise, the experts chosen are predominantly men. A man's view on society and politics may not be wrong, but a woman's view is certainly different from a man's view. Women surely have something to say when it comes to political reform and systemic transformation, and this may in some cases differ from what men have to say. In order to illustrate how women can function as agents of change, the example of two Southeast Asian states has been raised in which the women's movements have actively engaged in the national reform movements of the late 1990s.

In Malaysia, this engagement was strategically planned and members of the political elite were directly approached. The women's organizations themselves tried to enter parliament by running a candidate from their midst in the general elections of 1999. Although they did not succeed in pushing their agenda through, the state was responsive. The state's readiness to attend to women's concerns was largely driven by the wish to secure women's votes. Women capitalized on this and the state cannot draw back from the set standard too easily. The women's movement has won a respected, if small, political leverage. It would not have succeeded in this, though, without the support of allies and persons sympathetic to its demands within the ruling as well as opposition elite.

In Indonesia, political liberalization took place at a rapid pace since the fall of Suharto in 1998. One would thus expect the women's movement to be among the main change agents. However, the contribution of the women's movement to the genesis and vitality of the reform movement did not enter the public perception in a way one would wish for. When the political climate had changed and women's (political) concerns could have had a chance to enter the circles of policy formulation, the succeeding (including one female) presidents' responsiveness was rather disappointing. Moreover, the political elite are still significantly influenced by the military—which has other priorities in mind than promoting women's political activism. In addition to this, many of the progressive female voices have been publicly blamed and attacked by representatives of a retrograde Islam. A stronger connection between open-minded elite members and movement activists would surely facilitate the women's struggle for change.

As for the measurement of transformation and change in the two countries, Malaysia has received lower scores for political transformation than Indonesia in the BTI of 2003. It may be questioned whether a gender sensitive expert team would fully subscribe to such a ranking. However, a gender perspective should at least become a component of any research design that aims at measuring transition and change.

NOTES

1. The terms transition and transformation are used as synonyms. While aware of the differences, for the purpose of this chapter it is considered legitimate to treat them equally.
2. Bertelsmann Stiftung, ed. *Bertelsmann Transformation Index 2003* (Gütersloh: Verlag Bertelsmann Stiftung, 2004). The index and the book interpreting the results are also published on the internet. For an English language version see http://www.bertelsmann-transformation-index.de/11.0.html?&L=1,—In 2006, the second BTI was published. The BTI of 2003 is focused on because it covers the peak period of Malaysia's and Indonesia's political transition, hence the period under examination.
3. See http://www.bertelsmann-transformation-index.de/11.0.html?&L=1. [14 September 2005].
4. See Bertelsmann Stiftung, *Transformation Index 2003*, 377.
5. For a discussion of Inul Daratista's case see Mulligan, Diane. 'The discourse of Dangdut,' In *Gender and Civil Society*, ed. Jude Howell and Diane Mulligan (London and New York: Routledge, 2005), 117-38.
6. Ibid., 121f.
7. Ibid., 121.
8. Ibid.
9. See http://www.humantrafficking.org/countries/eap/indonesia/ngos/national/komnas.html. [21 September 2005].
10. Ibid.
11. Mulligan, 'Dangdut,' 123.
12. For more on this see also Noerdin, Edriana. 'Customary Institutions, syariah law and the marginalization of Indonesian Women,' In *Women in Indonesia. Gender, Equity and Development*, ed. Kathryn Robinson and Sharon Bessell (Singapore: Institute of Southeast Asian Studies, 2002), 179-86.
13. For further information see www.humantrafficking.org/countries/eap/indonesia [15 September 2005]
14. For further information see www.kalyanamitra.or.id/profile.php [21 September 2005].
15. Interview with Titi Sumbung, 15 Feb. 2006.
16. http://www.bertelsmann-transformation-index.de/127.0.html, accessed 8 June 2006.
17. Interviews with Nurul Arifin, 15 Feb. 2006, and Smita Notosusanto, 22 Feb. 2006.
18. Interview with Titi Sumbung, [15 Feb. 2006].
19. Interview with Smita Notosusanto, [22 Feb. 2006].
20. Kristiansen, Stein and Lambang Trijono. 'Authority and Law Enforcement; Local Government Reforms and Security Systems in Indonesia,' In *Contemporary Southeast Asia* 27(2005)2: 242.
21. Ibid.
22. With the term 'local' reference is made to the provincial and the district level.
23. Kristiansen/Trijono, '*Authority and Law Enforcement*', 244.

24. Adriana Venny, Executive Director of *Jurnal Perempuan* (Women's Journal), personal interview, [15 Feb. 2006].

25. Hng, Hung Yong. CEO Malaysia, *Strategy in Nation-Building* (Subang Jaya: Pendaluk, 1998), p. 39.

26. Ibid., 39f.; Mahathir Mohamad. *Multimedia Super Corridor* (Subang Jaya: Pendaluk, 1998), 16f.

27. Malaysia was not among the countries of the WGS sample.

28. Anwar Ibrahim is the former Deputy Prime Minister of Malaysia. He was sacked in 1998 by then PM Mahathir Mohamad and charged for corruption. He was released from prison in 2004, after allegations of sexual impropriety were turned down. His sacking and subsequent detention caused the formation of the reform movement *Reformasi.*

29. http://www.bertelsmann-transformation-index.de/128.0.html?&L=1. [20 September 2005].

30. For the whole text of this agenda see http://wa4change.tripod.com/english.htm. [20 September 2005].

31. http://wa4change.tripod.com/english.htm. [20 September 2005].

32. http://wa4change.tripod.com/english.htm. [20 September 2005].

33. For detailed information on this candidate see Hassan, Saliha, 'Malaysia: Transformative not Alternative,' In *Seethings and Seatings. Strategies for Women's Political Participation in Asia Pacific*, ed. Rashila Ramli, Elisa Tita Lubi and Nurgul Djanaeva (Chiang Mai: Asia Pacific Forum on Law, Women and Development, 2005), pp. 91-124.

34. Martinez, Patricia. 'Complex Configurations. The Women's Agenda for Change and the Women's Candidacy Initiative,' In *Social Movements in Malaysia. From moral communities to NGOs*, ed. Meredith L. Weiss and Saliha Hassan (London and New York: Routledge 2003), pp. 75-98 [80].

35. Ibid., p. 87.

36. Goetz, Anne Marie and Shireen Hassim. 'Introduction: Women in Power in Uganda and South Africa,' In *No Shortcuts to Power*, ed. Anne Marie Goetz and Shireen Hassim (London and New York: Zed Books, 2003), pp. 1-28 [27].

37. See e.g. McAdam, Doug; John D. McCarthy and Mayer N. Zald, eds. Comparative Perspectives on Social Movements, Political Opportunities, Mobilizing Structures, and Cultural Framing, (Cambridge: Cambridge University Press, 1996).

38. Indonesia had four presidents between 1998 and 2004.

39. Surbakti, Soedarti. 'Gender mainstreaming and sex-disaggregated data,' In *Women in Indonesia. Gender, Equity and Development*, ed. Kathryn Robinson and Sharon Bessell (Singapore: Institute of Southeast Asian Studies, 2002), pp. 209-18 [214].

40. Sadli, Saparina. 'Feminism in Indonesia in an international context,' In *Women in Indonesia. Gender, Equity and Development*, ed. Kathryn Robinson and Sharon Bessell (Singapore: Institute of Southeast Asian Studies, 2002), pp. 80-91 [90].

41. Ibid.

42. Original wording in http://www.bertelsmann-transformation-index.de/fileadmin/ pdf/BERT_Brosch_re_ENG.pdf. p. 5. [20 September 2005].

References

Bertelsmann Stiftung, ed. *Bertelsmann Transformation Index 2003*, Gütersloh: Verlag Bertelsmann Stiftung, 2004.

Goetz, Anne Marie and Shireen Hassim. 'Introduction: Women in Power in Uganda and South Africa,' In *No Shortcuts to Power*, ed. Idem, 1-28. London and New York: Zed Books, 2003.

Hassan, Saliha, 'Malaysia: Transformative not Alternative,' In *Seethings and Seatings. Strategies for Women's Political Participation in Asia Pacific*, ed. Rashila Ramli, Elisa Tita Lubi and Nurgul Djanaeva, pp. 91-124. Chiang Mai: Asia Pacific Forum on Law, Women and Development (APWLD), 2005.

Hng, Hung Yong. CEO Malaysia. *Strategy in Nation-Building*, Subang Jaya: Pendaluk, 1998.

Howell, Jude and Diane Mulligan, eds. *Gender and Civil Society*, London and New York: Routledge, 2005.

Martinez, Patricia. 'Complex Configurations. The Women's Agenda for Change and the Women's Candidacy Initiative,' In *Social Movements in Malaysia. From moral communities to NGOs*, ed. Meredith L. Weiss and Saliha Hassan, pp. 75-98. London and New York: Routledge 2003.

McAdam, Doug; John D. McCarthy and Mayer N. Zald, eds. *Comparative Perspectives on Social Movements. Political Opportunities, Mobilizing Structures, and Cultural Framing*, Cambridge: Cambridge University Press, 1996.

Mulligan, Diane. 'The discourse of Dangdut.' In *Gender and Civil Society*, ed. Jude Howell and Diane Mulligan, pp. 117-38, London and New York: Routledge, 2005.

Noerdin, Edriana. 'Customary Institutions, syariah law and the marginalization of Indonesian Women,' In *Women in Indonesia. Gender, Equity and Development*, ed. Kathryn Robinson and Sharon Bessell, pp. 179-86. Singapore: Institute of Southeast Asian Studies, 2002.

Robinson, Kathryn and Sharon Bessell, eds. *Women in Indonesia. Gender, Equity and Development*, Singapore: Institute of Southeast Asian Studies, 2002.

Robinson, Kathryn. 'Islam, Gender and Politics in Indonesia,' In *Islamic Perspectives on the New Millennium*, ed. Virginia Hooker and Amin Saikal, pp. 183-96. Singapore: Institute of Southeast Asian Studies, 2004.

Sadli, Mohammad. 'Further comments on the economy, with a gender perspective,' In *Women in Indonesia. Gender, Equity and Development*, ed. Kathryn Robinson and Sharon Bessell, pp. 61-67. Singapore: Institute of Southeast Asian Studies, 2002.

Sadli, Saparinah. 'Feminism in Indonesia in an international context,' In *Women in Indonesia. Gender, Equity and Development*, ed. Kathryn Robinson and Sharon Bessell, pp. 80-91, Singapore: Institute of Southeast Asian Studies, 2002.

Sen, Krishna. 'The Mega factor in Indonesian politics: A new president or a new presidency?' In *Women in Indonesia. Gender, Equity and Development*, ed. Kathryn Robinson and Sharon Bessell, pp. 13-27. Singapore: Institute of Southeast Asian Studies, 2002.

Surbakti, Soedarti. 'Gender mainstreaming and sex-disaggregated data.' In *Women in Indonesia. Gender, Equity and Development*, ed. Kathryn Robinson and Sharon Bessell, pp. 209-18. Singapore: Institute of Southeast Asian Studies, 2002.

Weiss, Meredith L. and Saliha Hassab, eds. *Social Movements in Malaysia. From moral communities to NGOs*, London and New York: Routledge 2003.

Unauthored websites
Bertelsmann Transformation Index 2003. http://www.bertelsmann-transformation-index.de/11.0.html?&L=1. 20 September 2005.
Women's Agenda for Change. http://wa4change.tripod.com/english.htm. 20 September 2005.
Human trafficking (Indonesia). 2ww.humantrafficking.org/countries/eap/indonesia. 15 September 2005.
Kalyanamitra. 2ww.kalyanamitra.or.id/profile.php. 21 September 2005.
Komnas Perempuan. http://www.humantrafficking.org/countries/eap/indonesia/ngos/national/komnas.html. 21 September 2005.

3

The Effect of Electoral Gender Quotas— 'Quota Women' in Politics

Drude Dahlerup

Introduction

Many countries all over the world have recently introduced electoral gender quotas even though quotas for women are very controversial, in order to enhance women's political representation. In this article some of the results from a larger research project about the recent introduction of electoral gender quotas world-wide are presented.[1] First, this chapter gives an overview of the widespread use of gender quotas in politics. Second, the concepts of a 'fast track' versus an 'incremental track' to political empowerment of women are presented. It is argued that the Scandinavian countries—for so long alone on the top of the world rank order in terms of women's parliamentary representation—are not the only model for increasing women's representation. Third, the chapter discusses the question of 'tokenism' or 'proxy women', which is very central to the discussion of women's empowerment, especially in South Asia.

It is a widespread worry that 'quota women' will merely have token value. However, double standards seem to be at work, when only women are blamed for being tokens or proxy. Male politicians too are highly dependent on party leaderships and family connections. Four different aspects of 'tokenism' are identified and discussed.

Electoral gender quotas—a new global trend

Only 17 per cent of the parliamentarians of the world are women, which implies that men still occupy the overwhelming majority of the elected seats in parliaments around the world.[2] Many different strategies are being used to enhance women's political representation and some strategies have proven successful, while others are merely symbolic. However, the effects of such strategies are interesting fields of research.

In the book, *Women, Quotas and Politics,* which is the first world-wide comparative analysis of the introduction of gender quotas in politics, based on research in almost all major regions of the world, the following are analysed:

1) the quota discourses,
2) the actual quota rules (different quota regimes),
3) the often troublesome implementation of quotas,
4) the effects of quotas in both quantitative terms (numbers) and qualitative terms (empowerment).[3]

In co-operation with International IDEA, the first world-wide website has been constructed with information about all countries in the world applying electoral gender quotas.[4] During just the last one and a half decade, almost fifty countries in the world have introduced *legal quotas,* e.g. quota rules inscribed in the constitution or the electoral law. In another fifty countries, major political parties have introduced gender quotas for their own list for public elections, such as *voluntary party quotas.* This is a new development which challenges previous theories that improvement in women's education and women's labour market participation are a prerequisite for increase in women's political representation. Today, historical jumps in women's representation are witnessed, most often in post-conflict societies and in countries in transition to democracy. The previous world record in women's representation of Scandinavian countries is being challenged by South Africa, Costa Rica, Mozambique, Argentina, as well as Rwanda, which now has the highest share of women in parliament in the whole world, (48.8 per cent). Various types of electoral gender quotas are part of the explanation behind the exceptional historical leaps in women's representation in all the mentioned countries.

Table 1 shows the top of the world rank order in terms of women's representation. Three main conclusions can be drawn from this table. Firstly, the five Scandinavian countries, for so long solely on the top of the world rank order in terms of women's representation, are as mentioned now being challenged by several countries from the Global South. Secondly, many of those countries who have more than 30 per cent women in parliament do make use of some kind of quotas, be it legal or voluntary party quotas. However, the table also reveals that quotas are not a necessary condition for high representation for women as the cases of the Scandinavian countries of Denmark and Finland show. Thirdly, the table shows that most of the countries with the highest women's representation elect its representatives under a proportional representation electoral system.

Table 1: The Top of the World Rank Order of Women in Parliament

Country	Women in National Parliament (%)	Quota Type	Electoral system
Rwanda	48.8 (2003)	Legal quotas (C)	List PR
Sweden	47.3 (2006)	Party quotas	List PR
Costa Rica	38.6 (2006)	Legal quotas (L)	List PT
Norway	37.9 (2005)	Party quotas	List PR
Finland	37.5 (2002)	No quotas	List PR
Denmark	36.9 (2005)	No quotas	List PR
Netherlands	36.7 (2003)	Party quotas	List PR
Cuba	36.0 (2003)	No quota	Two Rounds
Mozambique	36.0 (2004)	Party quotas	List PR
Spain	36.0 (2004)	Party quotas	List PR
Argentina	35.0 (2003)	Legal quotas (C)	List PR
Belgium	35.3 (2003)	Legal quotas (L)	List PR
Austria	33.3 (2002)	Party quotas	List PR
South Africa	32.8 (2004)	Party quotas	List PR
New Zealand	32.2 (2005)	Party quotas	List PR
Germany	31.8 (2005)	Party quotas	MMP
Burundi	30.5 (2005)	Legal quotas	List PR
Iceland	30.2 (2003)	Party quotas	List PR

Key to electoral systems: List PR: Proportional Representation. MMP: Mixed Member Proportional.
Key to quota types, the mandate: Legal quotas: Constitutional (C) or Law (L). Party quotas: voluntary party quotas by some or all parties in a country.
Source: International IDEA and Stockholm University (2006); official statistics. Changes after last election not included.

Types of quota regimes

Electoral gender quotas come in many different forms today. In order to understand the effect of quotas, it is crucial to analyse how different quota systems match—or do not match—with various electoral systems. While quotas may be mandated by legal means (constitutions and electoral law) or be voluntarily regulated in a political party's own statutes, the quota requirement may also target various steps in the nominations process: First, women's share of the aspirants, that is the pool of potential candidates; second, the gender composition of the candidates lists for the election; and third a minimum number of women to be elected. In the last case are the 'reserved seats' as in Uganda, Rwanda and Burundi, or at the local level in India, Pakistan and Bangladesh. Today, many reserved seat systems are not based on appointment, but on competitive elections, like in Uganda, where one parliamentary seat is reserved for a woman in each of the 56 electoral districts.[5]

The actual quota percentage varies from five per cent in Nepal over Brazil's and Uzbekistan with 30 per cent and Sweden and France with 50 per cent. The French case, however, shows that without rules about the rank order of women and men on the lists or about their share of the safe seats, and without sanctions for non-compliance, even a very high quota requirement may not have any real effect.

Regional differences

In all the Scandinavian parliaments, women's representation exceeds 35 per cent. The rest of Europe, the Americas, Asia and Sub-Saharan Africa are all close to the world average, while the figure for the Pacific is only 10.9 per cent and the average in Arab countries is 6.8 per cent. However, there are considerable variations within the world's regions, and today countries like Costa Rica, South Africa, Rwanda and Mozambique have overtaken industrialized nations like the United States and the United Kingdom, which in the House of Representatives and the House of Commons only have 15 and 19 per cent women, respectively.

In the debate in Latin America, in South Africa and in many other countries, the extraordinarily high representation of women in Scandinavian parliaments has been used as an argument in support of the introduction of electoral gender quotas. This argument is, however, somewhat misleading, since the real boom in women's representation in Denmark, Finland, Norway and Sweden occurred in the 1970s and in Iceland in the 1980s, all before the introduction of any quotas. Gender quotas were introduced when women already comprised twenty to thirty per cent in the parliaments of these small Northern countries. Moreover, in the Scandinavian countries electoral quotas have always been voluntary, never a legal requirement, and are only used by some of the political parties, mainly by parties at the centre and the left.[6]

In general, the Scandinavian countries come close to what we label *the incremental track* towards equal political representation for women and men. It took approximately sixty years since women's enfranchisement for Denmark, Norway and Sweden to cross the 20 per cent threshold and seventy years to reach 30 per cent. This means that the Scandinavian countries, in spite of the high level of women's representation, can no longer be considered the model, or at any rate the only model, for increasing women's representation.

The 'Fast Track' versus the 'Incremental Track' to Gender Balance in Politics

Dahlerup and Freidenvall have identified two current tracks to gender balance in politics.[7] Constructed as an analytical distinction between discourses, the two tracks include different assumptions about the historical development, different problem identifications with regard to the causes of women's under-representation as well as differences in choice of strategy.

Why are women under-represented? The primary problem, according to the *incremental track* discourse, is that women do not have as good resources, and/or not the same political resources as men. While prejudice against women is recognized, it is assumed that this will eventually disappear as society develops. There is thus an inherent notion of gradualism, often embedded in an optimistic, linear view of progress.

In contrast, the *fast track discourse* rejects the idea of gradual improvement in women's representation. It is assumed that an increase in resources might not automatically lead to equal representation. And backlash may even occur. Based on a new diagnosis of the problem associated with the fast track discourse, according to which gender balance will not come about 'by itself', there is a growing impatience among contemporary feminists, who are not willing to wait decade after decade for gender balance in politics. Discrimination and mechanisms of exclusion are identified as the core problem, the solution to which could very well be affirmative action. Consequently, the main responsibility for changing the under-representation of women rests with the political institutions themselves. It follows from this understanding of women's under-representation, that measures like electoral gender quotas are seen as a legitimate type of intervention.

Electoral gender quotas represent the '*fast track*' to equal representation of women and men in politics in contrast to the '*incremental track*'. The notion of the *fast track* versus the *incremental track* can be viewed as involving not just the two different discourses discussed above, but also different types of actual equality policies, and finally an account of the actual speed of historical development in women's representation.[8] The distinction between the two tracks may be relevant for many other policy areas but has been developed with respect to gender and political institutions.

The Beijing Platform for Action

The Beijing Platform represents a *fast track* discourse. In 1990 the United Nation's Economic and Social Council endorsed a target of 30 per cent women in decision-making positions in the world by 1995.[9] This target was far from met, since in 1995, only 10 per cent of the parliamentarians in the world were women. In the Beijing Platform, affirmative action is suggested as a possible means of attaining the goal of gender balance in political decision-making, although the controversial word 'quotas' is not used.[10] For governmental and public administration positions, it is recommended that the world's governments use 'specific targets and implementing measures … if necessary through positive action' (art.190.a). Concerning elections, it is stated that governments should commit themselves to 'take measures, including, where appropriate, in electoral systems that encourage political parties to integrate women in elective and non-elective public positions in the same proportion and at the same levels as men' (art.190.b). Political parties should 'consider examining party structures and procedures to remove all barriers that directly or indirectly discriminate against the participation of women' (art.191.a).[11]

Even if the language is cautious, the Beijing Platform represents on the whole a new discourse, by focusing on the mechanisms of exclusion through institutional practices, by setting *gender balance*—and not just 'women in politics'—as the goal, and by demanding that governments and political parties commit themselves to affirmative action.

Are gender quotas discrimination against men?

If the actual exclusion of women is taken as the starting point, that is, if it is recognized that many barriers exist that prevent women from entering the realm of politics, then quotas are not to be seen as discriminating (against men), but rather as compensation for all the obstacles that women meet. When all of these impediments are removed, quotas will no longer be necessary, it is often argued. In this respect, quotas are a temporary measure. It may take decades, though, before all social, cultural and political barriers preventing equal female representation are eradicated. Today, the very concept of a linear progressive development toward gender equality is challenged by actual experiences of backlash and stand still when it comes to women's representation in formal political institutions.

In order to answer the question of whether electoral gender quotas are in fact discrimination of men, how political systems function needs to be looked at. The gatekeepers to the political arena are usually the political parties, because in most countries they control the nomination process. The role of voters is often not as decisive as one would imagine. Who will be elected is mostly decided by the nomination committees of the political parties, because they select the candidates and place them in a good or a bad constituency in terms of the chances of actually being elected. Prior to the election, the political parties usually know which seats are 'safe'. In all systems, it is important to examine who actually exercises control over the nomination process. In countries with a high level of female representation, women's organizations have successfully asked who controls the nomination process and consequently asked for more women at the nominations committees.

Do 'quota women' become tokens?

In many parts of the world, but maybe most outspoken in South Asia, women in politics are accused of being just tokens. Such accusations seem to be most severe, when women are elected under some kind of quota system and referred to as 'quota women'! In India the many women elected to the local councils, the *panchayats*, are frequently named 'proxy women'.[12] Such accusations may come from opponents of any measure to increasing women's political representation. But it is important to note that many feminists also fear that the elected 'quota women' will be just tokens in the political game. 'Tokenism' is especially feared when quotas are introduced as reserved seats, but also voluntary party quotas are sometimes met with suspicion.

In an African context, many critics of quotas are found, also among feminists, many of whom believe the practice leads to tokenism and can become yet another mechanism in the service of patronage politics. There is also a worry that the elected women will not be qualified and therefore unable to work the system.[13] In Egypt where gender quotas were in practice for a shorter period of time in the 1970s and 80s, the women elected on quotas were heavily criticized, not least by the women's movement.[14]

The debate about token women does need clarification. At least four different aspects seem to be at play here, which need to be discussed separately. They are related to different stages of the nomination and election process.

When women are substitutes for their husbands or fathers

When 33 per cent quotas for women were introduced in India, examples of women elected as substitutes for their husbands were seen. In such cases the husband had been elected previously, but now had to step down because of the new quota regulation, and consequently he placed his wife in the seat. In many of these cases it was reported that the husband remained the real decision-maker behind the scene. In some cases, the husbands even went to the meetings instead of the elected wives. In such cases, the concept of tokenism seems highly appropriate. However, it has been reported that the elected women in several cases after some time claimed their own seat.[15] This kind of tokenism has some resemblance with the tradition known from, for instance the United States, when widows have been elected to Congress as substitutes for their deceased husbands. In all these instances the election of the woman was purely symbolic, but she may, however, later prove to be a competent politician.

Dependency on networks and family ties

A second type of problem for women politicians has to do with recruitment through networks and family ties. The outstanding number of women leaders in South Asia and South East Asia are often met with the comment that these women have just obtained their positions because of their family ties. This may be accurate, but double standards are nevertheless at play here. These commentators seem to forget that most male politicians have also earned their positions through connections or even them through close family ties. Why did Rajiv Gandhi become prime minister? In the Philippines, it is even possible to name those families that for ages have controlled the various provinces.[16] The conclusion is that in clientalist political systems both men and women politicians are heavily dependent of their connections, and consequently it is an expression of double standards only to blame the women politicians for this.

In the same way, women elected on quota provisions such as the reserved seats in Uganda and the 'National List' in Morocco are accused of being too dependent on the political parties and the party leadership which nominated them. Even here double standards are involved in such accusations. It is a fact, that in every political system, in which the political parties control the nominations, all candidates are dependent on the party leadership, be it local or national, for their nomination. The political parties are the gatekeepers to political representation—also for men. In these cases women politicians are no more independent of party leadership than their male colleagues, and quotas do not alter this. That there are many incumbents and many safe seats in most electoral systems, and most of these seats are occupied by male candidates should not be.

The effectiveness of elected women

A third dimension to be discussed here is the performance of women politicians. One might define the 'effectiveness' of women politicians as the ability to perform their task as elected representatives the way they want. While Goetz and Hassim define women's 'effectiveness' as their ability to make reforms which will benefit women,[17] I define 'effectiveness' as women politicians' ability to make the reforms they want, be it feminist or not. Under what conditions will women politicians be able to make use of their positions as elected politicians? What are the obstacles? Seen from this perspective, the focus shifts to the electoral system and to political institutions seen as workplaces, that is the institutional routines, norms and culture that frame the abilities of women and men to actually work as politicians. Significantly, in these contexts women are often met with another double standard: women politicians are accused of lacking knowledge and education but at the same time criticized for only representing a small group of educated elite women!

Ever since the enfranchisement, women's movements have criticized female politicians. This critique has been based on feminist goals—they want women's politicians to represent women and not adapt so much to the party line. This criticizm is reasonable from the point of view of the feminist movement. However, women politicians are often squeezed behind two conflicting sets of expectations: On the one hand they are expected to show that they are just as good—just like the male politicians, who have the benefit of operating in a culture formed by men with women everywhere in a minority. On the other hand, the feminist movements want women politicians to promote feminist goals, and consequently accuse them of not fighting sufficiently hard for women's issues.

When quota women lack a power base of their own

The most serious cases of stigmatization of 'quota woman' seem to occur when only few women are elected, and mostly in countries marked by general hostility against women politicians. However, the very construction of the quota regulation may in fact influence the status of women politicians. If the quota system is constructed in such a way that the 'quota women' do not have a constituency of their own, their status may diminish.

The local gender quotas in India, reserving 33 per cent of the seats for women and—in combination—for scheduled castes constitute severe problems for women. This system functions on a rotation basis, which implies that the elected women usually only serve one period, if they do not choose to stand for one of the 'free' seats in the following election. In contrast, in Bangladesh, the reserved seats for women cover three constituencies (wards), but this system deprives the elected women a constituency base of their own, and force them in their political work to compete with the men elected from the wards.[18] Thus some quota systems imply that the elected women lack a power base of their own which may damage their effectiveness. Consequently, it is crucial to analyse the effect of different quota arrangements.

In conclusion, quota provisions do not solve all problems for women in politics and they may even create new ones. If there is prejudice against women in a society, as is often the case, quotas do not remove these barriers for women's route to full citizenship. If women have trouble combining family responsibilities and political work, quotas do not in themselves overcome these difficulties. However, quota provisions might make it possible for women to surmount some of the barriers that prevent gender balance in politics. These can enable a 'jump start' in places where women had almost no representation before. Quotas can also lead to an increase in women's representation in cases of standstill or even backlash. Gender quotas thus represent a window of opportunity for women, but only if the quota system is designed to match the electoral systems in the individual countries.

NOTES

1. Stockholm University, *The Research Program on Gender Quotas*. [Online]. Available: www.statsvet.su.se/quotas [19 October 2006].
2. www.ipu.org [19 October 2006].
3. Drude Dahlerup, ed., *Women, Quotas and Politics* (London: Routledge, 2006).
4. International IDEA and Stockholm University, *Global Database of Quotas for Women*, [Online], Available: http://www.quotaproject.org. [19 October 2006].
5. For different types of quotas and their use, see Dahlerup, *Women, Quotas and Politics*, 2006.
6. Freidenvall, Lenita, Drude Dahlerup and Hege Skjeie, 'The Nordic Countries: An incremental model,' in *Women, Quotas and Politics,* ed. Drude Dahlerup (London: Routledge, 2006), pp. 55-82.
7. Drude Dahlerup and Lenita Freidenvall, 'Quotas as a "Fast Track" to Equal Political Representation for Women: Why Scandinavia is No Longer the Model,' paper presented at the IPSA World Congress in Durban, July 2003 and at the APSA Annual Meeting, Philadelphia, August 2003.
8. Dahlerup and Freidenvall, 'Quotas as a "Fast Track";'; Drude Dahlerup and Lenita Freidenvall, 'Quotas as a Fast Track to Equal Representation for Women,' *International Feminist Journal of Politics* 7, (1 March 2005): pp. 26-48.
9. United Nations Commission on the Status of Women, *Monitoring the Implementation of the Nairobi Forward-looking Strategies for the Advancement of Women*. E/CN.6/1995/3/Add.6, 1995, [Online]. Available: http://www.un.org/documents/ecosoc/cn6/1995/ecn61995-3add6.htm. [19 October 2006].
10. United Nations Fourth World Conference on Women. *Beijing Declaration and Platform for Action.* 1995, [Online]. Available: http://www.unesco.org/education/information/nfsunesco/pdf/BEIJIN_E.PDF. [19 October 2006].
11. Some of these new formulations may in fact be found in the CEDAW convention from 1979. The convention recommends the states to adopt 'temporary special measures' (United Nations, 'Convention on the Elimination of All Forms of Discrimination Against Women'. UN Treaty Series, 1979, 1249: 13, Art. 4). Also, the Interparliamentary Union, IPU, and other international and regional organizations formulated new claims for women's representation early on. However, it is the Beijing Platform that is most often referred to in the quota debate.

12. International IDEA, The Implementation of Quotas: Asian Experiences, Quota Workshop Report Series no. 1 (Stockholm: International IDEA, 2003); Shirin M. Rai, Farzana Bari, Nazmunnessa Mahtab and Bidyut Mohanty, 'South Asia: Gender Quotas and the Politics of Empowerment: A comparative study.' in *Women, Quotas and Politics*, ed. Drude Dahlerup (London: Routledge, 2006), pp. 222-45.

13. Aili Tripp, Dior Konate, and Colleen Lowe-Morna, 'Sub-Saharan Africa: On the Fast Track to Women's Political Representation,' In *Women, Quotas and Politics*, ed. Drude Dahlerup (London: Routledge, 2006), pp. 112-37; see also International IDEA, *The Implementation of Quotas: African Experiences*, Quota Workshop Report Series no. 3 (Stockholm: International IDEA, 2004).

14. Gihan Abou-Zeid, 'The Arab Region: Women's Access to the Decision-Making Process Across the Arab Nation,' in *Women, Quotas and Politics*, ed. Drude Dahlerup (London: Routledge, 2006), pp. 168-93.

15. Rai, Bari, Mahtab and Mohanty, 'South Asia: Gender Quotas and The Politics of Empowerment'.

16. Edna E.A. Co et al, *Philippine Democracy Assessment* (Friedrich-Ebert Stiftung and National College of Public Administration and Governance, University of Philippines, 2005).

17. Anne Marie Goetz and Shireen Hassim, 'Introduction: Women in Power in Uganda and South Africa,' in *No Shortcuts to Power: African Women in Politics and Policy Making*, eds. A. M. Goetz and S. Hassim (London: Zed Books, 2003), pp. 1-28.

18. Rai, Bari, Mahtab and Mohanty, 'South Asia: Gender Quotas and The Politics of Empowerment,'; Emma Frankl, 'Quotas as Empowerment. The Use of Reserved Seats in Union Rai Parishad as an Instrument for Women's Political Empowerment in Bangladesh,' Working Paper Series 2004: 3 (Stockholm University: The Quota Project).

References

Abou-Zeid, Gihan. 'The Arab Region: Women's Access to the Decision-Making Process Across the Arab Nation.' In *Women, Quotas and Politics*, ed. Drude Dahlerup, pp. 168-93. London: Routledge, 2006.

Co, Edna E.A. et al. *Philippine Democracy Assessment*. Friedrich-Ebert Stiftung and National College of Public Administration and Governance, University of Philippines, 2005.

Dahlerup, Drude, ed. *Women, Quotas and Politics*. London: Routledge, 2006.

Dahlerup, Drude and Lenita Freidenvall. 'Quotas as a "Fast Track" to Equal Political Representation for Women: Why Scandinavia is No Longer the Model,' Paper presented at the IPSA World Congress in Durban, July 2003 and at the APSA Annual Meeting, Philadelphia, August 2003.

Dahlerup, Drude and Lenita Freidenvall. 'Quotas as a Fast Track to Equal Representation for Women,' *International Feminist Journal of Politics* 7, 1 (March 2005): pp. 26-48.

Frankl, Emma. 'Quotas as Empowerment. The Use of Reserved Seats in Union Rai Parishad as an Instrument for Women's' Political Empowerment in Bangladesh,' Stockholm University: The Quota Project. Working Paper Series 2004: 3.

Freidenvall, Lenita, Drude Dahlerup and Hege Skjeie. 'The Nordic Countries: An incremental model,' in *Women, Quotas and Politics,* ed. Drude Dahlerup, 55-82. London: Routledge, 2006.

Goetz, Anne Marie and Shireen Hassim, 'Introduction: Women in Power in Uganda and South Africa.' In *No Shortcuts to Power: African Women in Politics and Policy Making,* eds. A. M. Goetz and S. Hassim, pp. 1-28, London: Zed Books, 2003.

International IDEA. *The Implementation of Quotas: Asian Experiences*, Quota Workshop Report Series no 1. Stockholm: International IDEA, 2003.

International IDEA. *The Implementation of Quotas: African Experiences*, Quota Workshop Report Series no 3. Stockholm: International IDEA, 2004.

International IDEA and Stockholm University. *Global Database of Quotas for Women,* Online. Available: http://www.quotaproject.org. 19 October 2006.

Rai, Shirin M., Farzana Bari, Nazmunnessa Mahtab and Bidyut Mohanty, 'South Asia: Gender Quotas and the Politics of Empowerment: A comparative study,' In *Women, Quotas and Politics,* ed. Drude Dahlerup, pp. 222-45. London: Routledge, 2006.

Stockholm University. *The Research Program on Gender Quotas.* Stockholm University: Department of Political Science, Online. Available: www.statsvet.su.se/quotas. 19 October 2006.

Tripp, Aili, Dior Konate, and Colleen Lowe-Morna. 'Sub-Saharan Africa: On the Fast Track to Women's Political Representation,' In *Women, Quotas and Politics,* ed. Drude Dahlerup, pp. 112-37, London: Routledge, 2006.

United Nations. 'Convention on the Elimination of All Forms of Discrimination Against Women', UN Treaty Series, 1979, 1249: 13.

United Nations Commission on the Status of Women. *Monitoring the Implementation of the Nairobi Forward-looking Strategies for the Advancement of Women*, E/CN.6/1995/3/Add.6, 1995. Online. Available: http://www.un.org/documents/ecosoc/cn6/1995/ecn61995-3add6.htm. 19 October 2006.

United Nations Fourth World Conference on Women. *Beijing Declaration and Platform for Action.* (1995) Online. Available: http://www.unesco.org/education/information/nfsunesco/pdf/BEIJIN_E.PDF. 19 October 2006.

4

The Politics of Quotas around the World: Asia in Perspective

Manon Tremblay and Jackie F. Steele

It is not a coincidence that gender quotas in politics have recently flourished around the world. This can in part be linked to the spread of liberal democracy worldwide, a phenomenon accentuated with the fall of communism. Democracy and the feminization of parliaments have become increasingly associated. The *Beijing Platform for Action* (1995) also establishes this link and pleads in favour of an increased presence of women in decision-making bodies, going as far as to encourage governments to 'take measures [...] in electoral systems that encourage political parties to integrate women in elective and non-elective public positions in the same proportion and at the same levels as men.'[1] In the same vein, Section 4 of the *Universal Declaration on Democracy* (1997) states that: 'The achievement of democracy presupposes a genuine partnership between men and women in the conduct of the affairs of society [...].'[2]

Innovative research at the international level has provided important indicators of women's representation in the form of the Inter-Parliamentary Union's ranking of countries,[3] or in the form of the Database of Quotas developed by International IDEA and the University of Stockholm.[4] While a substantial amount of country-specific research on women's representation over the past thirty years has concentrated on the concept of critical mass and the relationship between the descriptive and substantive representation of women,[5] emerging interest among Western feminist political theorists points increasingly to the more philosophical, if less tangible, meaning of political representation as an indicator of inclusion and equal citizenship.[6]

More recently, the focus of political theorists, feminist activists, and politicians has been on exposing the contradictions between professed commitments to gender equality and the ongoing exclusion of women from formal democratic institutions. Although the association of the concept of representation with democratic practices of self-government is not new, as Pitkin has rightly observed, 'no doubt the contemporary popularity of the concept [of representation] depends much upon its having become linked with the idea of democracy, as well as with ideas of liberty and justice.'[7] Indeed, in *Inclusion and Democracy*, Young asserts that 'calls for inclusion arise from experiences of exclusion—from basic political rights, from opportunities to participate, from the hegemonic terms of debate,'[8] and that inclusion is a norm invoked by 'those seeking to widen and deepen democratic practices.'[9] In short, the political representation of women and gender quotas have been increasingly of interest, not only for the 'efficient' role they play as an empirical indicator of the effectiveness of mechanisms destined to ensure the election of women to national parliaments in proportions equivalent to their socio-demographic presence, but also for the 'symbolic' role they play as normative indicators of the degree to which the idea of gender equality has been incorporated into the definition of democratic self-government and full citizenship.

What is to follow is an empirical description and qualitative evaluation of the practical experiences of positive action in Asia. First the main theoretical and conceptual elements that inspire this analysis in relation to the evolving definitions of 'inclusion' and 'democratic citizenship' will be outlined. Second the presence and application of quotas in Asia in comparison with other continents will be described. Third, analysis of the use of quotas from the perspective of five variables: the historical context of their adoption, the opportunity structure of the electoral system, the type of positive action, the level of implementation, the parameters of the quota measure will be undertaken. In conclusion, the Asian experience of quotas in light of the symbolic or rhetorical function versus their practical, efficient performance in feminizing the legislatures under study will be reflected upon.

Positive Action and the Politics of Inclusion

The core assumption about the role of law within modern democratic theory, and namely, the idea that legally binding agreements, adopted by means of a democratic process, form the normative blueprint, or social contract of any society considered to be enjoying democratic self-government. Legally binding agreements may include the general values and principles, such as equality, liberty and justice, as well as the concrete practices that are enshrined in a constitution or in the panoply of laws adopted by the national legislature. As such, quotas or positive action inscribed in a constitution, within an electoral law, or adopted as a separate law, serve a practical mechanical purpose in terms of advancing women's representation, as well as an ideological or normative purpose in terms of advancing the ideal of inclusion for women, or gender equality. As a normative idea, the standard of *inclusion* necessarily varies from one country to another. Inspired by Kanter,[10] the ideal of inclusion, as reflected by the descriptive presence of women in parliaments, according to a spectrum, whereby zero per cent women in national legislatures illustrates the exclusion of women from democratic citizenship, 15 per cent signifies the partial inclusion of women, 30 per cent represents more substantial inclusion, and 45 per cent and higher signifies the full inclusion of women in democratic citizenship is evaluated.

Fig. 1: Democratic Inclusion and Women's Descriptive Representation

(0%) Exclusion   Partial (15%)   Substantial (30%)   Full (45%+)

To be sure, by defining the achievement of 45 per cent+ women in a national legislature as full inclusion of women in terms of democratic citizenship is not to suggest that women will enjoy equal amounts of political power and influence, nor that women as a group or as individuals will immediately achieve equal socioeconomic and political standing with men inside democratic institutions or in society more generally. The analysis here is therefore limited to the concepts of symbolic and descriptive representation of women.[11]

Historically, the inclusion of all parts of a population within the electoral process was not a prerequisite for the assertion of democratic citizenship. Rather, democratic citizenship was defined in law as excluding women's, groups among others.[12] From the affirmations of Condorcet, Olympe de Gouges and Mary Wollstonecraft to the present, feminist theorists and activists worldwide have challenged and defeated this assumption with varying degrees of success.[13] The last thirty years has seen the promotion of gender equality strategies aimed at closing the gap between the formal guarantee of political rights for women, and the actual reality of women's ongoing exclusion from participation as elected representatives within democratic institutions of self-government. In particular, Norris identifies three kinds of gender equality strategies with respect to women's political representation. She identifies:

1) *Rhetorical strategies* as 'exemplified by signature of international conventions on women's rights, and official speeches and statements applauding the principles of equal opportunities for women and men.'[14]
2) *Equal opportunity strategies*, such as training sessions, special conferences, financial assistance, and access to childcare facilities, which 'are designed

to provide a level playing field so that women can pursue political careers on the same basis as men.'[15]

3) *Positive action strategies*, such as reserved seats, statutory gender quotas and voluntary quotas, which 'are designed explicitly to benefit women as a temporary stage until such a time as gender parity is achieved in legislative bodies.'[16]

Given that here the focus is on the use of quotas in Asia, mostly of interest is this last gender equality strategy, or namely, positive action strategies. If one or more of these three types of gender equality strategies can be found in a substantial number of countries worldwide, their ability to increase the number of women in political spaces varies tremendously as evidenced by the broad range in the percentage of women elected to one parliament or another. For countries that have double-barrelled legal quotas (at both the constitutional and legislative level), the level that specifically outlines the percentage to be achieved have been counted .

Secondly, we advance here the perspective that all forms of positive action serve two purposes: 1) they serve a symbolic or rhetorical purpose in terms of advancing the ideals of a society with respect to the standard for inclusion, citizenship and democratic self-government; and, 2) they serve a practical purpose in terms of the efficiency with which they ensure the election of women, or the descriptive representation of women in the national legislature. Within the three gender equality strategies presented by Norris, rhetorical gender strategies and positive action strategies are more akin to water-tight concepts that do not intersect, whereas the aim here is to demonstrate the fluidity between these two concepts by evaluating the holistic impact of different positive action measures. Although Norris advances the idea that positive action will be more effective at feminizing legislatures than rhetorical strategies, in fact, quotas must also be scrutinized for both the symbolic and efficient role they play in advancing women's representation, or namely in order to expose the predominantly *rhetorical value* of certain positive action strategies, in Asia, as is also the case elsewhere.

Fig. 2: Two Roles of Positive Action Strategies

←————————————————————————————————————→

Rhetorical Inclusion (Symbolism)   Practical Inclusion (Efficiency)

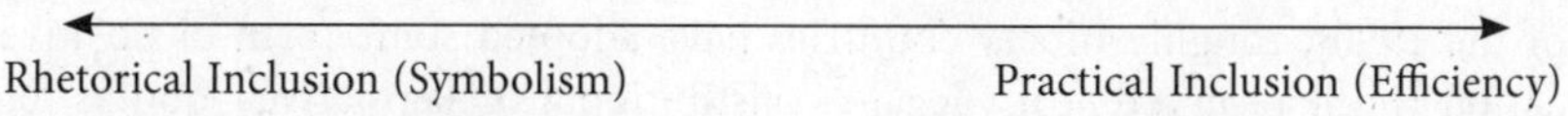

In addition to their practical or empirical role, it is suggested that positive action strategies must also be evaluated and understood for the rhetorical or symbolic vision of citizenship they reflect, given that many of them do not practically lead to the feminization of the legislature. The failure to feminize the legislature may occur as a result of faulty design (a proportion established at too low a level, lack of sanctions for non-compliance, etc.) or other technical concerns in evidence after several elections; however, the lack of feminization (towards the 15 per cent, 30 per cent, and 45 per cent level) of the legislature, despite several elections, may simply point to the normative ideal (however minimalist) of 'inclusion' behind the positive action strategy itself, and which may assume the non-necessity of women's active role in political representation. In short, to fully understand the effectiveness of certain positive action strategies in feminizing the legislature in some countries or continents, or the lack thereof, it is helpful to evaluate quotas for both the *efficient* practical role, as well as the *symbolic* rhetorical role they play in light of competing definitions of inclusion, citizenship and democratic self-government.

By further evaluating positive action measures according to a symbolism-efficiency spectrum, it is possible to evaluate a given quota according to which of the two elements predominates. The degree to which the symbolic or efficient parts yield concrete results depends on the construction of the positive action mechanism itself. As Goetz and Hassim[17] argue, institutional mechanisms can be evaluated as existing only to legitimize the state, or as a forum for women to put forth their needs and demand responses through policy. What follows is the presentation of an empirical and qualitative analysis of positive action strategies or quotas used in the Asian context.

Positive Action Strategies: Asia in Perspective

According to the Inter-Parliamentary Union, as of 31 May 2006, there was an average of 16.8 per cent women in lower and single houses of some 188 national parliaments. Depending on the continent, this proportion ranged between 40 per cent in the Nordic countries, about 19.4 per cent in European member countries of the OSCE, 20.5 per cent in the Americas, 16.7 per cent in Sub-Saharan Africa, 12.1 per cent in the Pacific countries, and 8.2 per cent in Arab States.[18] With 16.4 per cent of women in lower and single houses of parliaments, Asia is a little bit under the world average. Since the beginning of the 1990s, roughly ninety countries have adopted some form of positive action (be it reserved seats, legal—constitutional or legislative—quotas, or party quotas) to advance the presence of women within lower or single chambers of their parliaments. As shown in Table 1, these countries are spread out amongst all continents: there are 28 in Africa, 19 in Asia, 2 in North America, 7 in Central America and the Caribbean, 10 in South America, 29 in Europe and only one in Oceania (see Appendix p. 78 for a list of the countries). Proportionate to the total number of countries on the continent,[19] quotas (of any kind) are most present in Europe (29/44, 65.9 per cent), although their adoption on the subcontinent of South America has been most impressive—10 out of 12 countries or 83.3 per cent). On the other hand, quotas are almost completely absent in Oceania (1/14, 7.1 per cent) and remain marginal in Asia (19/49, 38.8 per cent) and in the subcontinent of Central America and the Caribbean (7/20, 35 per cent).

Table 1: Gender Quotas in Politics by Continent

Continent		Number of countries	Number of countries with gender quotas	% of countries with gender quotas
Africa		53	28	52.8
Americas		35	19	54.3
	North	(3)	(2)	(66.7)
Central and the Caribbean		(20)	(7)	(35.0)
	South	(12)	(10)	(83.3)
Asia		49	19	38.8
Europe		44	29	65.9
Oceania		14	1	7.1

Sources: www.quotaproject.org; en.wikipedia.org/wiki/List_of_countries_by_continent; both accessed July 2006.

Although positive action strategies, in the form of reserved seats, legal quotas, and party quotas are now present on all continents, they have not been used in the same ways; Table 2 reflects these specificities. For example, reserved seats are only used in Africa and in Asia, whereas legal (constitutional and/or legislative) quotas are present on all continents except Oceania, and party quotas exist everywhere around the world. In Asia more specifically, 17 of the 19 (or 89.5 per cent) countries of this continent have reserved seats and/or legal quotas. In comparison, only 14 of the 28 (50 per cent) African countries have reserved seats and/or legal quotas, and 6 out of the 29 (20.7 per cent) European countries only have legal quotas. Legal quotas as well as party quotas are also very present in South America (8 out of 10 countries of this sub-continent have legal and/or party quotas), as in Africa and Europe, be it in established democracies such as Iceland and Norway, or within newer democracies such as Poland, the Czech Republic or Macedonia.

Table 2: Gender Quotas in Politics by Continent and Type of Quotas

Continent	Types of gender quotas			
	Number of countries with gender quotas	Number with reserved seats (%)	Number with legal quotas (%)	Number with party quotas (%)
Africa	28	6 (21.4)	8 (28.6)	18 (64.3)
Americas	19	0 (0.0)	13 (68.4)	15 (78.9)
North	(2)	0 (0.0)	1 (50.0)	2 (100.0)
Central and the Caribbean	(7)	0 (0.0)	4 (57.1)	5 (71.4)
South	(10)	0 (0.0)	8 (80.0)	8 (80.0)
Asia	19	6 (31.6)	11 (57.9)	9 (47.4)
Europe	29	0 (0.0)	6 (20.7)	28 (96.6)
Oceania	1	0 (0.0)	0 (0.0)	1 (100.0)

Note: The breakdown of quotas by type exceeds the number of countries with quotas given that some countries have several types of gender quotas.
Source: www.quotaproject.org; accessed July 2006.

Prior to the 1990s, however, positive action had been implemented in only a few countries, and in particular, it found fertile ground in Asia. As such, the adoption of positive action in Asian countries began as early as 1953 with Taiwan's adoption of a 10 per cent reserved seat system for women in legislative bodies.[20] In Pakistan, the 1954, 1956, 1962, 1970, 1973 and 1985 Constitutions all provided for reserved seats for women in the National Assembly.[21] Beginning in 1972, Bangladesh introduced fifteen reserved seats in parliament (out of 315), which were in effect for a period of ten years; this modality was recently revived in 2004.[22] On other continents, Egypt reserved thirty seats (out of 360) for women in parliament between 1976 and 1986,[23] and in Argentina, roughly one-third of candidacies for the Peronist Party were reserved for women as early as the beginning of the 1950s.[24] How can we explain the weak performance of positive action strategies used in Asia despite the fact that reserved seats and legal quotas have been in place for over fifty years in some countries?

Interpreting the Asian Context

In this section, the objective is to analyse and interpret the situation on the Asian continent in light of five variables, namely, the historical context, the electoral system, the type of positive action, the level of implementation of the quota, and the content of the positive action strategy itself.

Variable 1: Historical context

According to Krook,[25] four 'causal stories' may explain why quotas are adopted:

- *Women's movements mobilize for the adoption of positive action to increase women's representation*: This interpretation posits women as strategic electoral actors who see quotas as an effective means of increasing their presence in the halls of power. According to this scenario, which is one of women's empowerment, it is the mobilizations of women that led to the adoption of quotas, rather than as a result of external forces that paternalistically granted quotas as a means of emancipating women.
- *Political elites recognized strategic advantages for pursuing gender quotas*: This interpretation essentially draws upon the idea of political parties as opportunistic agents wishing to maximize their electoral gains in the short, medium and long-term. As such, the adoption of quotas could be seen as a means of courting the feminine electorate, or of following the example of other parties so as to remain competitive. That said, as Krook has mentioned, parties can also be motivated to adopt quotas in order to appease internal tensions within their own ranks.
- *Quotas are consistent with existing or emerging notions of equality and representation*: This interpretation suggests that the adoption of quotas is simply the logical consequence of contemporary conceptions of the principle of equality and political representation. So framed, equality is achieved through the recognition of difference, rather than through its negation. For its part, political representation is understood as invoking a microcosmic vision of governance. It is a view that sees, in quotas, the potential to renew the very practice of democracy.
- *Quotas are supported by international norms and are spread through transnational sharing*: According to this fourth interpretation, quotas would be the consequence of international instruments such as the *Convention on the Political Rights of Women* (1952), the *Convention on the Elimination of All Forms of Discrimination Against Women*, the *Beijing Platform for Action* (1979) and the *Universal Declaration on Democracy* (1997). This reading insists on the importance of collaboration between femocrats within international organization and national and transnational women's movements.

These four 'causal stories' offer a useful framework for understanding the developments in Asia. As concerns the first 'causal story,' the adoption in 2004 of the 30 per cent quota (single member district [SMD] tier), and of a 50 per cent quota (for list proportional representation [list PR]) for the legislative elections in the Republic of Korea is not foreign to the mobilization of the women's movement around electoral politics since the early 1990s.[26] The Indian case however points more strongly to the second explanation, and perhaps to the first explanation, however negatively. Although the 33 per cent quota of reserved seats within local *Panchayati Raj* (the local level of government) came 'from above' rather than as a result of women's mass mobilization, the energy expended by women in favour of adopting reserved seats within the *Lok Sabha* (the People's Chamber) has not successfully overcome resistance at the national level against these demands.[27] The third and fourth factors help illuminate the choices and democratic aspirations recently endorsed in Afghanistan and Iraq.[28]

Designed to serve a more modest and perhaps symbolic function in electing between 0–15 per cent women, the gender equality strategy of reserved seats and/or legal quotas that were historically adopted prior to the 1990s trend were likely aimed at rhetorically including women within democratic citizenship, corresponding with low levels (i.e., exclusion and partial inclusion according to Figure 1) of women's descriptive representation, and weak quotas with few sanctions for non-compliance. Although positive action strategies were successful in partially countering patriarchal ideologies by allowing for the election of a symbolic number of women, these partial measures also ensured that women did not threaten men's monopoly over political power within democratic institutions in practice. Moreover, these positive action strategies indirectly contributed to the portrayal of women as second-class competitors, or as political actors in need of assistance to participate in political life.

Variable 2: Opportunity structure of electoral system

A second variable worth exploring is the impact of the electoral system in shaping the types of positive action chosen in Asia versus that used elsewhere. It has largely been demonstrated that the electoral system influences the gender make-up of parliament. More specifically, list PR systems are said to be more favourable towards social minorities, such as women, than plurality/majority system.[29] However, this reading has become increasingly scrutinized and nuanced.[30]

Does the electoral system offer another explanation as to the importance of reserved seats and legal quotas, and the weak level of women's representation in Asia? The answer is in the negative. Of the fourteen Asian countries with reserved seats and/or legal quotas,[31] four have a plurality/majority system for their national legislative elections (Bangladesh and Nepal use the first-past-the-post [FPTP] and the Democratic People's Republic of Korea and Uzbekistan have a two-round system [TRS]), five countries (Armenia,

Pakistan, Philippines, Republic of Korea, Taiwan) use a parallel (that is, non compensatory) mixed-member system, two (Indonesia and Iraq) use a list PR system, two (Afghanistan and Jordan) use the single non transferable vote (SNTV), and the last one (the Palestinian Territory) uses the block vote (BV). That said, a closer look reveals the dominance of plurality/majority systems amongst those countries that have adopted reserved seats and/or legal quotas. First, the five mixed-member systems are in fact majoritarian because they have a strong plurality/majority component (notably the FPTP in four of the cases, and the SNTV in Taiwan), representing between 57 per cent and 90 per cent of the total available seats in each respective parliament. Second, the SNTV system may be considered a cousin of plurality/majority systems[32] and the BV is a plurality system.[33]

An examination of the other continent for which reserved seats and/or legal quotas are important, notably in Africa, supports our observation of a certain relationship between gender quotas and the plurality/majority systems: of the 11 African countries with reserved seats and/or legal quotas,[34] six use a form of plurality/majority system (the FPTP and the party block vote [PBV] in Djibouti) and three (Burundi, Niger and Rwanda) use a list PR system. The remaining two have transitional governments and have not confirmed their electoral system. In sum, however, even if reserved seats and/or legal quotas seem to combine often with plurality/majority systems, this relationship is nonetheless inconclusive.

Variable 3: Type of positive action

A third element relates to the types of positive action used in Asia. As identified earlier, there are three main types of positive action strategies used worldwide: reserved seats, legal quotas (that is constitutional or legislative quotas); and party-based quotas. What is striking in the case of Asia is the predominant use of reserved seats and/or legal quotas, as compared to voluntary quotas. What also stands out is the weak proportion of voluntary party quotas, relative to their significant presence on other continents, such as Africa. For example, voluntary party quotas are present in 71.4 per cent (5 out of 7 countries) of Central American and Caribbean countries, and in 96.6 per cent (28/29) of European countries. This leads to the belief that reserved seats and legal quotas can serve to reduce the pressure on political parties to open their doors to women through internal mechanisms that would guide the composition of party lists. However, this point of view does not totally account for the situation in South America where party quotas and legal quotas are equally important. It is important at this point to take into consideration the role of contextual factors (such as the political culture and/

or the mechanical and psychological effects of voting systems) in shaping the mechanisms most likely to be adopted.

Variable 4: Level of implementation

One might think that in light of the fact that they are both inscribed in law, reserved seats and legal quotas would translate into a more significant proportion of female parliamentarians than is the case in countries with quotas internal to the parties who remain independent political actors that respond according to their private and corporate interests. Yet, as seen by the analysis here, the inscription of quotas in law does not guarantee the feminization of legislative assemblies. For example, among the Asian countries with reserved seats and/or legal quotas, the range of female members of parliament (MPs) spans from only 5.3 per cent (Armenia) to 27.3 per cent (Afghanistan), whereas in Europe where party quotas are dominant, the range varies from 9.2 per cent (Malta) to 45.3 per cent (Sweden).

As shown in Table 3, by polarizing countries with reserved-seats and/or legal quotas against those with party quotas only,[35] it becomes apparent that the performance of party quotas in electing women cannot be seen as systematically inferior to reserved-seats and/or legal quotas, as in evidence in several European countries (such as Spain [36 per cent], Sweden [45.3 per cent] and the Netherlands [36.7 per cent]) and African countries (notably in Mozambique [34.8 per cent of women MPs] and South Africa [32.8 per cent]). This interpretation warrants further analysis given that the various subtleties surrounding the use of reserved-seats and legal quotas on the one hand, and party-based quotas on the other has not been taken into account. In fact, the adoption of reserved-seats and/or legal quotas does not prevent countries from continuing to yield a low proportion of women legislators, as in Jordan (5.5 per cent) in Asia, Brazil (8.6 per cent) in South America despite a legislated quota of 30 per cent, or on the African continent in Kenya, where 7.3 per cent, or 6 of the 224 seats are informally[36] reserved for women. It must therefore be admitted that the adoption of reserved seats and/or legal quotas is not a guarantee that more women will sit in parliament or that party quotas are necessarily less efficient.

**Table 3: Proportion of Women in Parliament according to the
Types of Quotas, May 2006***

Continent	Reserved-seats and legal quotas (%)	Party quotas (%)
Africa	7.3-48.8	6.2-34.8
Americas	8.6-38.6	2.0-20.8
North	(25.8)	(20.8)
Central and Caribbean	(16.7-38.6)	(2.0-20.7)
South	(8.6-35.0)	(11.1-18.0)
Asia	5.3-27.3	0.0-14.3
Europe	7.9-34.7	9.2-45.3
Oceania	N/A	24.7

*: At the time of compiling this data, the proportions of elected women were not available for the Dominican Republic, the Palestinian Territory (occupied), Taiwan and Thailand.
Source: www.ipu.org/wmn-f/world.htm; accessed July 2006.

Several nuances must be made. Earlier it was argued that plurality/majority systems dominate in Asia, be it in the pure form of FPTP or of the TRS and BV, or derived by mixed-member parallel systems and the SNTV. As previously mentioned, a series of studies have demonstrated that, generally speaking, list PR systems are more favourable to the election of women than plurality/majority systems. In fact, the low proportion of women is perhaps less a function of the nature of the gender quotas (that is, reserved seats or legal quotas) than the actual electoral system within which these measures are functioning, namely, plurality/majority systems. This hypothesis must be further explored. Moreover, this inquiry would be further strengthened by consideration of political parties, the primary actors charged with the implementation of quotas. Recalling the four explanations proposed by Krook that help explain the emergence of quotas, in the absence of significant short, medium or long term electoral gains, political parties are likely to at best adopt a *laissez faire* attitude towards quotas, and at worst, they may act in bad faith; the non-compliance (with gender parity) of the largest parties in France for the national elections is telling. In short, the implementation of gender quotas and their impact upon political parties are inextricably linked to the voting system.

Variable 5: Content of positive action (the established percentage)

Two other elements must be taken into consideration before any conclusions are derived as to the potential of reserved seats and/or legal quotas to attain an acceptable proportion of women elected to office: 1) the proportions inscribed in the law; and, 2) the modalities relating to enforcement or compliance by political parties with the proscribed modalities. The capacity of reserved seats and/or legal quotas to feminize the legislative assemblies depends in part on the proportion that has been set. In this regard, Krook[37] distinguishes between two concepts, notably between 'implementation,' which indicates compliance with specific quota provisions, and 'impact,' which refers to the contribution of quotas to higher levels of women in parliaments. For example, Nepal, which has a legal quota of 5 per cent but has achieved 5.9 per cent women parliamentarians, experiences a high rate of *implementation* but a relatively low *impact* on the overall percentage of women legislators. Conversely, a country with a 50 per cent gender quota and only 40 per cent women MPs can be said to experience a medium-high rate (40 per cent would be an 80 per cent performance so perhaps this can be called medium rather than low) of *implementation,* and a relatively high *impact* of the quota on the overall percentage of women in parliament. For example, the 50 per cent legislative quota that applies to PR seats in South Korea enjoys a high level of *implementation*, but given that the 81 per cent of FPTP seats in this parallel mixed-PR system are not affected by the positive measure, the overall *impact* of the 50 per cent quota upon the feminization of parliament will be low to moderate.

As indicated in Table 4, in the case of fourteen Asian countries using reserved seats and/or legal quotas, the proportion varies between 5 per cent (in Armenia and Nepal) and 50 per cent for the list PR seats in South Korea. Together, the Asian gender quotas averaged 19.7 per cent. At the same time, only three of the fourteen countries set the critical threshold amount of 30 per cent (what is defined as 'substantial descriptive representation' in Figure 1), and none of these three countries have reached this rate of feminization of their parliament. The measures adopted in Asia lag significantly behind those adopted in Central America, the Caribbean and South America, where the proportions of legal quotas vary between 20 and 40 per cent, yielding an average of 29 per cent, and Europe where they vary between 30 and 50 per cent, producing an average of 34.6 per cent. Nonetheless, the Asian profile is close to that in Africa where percentages established in law vary between 5 and 40 per cent, with an average of 18.1 per cent.

Table 4: Reserved-seats and Legal Quotas in Asia: Some Traits, May 2006

Country	Type	Year of adoption	% of quotas	% of women (last election)	Diff. quotas/ % of women	Sanctions for non-compliance
Afghanistan	RS/L	2004	27.0	27.3 (2005)	+0.3	Yes
Armenia	L	1999	5.0	4.6 (2003)	-0.4	Yes
Bangladesh	RS	2004	13.0	14.8* (2001)	+1.8	N/A
Indonesia	L	2003	30.0	11.1 (2004)	-18.9	No
Iraq	L	2004	25.0	25.5 (2005)	+0.5	N/A
Jordan	RS	2003	5.45	5.5 (2003)	0.0	N/A
Korea (Democratic People's Republic of Korea)	RS	Prior 1998	20.0	20.1 (2003)	+0.1	N/A
Korea (Republic of)	L	2004	30.0 (FPTP) 50.0 (List)	13.0 (2004)	-17.0 to -37.0	N/A
Nepal	RS/L	1990	5.0	5.9 (1999)	+0.9	Yes
Pakistan	RS	2002	17.5	21.3 (2002)	+3.8	N/A
Palestinian Territory	L	2005	20.0	12.9 (2006)	-7.1	N/A
Philippines	RS**/L	1995	≈20.0**	15.3 (2004)	-4.7	N/A
Taiwan	RS	1997	10.0 to 25.0	22.2 (2001)	+12.2 to -2.8	N/A
Uzbekistan	L	2004	30.0	17.5 (2005)	-12.5	No

Source: www.quotaproject.org/; accessed July 2006.

*: According to the Inter-Parliamentary Union, '[i]n 2004, the number of seats in parliament was raised from 300 to 345, with the addition of 45 reserved seats for women. These reserved seats were filled in September and October 2005, being allocated to political parties in proportion to their share of the national vote received in the 2001 election.'; www.ipu.org/wmn-e/classif.htm#4; accessed July 2006.

**: The Filipino law is not limited to women: '[t]he Party List Law (RA 7941) passed in 1995 makes it compulsory to include women on political party lists. The law provides for the election of party list representatives from different sectors. The law allocates 20 per cent of the 250 seats in the Philippines House of Representatives (Lower House) for marginalized sectors of society including women.'; www.quotaproject.org/displayCountry.cfm?CountryCode=PH; accessed July 2006.

Table 4 also shows that as often as the proportion of women in parliament surpasses the percentage inscribed through reserved seats and/or legal quotas, just as often the proportion falls below these fixed percentages. According to Krook's language, in the first case the countries experience a high level of implementation, and in the second they experience a low rate of implementation. Moreover, the percentage points surpassing the proscribed percentage are inferior to the percentage points demarking a deficit below the proscribed target, and this cannot be explained as a result of an overly high threshold if one considers the cases of Bangladesh, Armenia and the Philippines. One means of explaining this rather negative portrait resides in the fact that, Nepal aside, reserved seats and/or legal quotas have all been adopted over the course of the past decade, as in the case of other continents, and according to Dahlerup,[38] at least three elections are required for quotas to take full effect.

Conclusion

In sum, the Asian continent has had a weaker proportion of gender quotas relative to other continents. It has demonstrated a preference for a conservative number of reserved seats that has not increased substantially over the course of the past thirty years. It has a significantly lower presence of voluntary parties quotas than all other continents. Finally, the legal quotas in Asia, when adopted, have established low percentages and have had few consequences for non-compliance by political parties. Consequently, although many of the positive measures in Asia were adopted as early as the early post-Second World War period, positive action in Asia has not constituted an accelerated, or efficient path for feminizing parliaments. Of the fourteen Asian countries that have reserved seats and/or legal quotas, only Afghanistan, Armenia and Indonesia include penalties for non-compliance, making many reserved seats and legal quotas in Asia primarily a symbolic or rhetorical, rather than a practical measure to promote gender equality through the feminization of legislatures.

That being said, these Asian realities cannot be simplistically read according to international legal norms alone. Rather, empirical data on women's representation, positive action strategies, and international legal conventions in dialogue with the different cultural contexts and local specificities must also be placed alongside. As has been demonstrated by Inglehart and Norris,[39] attitudes towards gender roles for women, be they traditional or egalitarian, constitute one of the most important indicators of the feminization of parliaments. For societies where there is a strong patriarchal or religious presence, and where there are low political participation rates for women, even minimal gender quotas that allow for a modest access for women to political representation can be interpreted as progressive, given that they allow for the political inclusion of women, albeit tentative and symbolic. As illustrated by the use of reserved seats in the *Panchayat Raj* in India, despite the reasons for their initial adoption by political elites, over time, positive action measures can significantly contribute to the political socialization of women, fuelling women's mobilization within electoral politics, and further claims for inclusion within democratic citizenship.[40] Indeed, the Asian continent has not escaped the more recent trend of gender quotas since the 1990s.[41] The adoption of positive measures in countries such as Afghanistan and Iraq, where women's mobilizing maximized pressure from the international community for more meaningful inclusion of women[42] point to the use of positive measures to both project the image of inclusion, and lead to more genuine compliance with the international consensus on women's human rights, as enshrined in the *Convention on the Elimination of All Forms of Discrimination against Women* (1979), the *Beijing Platform for Action* (1995) and the *Universal Declaration on Democracy* (1997). In short, future research would do well to explore the larger impact of the symbolic and practical effects of gender quotas upon governance, and the advancement of gender equality as a core foundation of democratic self-government.

Appendix: List of the countries with some form of gender positive action for the election to the national parliament, as of July 2006.

Africa (28/53): Algeria, Botswana, Burkina Faso, Burundi, Cameroon, Côte d'Ivoire, Djibouti, Equatorial Guinea, Eritrea, Ethiopia, Kenya, Liberia, Malawi, Mali, Morocco, Mozambique, Namibia, Niger, Rwanda, Senegal, Sierra Leone[1], Somalia[2], South Africa, Sudan, United Republic of Tanzania, Tunisia, Uganda, Zimbabwe.

Americas (19/35): *North* (2): Canada, Mexico; *Central and the Caribbean* (7): Costa Rica, Dominican Republic, El Salvador, Haiti, Honduras, Nicaragua, Panama; *South* (10): Argentina, Bolivia, Brazil, Chile, Ecuador, Guyana, Paraguay, Peru, Uruguay, Venezuela.

Asia (19/49): Afghanistan, Armenia, Bangladesh, Cyprus, Democratic People's Republic of Korea, India, Indonesia, Iraq, Israel, Jordan, Kyrgyzstan, Nepal, Pakistan, Palestinian Territory (occupied), Philippines, Republic of Korea, Taiwan, Thailand, Uzbekistan.

Europe (29/44): Austria, Belgium, Bosnia and Herzegovina, Croatia, Czech Republic, France, Germany, Greece, Hungary, Iceland, Ireland, Italy, Lithuania, Luxembourg, Macedonia, Malta, Netherlands, Norway, Poland, Portugal, Republic of Moldova, Romania, Slovakia, Slovenia, Spain, State Union of Serbia and Montenegro, Sweden, Switzerland, United Kingdom.

Oceania (1/14): Australia.

Source: www.quotap

1. The Movement for Progress Party (MOP) has a target of 50 per cent candidates for election; see www.quotaproject.org/displayCountry.cfm?CountryCode=SL; accessed July 2006.
2. Article 29 of the 2004 Transitional Federal Charter states that the 'Transitional Federal Parliament of the Somali Republic shall consist of two hundred and seventy five (275) Members of which at least twelve per cent (12%) shall be women,' see www.quotaproject.org/displayCountry.cfm?CountryCode=SO; accessed July 2006.roject.org; accessed July 2006.

NOTES

1. See paragraphs 190-1 at http://www.un.org/womenwatch/daw/beijing/platform/ decision.htm; accessed June 2006.
2. See www.ipu.org/cnl-e/161-dem.htm; accessed June 2006.
3. See www.ipu.org/wmn-e/world.htm; accessed June 2006.
4. See www.quotaproject.org; accessed June 2006.
5. Kathleen A. Bratton, 'Critical Mass Theory Revisited: The Behavior and Success of Token Women in State Legislatures,' Politics and Gender 1 1/2005): 97-125; Sarah Childs, New Labour's Women MPs. Women representing women (London: Routledge, 2004); Sandra Grey, 'Does Size Matter? Critical Mass and New Zealand's Women MPs,' Parliamentary Affairs 55 1/2002), 19-29; Donley T. Studlar and Ian McAllister, 'Does a Critical Mass Exist? A comparative analysis of women's legislative representation since 1950,' European Journal of Political Research 41 2/2002): 233-53; Ann Towns, 'Understanding the Effects of Larger Ratios of Women in National Legislatures: Proportions and Gender Differentiation in Sweden and Norway,' Women and Politics 25 1-2/2003): 1-29; Manon Tremblay, 'The Substantive Representation of Women and PR: Some Reflections on the Role of Surrogate Representation and Critical Mass,' Politics and Gender 2 4/2006; Laurel S. Weldon, 'Beyond Bodies: Institutional Sources of Representation for Women in Democratic Policymaking,' Journal of Politics 64 4/2002): 1153-74.
6. Bérengère Marques-Pereira, La citoyenneté politique des femmes (Paris: Armand Colin, 2003); Anne Phillips, The Politics of Presence (Oxford: Clarendon Press, 1995); Birte Siim, Gender and Citizenship (Cambridge: University of Cambridge Press, 2000); Rian Voet, Feminism and Citizenship (London: Sage, 1998); Melissa S. Williams, Voice, Trust, and Memory. Marginalized Groups and the Failings of Liberal Representation (Princeton: Princeton University Press, 1998); Iris Marion Young, Justice and the Politics of Difference (Princeton: Princeton University Press, 1990); Iris Marion Young, Inclusion and Democracy (Oxford: Oxford University Press, 2000).
7. Hanna F. Pitkin, The Concept of Representation (Berkeley: University of California Press, 1967), 2.
8. Young, Inclusion, 6.
9. Young, Inclusion, 5.
10. Rosabeth Moss Kanter, 'Some Effects of Proportions on Group Life: Skewed Sex Ratios and Responses to Token Women,' American Journal of Sociology 82 5/1977): 965-90.
11. Pitkin, Concept, 60-111.
12. Carole Pateman, The Disorder of Women: Democracy, Feminism and Political Theory (Cambridge: Polity Press, 1989); Joan W. Scott, Parité! Sexual Equality and the Crisis of French Universalism (Chicago: University of Chicago Press, 2005).
13. Marques-Pereira, La citoyenneté, p. 40.
14. Pippa Norris, Electoral Engineering. Voting Rules and Political Behavior (Cambridge: Cambridge University Press, 2004), 190.
15. Norris, Electoral Engineering, p. 190.
16. Norris, Electoral Engineering, p. 191.

17. Anne Marie Goetz and Shireen Hassim, 'Introduction: Women in Power in Uganda and South Africa,' in *No Shortcuts to Power: African Women in Politics and Policy Making*, eds. Anne Marie Goetz and Shireen Hassim (London: Zed Books, 2003), pp. 1-28.

18. www.ipu.org/wmn-f/world.htm; accessed July 2006.

19. In the absence of any authoritative typology for regional composition by continent, for the purposes of this article, Wikipedia's regional categorization was chosen to be used; see en.wikipedia.org/wiki/List_of_countries_by_continent; accessed July 2006.

20. André Laliberté, 'Taiwan: Mobilization des ONG, démocratisation et représentation parlementaire des femmes,' in *Femmes et parlements: un regard international*, ed. Manon Tremblay (Montreal: Remue-ménage, 2005), pp. 369-94.

21. Mariam Abou Zahab, 'Pakistan: D'une rhétorique gouvernementale de façade à la mobilisation du mouvement des femmes en faveur des quotas,' in *Femmes et parlements: un regard international*, ed. Manon Tremblay (Montreal: Remue-ménage, 2005), pp. 275-88.

22. Najma Chowdhury, 'Bangladesh: Identités marginales et voix effacées des femmes au Jatiya Sangsad,' in *Femmes et parlements: un regard international*, ed. Manon Tremblay (Montreal: Remue-ménage, 2005), pp. 175-203.

23. Nadia Rifaat, 'Égypte: Une conjoncture défavorable à la représentation parlementaire des femmes,' in *Femmes et parlements: un regard international*, ed. Manon Tremblay (Montreal: Remue-ménage, 2005), pp. 85-110.

24. N. Guillermo Molinelli, 'Argentina: The (No) Ceteris Paribus Case,' in *Electoral Systems in Comparative Perspective. Their Impact on Women and Minorities*, eds. Wilma Rule and Joseph F. Zimmerman (Westport: Greenwood Press, 1994), pp. 197-202.

25. Mona Lena Krook, 'Politicizing Representation: Campaigns for Candidate Gender Quotas Worldwide' (Ph. D. diss., Columbia University, 2005), pp. 60-62. Available: krook.wustl.edu/pdf/krook-dissertation.pdf [22 September 2006].

26. Bang-Soon L Yoon, 'Corée du sud: La représentation des femmes à l'Assemblée nationale dans une société androcentriste et militariste,' in *Femmes et parlements: un regard international*, ed. Manon Tremblay (Montreal: Remue-ménage, 2005), pp. 327-50.

27. Medha Nanivadekar, 'Inde: Les quotas et la représentation politique des femmes: un tour d'horizon,' in *Femmes et parlements: un regard international*, ed. Manon Tremblay (Montreal: Remue-ménage, 2005), pp. 205-24.

28. Pippa Norris, 'Opening the Door: Women leaders and constitution building in Iraq and Afghanistan,' Paper delivered at the 20th International Political Science Association Congress, Fukuoka (Japan), 2006.

29. Among others: Norris, Electoral Engineering; Pamela Paxton, 'Women in National Legislatures: A Cross-National Analysis,' *Social Science Research* 26 4/1997): 442-64; Andrew Reynolds, 'Women in the Legislatures and Executives of the World: Knocking at the Highest Glass Ceiling,' *World Politics* 51 4/1999): 547-72; Andrew Reynolds, Ben Reilly and Andrew Ellis, *Electoral System Design: The New International IDEA Handbook* (Stockholm: International IDEA, 2005), 37, 60–1; Wilma Rule, 'Electoral Systems, Contextual Factors and Women's Opportunity

for Election to Parliament in Twenty-Three Democracies,' Western Political Quarterly 40 3/1987): 477-98; Wilma Rule, 'Parliaments of, by, and for the People: Except for Women?' in *Electoral Systems in Comparative Perspective. Their Impact on Women and Minorities*, eds. Wilma Rule and Joseph F. Zimmerman (Westport: Greenwood Press, 1994), pp. 15-30; Wilma Rule and Pippa Norris, 'Anglo and Minority Women's Underrepresentation in Congress: Is the Electoral System the Culprit?,' in *Electoral Systems in Comparative Perspective*, eds. Wilma Rule and Joseph F. Zimmerman (Westport: Greenwood Press, 1992), pp. 41-54.

30. Karen Beckwith, 'Comparative Research and Electoral Systems: Lessons from France and Italy,' *Women and Politics* 12 3/1992): 1-33; R. Darcy, Susan Welch and Janet Clark, *Women, Elections, and Representation*, second ed. (Lincoln: University of Nebraska Press, 1994), 147; Sheri Kunovich and Pamela Paxton, 'Pathways to Power: The Role of Political Parties in Women's National Political Representation,' American Journal of Sociology 111 2/2005): 505-552; Mercedes Mateo Diaz, Representing Women? Female legislators in West European Parliaments (Colchester: ECPR Press, 2005), pp. 51, 81.

31. Some countries combined both reserved seats and legal quotas, hence a total from 17 countries (as shown in Table 2) to 14.

32. According to David M. Farrell, *Electoral Systems. A Comparative Introduction* (Houndmills: Palgrave, 2001), 46-7; Reynolds, Reilly and Ellis, *Electoral System Design*, 117; Norris, *Electoral Engineering*, p. 41.

33. Farrell, *Electoral Systems*, 44-5; Norris, *Electoral Engineering*, 41, Reynolds, Reilly and Ellis, *Electoral System Design*, p. 44.

34. Three countries have both reserved seats and legal quotas, hence a total from 14 (as shown in Table 2) to 11 countries.

35. Countries with both reserved seats and/or legal quotas and party quotas figure with the first group in light of the fact that they are subject to legal compliance.

36. In 1997, a constitutional amendment was passed which allows the President to appoint twelve nominated seats in parliament. In the past, six of these seats have been reserved for women (see www.quotaproject.org/displayCountry. cfm?CountryCode=KE; accessed July 2006).

37. Krook, *Politicizing Representation*, 38-41.

38. Drude Dahlerup, 'Quotas are Changing the History of Women,' in *The Implementation of Quotas: African Experiences. Quota Report Series No 3*, ed. International IDEA (Stockholm: International IDEA, 2004), pp. 16-20.

39 . Ronald Inglehart and Pippa Norris, *Rising Tide. Gender Equality and Cultural Change around the World* (Cambridge: Cambridge University Press, 2003), 141. See also Pippa Norris and Ronald Inglehart, 'Cultural Obstacles to Equal Representation,' Journal of Democracy 12 3/2001): 126-140.

40. Brigitte Geissel and Evelin Hust, 'Democratic Mobilization through Quotas: Experiences in India and Germany,' Journal of Commonwealth and Comparative Politics 43 2/2005): 222-244.

41. For an excellent overview of quota in South Asia see Shirin M. Rai, Farzana Bari, Nazmunessa Mahtab and Bidyut Mohanty, 'South Asia: gender quotas and the politics of empowerment—a comparative study,' in *Women, Quotas and Politics*, ed. Drude Dahlerup (London: Routledge, 2006), pp. 222-45.

42. See Norris, 'Opening the Door'.

References

Abou Zahab, Mariam. 'Pakistan: D'une rhétorique gouvernementale de façade à la mobilization du mouvement des femmes en faveur des quotas.' In *Femmes et parlements: un regard international*, ed. Manon Tremblay, pp. 275-88. Montreal: Remue-ménage, 2005.

Beckwith, Karen. 'Comparative Research and Electoral Systems: Lessons from France and Italy.' *Women and Politics 12* (3/1992): 1-33.

Bratton, Kathleen A. 'Critical Mass Theory Revisited: The Behavior and Success of Token Women in State Legislatures.' *Politics and Gender 1* (1/2005): 97-125.

Childs, Sarah. *New Labour's Women MPs. Women representing women.* London: Routledge, 2004.

Chowdhury, Najma. 'Bangladesh: Identités marginales et voix effacées des femmes au Jatiya Sangsad' in *Femmes et parlements: un regard international*, ed. Manon Tremblay, pp. 175-203. Montreal: Remue-ménage, 2005.

Dahlerup, Drude. 'Quotas are Changing the History of Women,' in *The Implementation of Quotas: African Experiences. Quota Report Series No 3*, ed. International IDEA, pp. 16-20. Stockholm: International IDEA.

Darcy, R., Susan Welch, and Janet Clark. *Women, Elections, and Representation* and second ed. Lincoln: University of Nebraska Press, 1994.

Farrell, David M. *Electoral Systems. A Comparative Introduction*, Houndmills: Palgrave, 2001.

Geissel, Brigitte, and Evelin Hust. 'Democratic Mobilization through Quotas: Experiences in India and Germany,' *Journal of Commonwealth and Comparative Politics 43* (2/2005): 222-244.

Goetz, Anne Marie, and Shireen Hassim. 'Introduction: Women in Power in Uganda and South Africa.' In *No Shortcuts to Power: African Women in Politics and Policy Making*, eds. Anne Marie Goetz and Shireen Hassim, pp. 1-28. London: Zed Books, 2003.

Grey, Sandra. 'Does Size Matter? Critical Mass and New Zealand's Women MPs,' *Parliamentary Affairs 55* (1/2002): 19-29.

Guillermo Molinelli, N. 'Argentina: The (No) Ceteris Paribus Case,' in *Electoral Systems in Comparative Perspective. Their Impact on Women and Minorities*, eds. Wilma Rule and Joseph F. Zimmerman, 197-202. Westport: Greenwood Press, 1994.

Inglehart, Ronald, and Pippa Norris. *Rising Tide. Gender Equality and Cultural Change around the World*, Cambridge: Cambridge University Press, 2003.

Kanter, Rosabeth Moss. 'Some Effects of Proportions on Group Life: Skewed Sex Ratios and Responses to Token Women,' *American Journal of Sociology 82* (5/1977): 965-990.

Krook, Mona Lena. 'Politicizing Representation: Campaigns for Candidate Gender Quotas Worldwide,' Ph.D. diss., Columbia University, 2005 (available at krook.wustl.edu/pdf/krook-dissertation.pdf).

Kunovich, Sheri, and Pamela Paxton. 'Pathways to Power: The Role of Political Parties in Women's National Political Representation,' *American Journal of Sociology 111* (2/2005): 505-552.

Laliberté, André. 'Taiwan: Mobilization des ONG, démocratization et représentation parlementaire des femmes.' In *Femmes et parlements: un regard international*, ed. Manon Tremblay, 369-394. Montreal: Remue-ménage, 2005.

Marques-Pereira, Bérengère. *La citoyenneté politique des femmes*. Paris: Armand Colin, 2003.

Mateo Diaz, Mercedes. *Representing Women? Female legislators in West European Parliaments*. Colchester: ECPR Press, 2005.

Nanivadekar, Medha. 'Inde: Les quotas et la représentation politique des femmes: un tour d'horizon.' In *Femmes et parlements: un regard international*, ed. Manon Tremblay, pp. 205-24. Montreal: Remue-ménage, 2005.

Norris, Pippa. 'Opening the Door: Women leaders and constitution building in Iraq and Afghanistan,' paper delivered at the 20th International Political Science Association Congress, Fukuoka, Japan, 2006.

Norris, Pippa. *Electoral Engineering. Voting Rules and Political Behavior*, Cambridge: Cambridge University Press, 2004.

Norris, Pippa, and Ronald Inglehart. 'Cultural Obstacles to Equal Representation,' *Journal of Democracy 12* (3/2001): 126-140.

Pateman, Carole. *The Disorder of Women: Democracy, Feminism and Political Theory*, Cambridge: Polity Press, 1989.

Paxton, Pamela. 'Women in National Legislatures: A Cross-National Analysis,' *Social Science Research 26* (4/1997): 442-464.

Phillips, Anne. *The Politics of Presence*, Oxford: Clarendon Press, 1995.

Pitkin, Hanna F. *The Concept of Representation*. Berkeley: University of California Press, 1967.

Rai, Shirin M., Farzana Bari, Nazmunessa Mahtab, and Bidyut Mohanty, 'South Asia: gender quotas and the politics of empowerment—a comparative study,' In *Women, Quotas and Politics*, ed. Drude Dahlerup, pp. 222-45. London: Routledge, 2006.

Reynolds, Andrew. 'Women in the Legislatures and Executives of the World: Knocking at the Highest Glass Ceiling,' *World Politics 51* (4/1999): 547-572.

Reynolds, Andrew, Ben Reilly, and Andrew Ellis. *Electoral System Design: The New International IDEA Handbook*. Stockholm: International IDEA, 2005.

Rifaat, Nadia. 'Égypte: Une conjoncture défavorable à la représentation parlementaire des femmes,' in *Femmes et parlements: un regard international*, ed. Manon Tremblay, pp. 85-110. Montreal: Remue-ménage, 2005.

Rule, Wilma. 'Parliaments of, by, and for the People: Except for Women?' In *Electoral Systems in Comparative Perspective. Their Impact on Women and Minorities*, eds. Wilma Rule and Joseph F. Zimmerman, pp. 15-30. Westport: Greenwood Press, 1994.

Rule, Wilma. 'Electoral Systems, Contextual Factors and Women's Opportunity for Election to Parliament in Twenty-Three Democracies,' *Western Political Quarterly 40* (3/1987): 477-498.

Rule, Wilma, and Pippa Norris. 'Anglo and Minority Women's Underrepresentation in Congress: Is the Electoral System the Culprit?' In *Electoral Systems in Comparative Perspective*, eds. Wilma Rule and Joseph F. Zimmerman, pp. 41-54. Westport: Greenwood Press, 1992.

Scott, Joan W. *Parité! Sexual Equality and the Crisis of French Universalism*, Chicago: University of Chicago Press, 2005.

Siim, Birte. *Gender and Citizenship*. Cambridge: University of Cambridge Press, 2000.

Studlar, Donley T., and Ian McAllister. 'Does a Critical Mass Exist? A comparative analysis of women's legislative representation since 1950,' *European Journal of Political Research 41* (2/2002): 233-253.

Towns, Ann. 'Understanding the Effects of Larger Ratios of Women in National Legislatures: Proportions and Gender Differentiation in Sweden and Norway,' *Women and Politics 25* (1-2/2003): 1-29.

Tremblay, Manon. 'The Substantive Representation of Women and PR: Some Reflections on the Role of Surrogate Representation and Critical Mass,' *Politics and Gender 2* (4/2006).

Voet, Rian. *Feminism and Citizenship*, London: Sage, 1998.

Weldon, S. Laurel. 'Beyond Bodies: Institutional Sources of Representation for Women in Democratic Policymaking,' *Journal of Politics 64* (4/2002): 1153-1174.

Williams, Melissa S. *Voice, Trust, and Memory. Marginalized Groups and the Failings of Liberal Representation*, Princeton: Princeton University Press, 1998.

Yoon, Bang-Soon L. 'Corée du sud: La représentation des femmes à l'Assemblée nationale dans une société androcentriste et militariste,' in *Femmes et parlements: un regard international*, ed. Manon Tremblay, 327-350. Montreal: Remue-ménage, 2005.

Young, Iris Marion. *Inclusion and Democracy*, Oxford: Oxford University Press, 2000.

Young, Iris Marion. *Justice and the Politics of Difference*, Princeton: Princeton University Press, 1990.

5

Role of Women in Peace and Conflict: Suffering of Afghan Women

Khalida Ghaus

Introduction

Ever since the end of the Second World War, the world has experienced some of the worst conflicts within and between states. The multi-faceted nature of the conflicts has resulted in causing tensions both at the inter and intra-state level and carries within it the potential of escalation. These conflicts have in recent times resulted in posing new challenges to states, such as increased human, arms and drug trafficking, displacement of people, and the making of the refugee problem. The nature of the escalation emphasizes the need to improve the state-society equation[1] that prevails particularly within the developing societies.

Keeping the focus within the delineated parameters, the analysis is restricted to some of the recent trends seen in the international political arena with a particular focus on conflict—its various types and nature, the tendencies seen in the making of a conflict and its implications/consequences for the women and the overall security—related issues. The chapter also briefly refers to the role of the state, to issues of governance and development besides the crises of a soft-state. The consequences of the latter, in particular, are difficult to control, unlike the inter-state conflicts which can be avoided by use of preventive diplomacy. The understanding of the issues does not escape the challenges of international developments caused by the sudden demise of the Cold War, the collapse of command and control economies, the fiscal crisis of the welfare state[2] besides the crises of the failed states in Afghanistan and parts of Africa where the states failed in protecting their people. Human welfare in such cases was marginalized due to the weak and fractured state capability—which (in the case of Afghanistan) prevented the available capability being used for the society's benefit.[3] No focus, whatsoever, was given to improve the much needed state capability. Improvement which helps make the state more responsive to societal needs mainly by closing the gap between the people and the government by decentralizing the structures and encouraging broad-based participation, which in turn, helps private sector to strengthen, increases growth and consolidates development. This, however, was missing in the case of Afghanistan due to multiple reasons. Foremost in this regard was the nature of political governance, which, throughout its contemporary history has negated popular participation and strengthened totalitarianism by continued monarchism, warlordism and Talibanization besides the Soviet occupation. The other augmenting and causative factors are tribalism, violent ethnicity, absence of nation-state and an absence of conducive environment both for men and women. Seemingly, the hierarchy of low politics and high politics constructed by the realist did not hold swing and contributed to the surge of sectarianism, tribalism, warlordism and extremism in all its various forms and manifestations. In brief the developments were such that resulted in initially discontent, Discontent that was left unattended and which eventually graduated to the state level, tearing apart the very fabric of the nation and society. In Afghanistan and to some extent in Kashmir,[4] poverty, alongwith political and religious extremism became one of the major augmenting factor for making conflicts multifaceted in the two societies, thus pushing forward the issue of internal displacement besides institutionalizing inequalities and inequities as seen in the case of Afghanistan. The two consequential developments, contributed to the grievances and injustices and led to socio-political unrest and conflict.

In Afghanistan, the 'social gap' also widened and resulted in generating deprivation and marginalization, particularly of women in Afghan society. Unfortunately, the 'social exclusion'[5] not only resulted in excluding people of all ethnic communities from participating in the affairs of the society, it also led to gender disparities and political fragmentation of society. Particularly, the threat to societal security during the nineties was an outcome of religio-political and ethno-political strife in which religion became politicized, particularly during the Taliban rule. The consequence of the deterioration was the total and final collapse of the state system, paving the way for religiously motivated ideological conceptions and symbols which failed either to build or nurture any popular appeal primarily because of their exclusive and divisive nature. The politics of exclusivity[6] only moved Afghanistan towards centralization and personalization of political authority (during Taliban rule) and further pushed the state structure towards an intentional un-accommodation. Internal security could probably have been saved by preserving and consolidating 'social cohesion' which was fractured mainly because of the adversarial relations between and amongst ethnic communities on the one hand and the state on the other. The different exploited and oppressed Afghan sections perceived each other as an adversary and struggled to alter these relations. State policy, thus, generated intolerance and extremism of a volume that negated all civilized forms of rule.[7] Women no longer had access to a number of administrative and social services or to the education system in Afghanistan. Measures[8] brought about drastic reduction in the work of certain non-governmental organizations and United Nations agencies such as UNICEF and United Nations Children's Fund, while organizations, such as OXFAM and Save the Children (UK) had to entirely suspend their programmes in the south of the country. The developments changed the existing socio-political system and helped institutionalized violence[9] mainly by selling its self-conceived ideological justification to legitimize its acts and the changed social behavior.[10] Behaviour that sanctioned violence against women. Desporte[11] drawing attention towards criminal behaviour once stated that 'violence is consubstantial with war, which is a legitimate way of expressing violence. The primary instrument of war is the use of force in the form of organized violence, whether real or virtual. It is through violence or the threat of violence that the will of the adversary is subdued.' In Afghanistan it was the threat of punishment that forced a change in socio-cultural norms causing uncertainty and agony to Afghan women. Earlier in the nineties, the United Nations Office for Afghanistan (UNHCR) requested the United Nations High Commissions for refugees for an intra-agency emergency operation. The UNHCR till then had focused itself with the voluntary repatriation programme of the refugees from the two bordering countries of Afghanistan, namely, Pakistan and Iran. In its initial involvement with internally displaced persons,[12] UNHCR helped in providing shelter to the uprooted in newly set-up camps besides helping those who desired to be relocated in Kabul.

The contradictory developments of several years besides the indicators for future difficulties necessitated the reappraisal and reassessment of the continued relevance of established approaches to the present nature of problems of refugees as well as those displaced. The new strategies/concerns identified[13] and initiated by the UNHCR could not help evolve an engendered approach towards re-establishment and reintegration of the returnees. Repatriation needed to be accompanied by gender sensitive policies/plans both by the Afghan government and international agencies. The peculiar problem[14] demanded equal attention to both the humanitarian and strategic needs. Unfortunately, the type of protection which females required largely remained unaddressed. For instance, the design and management of refugee camps in Pakistan either did not take into account the practical needs of women[15] such as pregnant women or those having young children and their being at risk of sexual violence, or else they have proven exiguous. The absence of proper measures addressing their practical needs only resulted in marginalizing their position and made them vulnerable to all forms of discrimination and exploitation.[16] The protracted political violence thus had a multifaceted effect on young girls and women of Afghanistan, foremost being social transformation (which was not discreet) and which led to the eventual brutalization and criminalization of the very structure of Afghan society. While men were occupied with conflict and joining militias, women stayed either at home or were forced to flee. In the former situation, they feared compulsory abeyance by use of force[17] while, in the latter situation they feared physical abuse.[18] In both the cases, consequential developments forced women headed households, thus making the experience of the war/conflict different for women. The experience being contextual and shifting was reflective of the different phases of violence. Disaggregated data, unfortunately, is not available and whatever statistics are available on the nature of causalities that have occurred are unreliable.[19]

Due to the absence of an objective analysis of the Afghan conflict, a proper understanding of the motivation of the different players involved in the conflict and a holistic approach of the human conditions could not be built. The discourse adopted was political—which interprets the human interests purely in geo-political terms totally sidelining the people's perspective of the issue. The measures taken and the programmes initiated therefore necessitated a reconsideration of the approach. There is a need to probe into the linkages that exist between the decision-making and interests that exist at the local, national and international level. Moreover, in this particular case, the conflict, its repercussions and the responses adopted locally or by internationally humanitarian regime were not viewed in relation to gender/power relations.[20] The Afghan conflict brought into the forefront the element of subjugation—a consequence of restrictions on fundamental rights that forced women into displacement. Women forbidden to leave home without being escorted by men could not seek basic health care and food for their children. Doctors, invariably male, were prohibited from providing any reproductive healthcare to women, girls were prevented from schooling and widows forced to beg. All this pushed women out of public life and made this most vulnerable group yet more vulnerable.[21] According to the UNHCR, over a million refugees continue to live in camps[22] in the NWFP and Balochistan province while over a million are internally displaced. Those who have moved out of camps are not registered as refugees and live in cities in Pakistan. For refugees, the UNHCR provided some 55.6 million dollars in humanitarian aid in the early eighties; however, by 1995 the World Food Program and the UNHCR Care and Maintenance Program were shelved. The suspension of WFP assistance resulted in wheat shortage for refugees. According to Zohra Rasekh,[23] 'life in the refugee camps is a very unnatural kind of life for women. The basic needs of life are not being met; they are forced to live in makeshift tents or in mud houses which have no showers and are forced to observe *purdah*.' She complained of not being able to go home, for life without a man was difficult.

The victimization and marginalization was not limited to refugees in the camps alone. Many migrated out of camps over time, particularly after 1995, when general food distribution in camps ended. Some refugees settled in cities on arrival, many among them educated and professional Afghans. Urban refugees were generally ignored as the host government never wanted them in the city and barred UNHCR from registering or assisting refugees in urban centres. Social ills like crime, drugs, weapons and prostitution were blamed on refugees in urban areas.

Those who moved out of camps and settled in Karachi[24] are largely concentrated in Metroville and Gulshan-e-Iqbal. Practically all are involved in economic activities in the informal sector. The Shigri report also indicated their involvement in various types of crimes. Particularly over the last couple of decades, credible evidence is available of mafias involved in the trafficking of females and forcing women into prostitution. The organized racketeers working within Pakistan and collaborating with the regional network made the trade a risk minimum–maximum profit business. Unfortunately, women who become useless for the traffickers (because of disease/illness or age) also find their way into the informal sector to sustain themselves economically. Usually, whatever form of economic activity they are involved in, the element of coercion, exploitation and harassment is present. They all live in abject poverty and are grateful for whatever economic opportunities come their way. There is no assurance of continuity of work or wage and their vulnerability places them in a very exploitative position both by the employers and law enforcers. The presence of middlemen and the absence of any regulatory structures in the informal sector all contribute towards their suffering and exploitation. With restricted access to illegal women (including Afghan women) working in the informal sector, there exists a need to identify ways to provide relief to these women by looking into the issues confronted by them in a holistic manner. The government both at the federal and provincial level must acknowledge the presence of illegal women working in the sector and take appropriate remedial measures to prevent the exploitation of Afghan women. These women continue to live on a day to day basis in small and congested houses without proper ventilation, poor sanitary conditions, no running water and no access to healthcare. They are lonely, because of their alien status and because of cultural and social constraints. The situation definitely needs both preventive and protective measures. The number of Afghan women working in the sector is large, yet, their problems continue to be unattended. The most challenging problem is the crime network. Recognition of their presence besides some serious and concerted measures is required both at the governmental level and by civil society organizations. The initiatives taken so far are few, far apart and cosmetic in nature.

The Gender Differentials

Women globally and regionally continue to see violence and bloodshed as ritual. In addition, she is the head of a household with no idea how to 'head' it; she has lost her traditional anchor, her husband; she has lost her home; she has no idea about what the future holds and is insecure; decisions intimately impacting her life are being made by people and institutions she has never seen; and she can do nothing about it. She cannot reconstruct with material aid what she has lost—her family, home, community and security—all integral in forming her identity. She proceeds, therefore, by reconstructing her identity.

Mehr fled the Soviet occupation with her family, hoping to send her son to the United States for education once in Pakistan. Instead, her son was trained in artillery capability and sent back to Afghanistan as part of the Taliban force. In the face of a monolithic, homogenous 'refugee' identity, their voices and experience of conflict remained largely absent. This undifferentiated image of refugees formed the basis of humanitarian intervention, which consequently remained largely gender blind. Gender differences were crucial to address in order to understand the social process resulting from rapid changes witnessed by refugees and also to respond with well informed, equitable options. Societal flux could have been used to address historic and current gender gaps. There were widespread changes in gender roles, with many refugee women left to become household heads and bread earners, thus changing patterns of division of labour. For many women, this necessitated a foray into the public sphere—working outside the home for remuneration for the first time. Initially, their condition also compromised their access to food and basic services because of the international aid bodies' shortsightedness, which did not realize this as a barrier upfront. Many initial food distribution programmes targeted only male heads of households. The only jobs many were equipped to do were menial, domestic chores that they performed at home. This created a class structure, as these jobs are poorly paid. Many women, who were not as poor in Afghanistan but could not work outside the home for cultural reasons, were relegated to the lower income class by virtue of their jobs outside camps. Within camps, many women were provided training in skills to be midwives and do embroidery and stitching for livelihood.

In the face of monumental change, from being shut out of public domains to being sole providers, the traditional boundaries could have been further challenged and renegotiated to include women in other non-conformist types of work. It is becoming evident from accounts of returning refugees that women are expected to continue these activities on their return to Afghanistan. The social institution also in disarray, opened up for the reformulation of what defined family. Ill-equipped to deal with the scale of change, many women looked for support where they could. There was a marked increase in situational and economically driven marriages, sometimes of girls in early teens, as mothers wanted someone else to take on the 'responsibility'. Another manifestation was remarriages in age groups which women may not have considered before. Widowhood affected physical safety, identity and mobility of women as they were seen as women without 'protectors', and therefore became easier targets for crime and duplicity. Women as seen in the case of several post-conflict situations lose their traditional roles and responsibilities and support networks. Extended family, neighbourhood and community often provide women their security. The lack of safety that they face is usually because of altered social and familial structures that would otherwise have provided stability and protection. While home is a primary site of violence for many, it is also a positive locus of identity.

Donor organizations and the international community struggled to keep up and provide basic necessities, with little funds to venture beyond that. But with gender analysis, fine tuned interventions could have made them more responsive to women's needs. Gender based analysis was imperative in order to assess the experience of men and women in light of their different social realities, life expectations, and economic circumstances. Integration of these differences must be ensured, for it is crucial that the gender analysis is not focused just on outcomes but on the concepts, arguments and language used to justify the policy. How needs are interpreted and discussed is intrinsic to policy development. A feature that stands out in the case of Afghan refugees, as with women impacted by conflict elsewhere in the world, is their version and quest for peace. 'Men are more sensitive to whose bombs are raining on them—for women, bombs are bombs, Soviet, American, whatever'.[25] Most testimonials of Afghan women refugees, the Palestinians or even Iraqis reflect a deep rooted, intense wish that the fighting and war would stop. Each one has been intimately acquainted with and bereaved by loss of family, friends, jobs, security, home, and a way of life. However, the male members continue to be pulled in this dragnet of violence. The Afghan males were recruited to go back to Afghanistan to fight the *jihad* along with the *mujahideen*. Even the women who stayed behind were co-opted into power struggles. Each refugee camp had a power structure that each of the camp's households had to swear allegiance to as a precondition for eligibility to receive food, shelter and security. For example, Shamshatoo camp 'belonged' to Hizb-i-Islami, and allegiance had to lie with its head, warlord Gulbaddin Hikmatyar. The Jalozai camp was the power hold of warlord Abdul Sayyaf. Thus, homeland politics projected across the camps and many had to change loyalties out of compulsion as dissenters faced violence. The camp's inhabitants became sharply divided along religious and ethnic lines, mirroring ethnic and political conflicts within Afghan society. In these camps, Afghan refugee men received training and indoctrination from agencies, the most important being the CIA. Overriding women's concerns, the state of Pakistan allowed this for its own political purposes, as it needed this manpower to fight it's proxy war in Afghanistan. The international and the aid community overlooked this in the face of the ensuing geo-politics. Moreover, the different actors within the camps—Afghan political leadership, donor agencies and Pakistani administrative structures—manipulated particular images of the ideal family and the role of women. While men were fighting the war, women had to carry the 'noble' burden of culture and identity vested in their bodies and actions. They were thus 'vulnerable' to attacks from their own community for not conforming, as well as, targeted by enemies to subvert this very role.[26] For the Afghan women in camps, ultra conservative religious edicts were declared and circulated. One such *fatwa* stated 'Women, without necessity, do not have the right to go out in public and in the schools. We ask the leaders to forbid Muslim women, according to Sharia texts. If this action is not taken, the success of *jihad* will turn into failure and we will face harsh problems.'[27] The connection between this environment for women and success of *jihad* is clear. The checks on women's mobility and literacy gave Afghan men psychological assurance that their women would not be interacting with other men in person or in writing in their absence.[28] This was evidently against the interest and wishes of women—a factor which remained irrelevant. 'Afghan women refugees in Pakistan do not seem to enjoy any immunity from the consequences of Talibanization in their own country... the Talibanization of refugee camps in Pakistan was accomplished and the refugee women were clearly the main victims.'[29] Women's experiences centered on ensuring survival for their families. Women-headed households in particular were unequivocal about their need to live in a place where they could access food assistance and receive tents without violence or patronage. In hindsight, if women's perspective[30] and needs had been valued, the support for the *mujahideen* and training of Taliban may have been stopped in its ranks.

The Pushtun women suffered, as did ones from different ethnic groups, but the 'fear alleviation strategies' should have taken into account the need to have a fuller understanding of how security is different for females. This is testified by trends showing feminization of households in refugee camps across Pakistan. Encapsulated in these facts are ethnic, class and gender differences and within these threat perceptions are the variations in what they were fleeing from, what they were running to and what they were in search of. Such are the differences that make the issue of passivity (particularly among Asian refugee women) necessary for serious studies. All movies and documentaries portray them as passive victims, overlooking their agency and survival bids, in which they used whatever means were at their disposal. In the face of restrictive cultural and legal practices, 'defiance of these norms was not only a personal act but also a political rebellion against a state imposed institution of patriarchy... the refugee process did not recognize the doctrine of patriarchy as a political belief and thus relegated women's fight against it to the realm of personal actions'.[31] Similarly, a physician for Human Rights study[32] of Afghan women in Afghanistan and refugee camps in Pakistan found women's physical and mental health damaged. They attributed their poor mental health to Taliban's official policies towards women, besides living in armed conflict, devastating poverty and underdevelopment. For most part, for the international community, capacity building meant teaching them skills and organization, not encompassing or enabling them to cope psycho-socially. Neither did the healthcare providers have clear protocols for addressing violence and no psychosocial programmes existed for camp-based refugees that targeted gender based violence, even though UNFPA cooperated with United Nations High Commissioner for Refugees (UNHCR) in provision of refugee healthcare, of which prevention and response to Gender Based Violence is a stated objective. Research on domestic violence particularly against women in Gaza refugee camps has shown increase in physical, mental, psychological and sexual violence against women including incest and rape, in relation to the increasing 'external' violence, but no such investigative research was carried out in the Afghan refugee camps in Pakistan. The Afghan-women-related non-governmental organizations in the recent past developed informal mechanisms to address victims of violence, but 'the need to operate under the radar of the Taliban and their inability to provide anything other than emotional support has restricted their impact.

Nevertheless, it bears consideration that in a culture of silence, it was difficult to determine the extent of war-related sexual violence against Afghan women. Inspite of rape and abductions taking place generally, there was no corresponding attention extended to women refugees victimized by it. In the Balkan Wars and the Rwandan genocide, sexual violence did not go unnoticed, unlike the German crimes in the Soviet Union and the regime's relentless propaganda certainly contributed to the terrible violence against German women in East Prussia. An absolutely appalling example of vengeance being used as a justification is the reminder that the Red Army officers and soldiers also raped Ukrainian, Russian and Belarusian women and girls released from slave labour in Germany. The widespread raping of women undermines any attempts of justifying Red Army behaviour on the grounds of revenge for German brutality in the Soviet Union.[33]

In patriarchal constructs, prioritization of national concerns over gender rights is routine, pushing women further away from the public productive sphere into the domestic realm. Looking at the experiences of refugees, it can be said that experiences change on an extensive scale. The change is not just of physical location, but social institutions, identity, relations, land, culture and societal fabric. While the dislocation is at enormous cost, it also offers the chance to make certain positive changes, some permanently. In this reference, the case of Afghan women refugees was a tragic opportunity not seized the way it could have been. The overall structure of patriarchy was reconstituted in camps after migration, with minor alterations. Restrictions on women's mobility were maintained, decision-making powers held by Maliks or male household heads while women's needs and opinions remained sidelined and irrelevant; violence against them was tolerated and their status was elevated only in a narrow sense—as upholders of identity and culture. Men continued to be the main players outside the home domain and where women worked outside it was in keeping with tasks socially accepted as extension of the home domain. The division of labor also remained gendered and imbalanced and the system was allowed to self-perpetuate.

To say that the bulk of effort directed towards Afghan refugees in Pakistan were gender blind is not to say they were women blind. The refugees were recipients of many women specific initiatives, but the term gender encompasses the relations between women and men and with larger society. Those remained largely unaddressed. The levels of poverty were high and survival mechanisms low, so women had to work, and the world gave them options and skills to do it. Their status, however, remained beyond the world's scope when faced with more 'pressing needs'. Gender relations in pre-conflict situations often set the stage for women's and men's options during and after the conflict. The dominant socio-political and economic norms often influence the scope and potential women and men have for action in conflict and post-conflict situations particularly by when initiatives are designed to respond to a specific set of circumstances such as, the emergency relief measure undertaken to respond to conflict situations. As a result when the imperatives of necessity changed, so did their 'empowerment'. In the case of Afghan women, a large number of women became bread earners and decision makers in time of war while the 'men were away'. However in recent years with men returning from battlefield,[34] women were supposed to simultaneously 'withdraw' accordingly. Similarly, the Israeli forces using multiple strategies to suppress the unprecedented political mobilization of Palestinian women, have arrested and interrogated Palestinian women not only because of their political activities but also to put pressure on their families. Harassment and physical violence are not unheard of in the case of Palestinian struggle. During the last couple of decades, the organizations for Women Political Prisoners (WOFPP) in Tel Aviv and Jerusalem have received numerous complaints of physical violence committed by Israeli military forces against Palestinian women in the occupied territories. Such incidents occur not only during interrogation but also in connection with street patrols and the suppression of demonstrations. The Indian government in its effort to suppress the Kashmiri uprising also used rape as a weapon. The three examples cited are indicative of the fact that physical violence continues to be used as a means of targeting women whom the security personnel accuse of being 'militant sympathizers'. Rape, therefore, continues to be used as a tool.

Peace being inextricably linked with equality between women, men and development, the governments, international organizations and the public in recent times have become increasingly aware of the problems faced by women.[35] The present discourse therefore, is inclusive of the following changing dynamics:

1. Inter and intra-state Conflicts being an ongoing reality affects both women and men. Unfortunately gross and systematic violations continue to occur and international humanitarian law violated. The violations have specific bearing on the safety of women and children. The most debated are the massive violations of human rights as a strategy of war including systematic rape of women in war situations, mass exodus of population and internal displacement. In short, the impact of violence against women and violation of the human rights of women in such situations is experienced by women of all ages. Its impact on the economy and her economic conditions also puts women at a greater risk for having to engage in 'survival' sex or sexual bartering, exposing women to HIV. In the nineties, the US State Department noted that 'worldwide peacekeeping operations may pose a danger of spreading HIV.' Increasing concerns led to an unprecedented discussion in the Security Council in 2000 when US Ambassador Richard Holbrook introduced discussions on the relationship between HIV, conflict and security.[36] The United Nations Security Council resolution 1308, adopted in the year 2000, recognizing the urgency, recommended that HIV prevention be incorporated into all peacekeeping initiatives.[37] While Resolution 1325 adopted by the Security Council addressed the issues of women and armed conflict, the Security Council specifically called for 'training guidelines and materials on the protection, rights and particular needs of women, as well as on the importance of involving women in all peacekeeping and peace-building measures.'

2. The glaring gaps in women's protection over the years have exposed the systematic failure of the humanitarian community to reach women. Although women have benefited from humanitarian assistance, their specific needs are largely neglected, particularly, in relation to physical and psychosocial care, economic security, HIV/AIDS and displacement. Women continue to have the least access to protection and assistance provided by the state or

international organizations. In Afghanistan, for instance, women have not created a new era yet. Afghan women are neither secure nor safe. The status of Afghan women is as precarious as the stability of the country's transition to peace. Women's gains thus are lost through wars and conflicts. The second category consists of societies moving towards extremism where militarization has bred violence that have shattered women's life before, during and after conflict. Within Afghan society, conflicts have also emerged between the concepts of modernization and traditionalism, religion and modernity and the feudal mind-set and modernity.[38] The latter existing on ethnic lines are directly connected to issues of equal opportunities, distribution of resources and the process of decision making. All three categories of conflict have had its consequences for women in Pakistan. For example, the violence seen in the ethnic conflict in Karachi in 1980s caused large-scale internal displacement. With conceptual conflicts having its repercussions for women, it is important to bring conceptual clarity both at the governmental and societal levels. The present use of the two modalities of social engineering[39] have caused alarm and misgivings about the intentions and the strategy involved. Perhaps, it requires modalities that involves existence of buffer organizations between the ruler and the ruled, democratic procedures through which participation and governance is achieved, and use of dialogical reasoning between all stakeholders.

Realizing that violence will not abate while weapons are easy to acquire and that the easy flow of weapons in the community translate into violence against women in the home and on the street, women's movements globally worked for the broader emphasis on the issues of security—one that is inclusive of human security and not restricted to military security only. The developments thus emphasize the need to understand conflicts and its impact on women. Whereas, when there is talk about women's contribution to peace and security, the assumption is that, women by nature are more pacifist and peace loving. For women, peace building and peace preservation are intimately connected with issues of daily life and survival. They are, therefore, perceived as having a more honest and genuine interest in stopping conflict. With limited access to political participation and decision-making, they are less rigid and more open to listening and finding an equitable solution. They are viewed with less suspicion by the 'enemy' and are considered to have empathy—a quality that is necessary for managing conflict and conflict resolution. The problem, however, is that since women have a limited role in political decision-making, the solutions and programmes they propose are neither taken seriously nor implemented. Nevertheless, in recent times women have been at the forefront of activities for peace ranging from spontaneous demonstrations[40] to organized groups protesting against invasions, violence and civilian killings. Notable is the women's active participation in the anti-war demonstrations against the War on Terrorism[41] in Europe and elsewhere. Their peace-building campaigns have categorically stated their concerns regarding the perception of women as victims during violent conflict and that war obscures their role as peace-makers in reconstruction and peace building processes, besides their exclusion from decision-making processes in peace negotiations. In short, for any long term durable peace their inclusion as full partners in peace-building is increasingly gaining importance.

3. Women's empowerment in general needs to be ensured. The world at large needs to recognize the fact that the opinion of fifty per cent of the world population on security related issues cannot be kept in hibernation, and for this to happen, not only the approach towards peace needs to be changed but also the mindset of both men and women. During the last decade, a conscious effort has been made at the international level to include information on gender mainstreaming throughout peacekeeping missions and all other aspects relating to women and girls, such as inclusion of gender units/advisors in the peace-keeping operations in Kosovo and East Timor. The United Nations, however, continues to emphasize the need to protect women during and after the conflict and encourages women's participation in conflict prevention and peace building. The Security Council reaffirmed this in its Resolution 1366[42] on conflict prevention by calling for greater attention to a gender perspective in the implementation of peace keeping and peace-building mandates as well as in conflict prevention. While the importance of gender is well recognized, yet early warning information from and about women is missing. It is important that fact-finding missions to areas of potential conflict must include and consult the gender expertise. The 2001 statement by the Foreign Ministers of the G8 nations on 'Strengthening the Role of Women in Conflict Prevention' describes the opportunities available for supporting and identifying local women who represent an influential voice for peace, and delineates the resources needed to carry this out. The G8 statement emphasis is on the importance of systematic involvement of women in the prevention and resolution of conflicts and in peace building, as well as their full and equal participation in all phases of conflict prevention, resolution and peace-building. It also encourages the participation of all actors of civil society, including women's organizations, in conflict prevention and conflict resolution, and encourages the sharing of experiences and best practices. However, all of this should have been followed by the implementation of policies both at the international and domestic level, thus turning policies into action.

4. Justice for female victims of gender based violence in armed conflict is a matter of international and local concern and must include a detailed consideration of such programme and services that take into account the reintegration of victims in the community. Too often in post-conflict settings, female survivors of assault are left with little community support, insufficient economic means to sustain themselves, and with profound physical and psychological trauma. Communities often blame women and girls abducted by members of warring factions for what happened to them. When conflict ends, such women and girls often do not return home for fear of being rejected by their families primarily because of the stigma attached to physical violence. Victims feel discouraged from coming forward to seek help. It would be a gross injustice if women continue to suffer in peaceful times as well. Governments need to review laws and customary practices to eliminate all impediments to women's equal and autonomous decision-making. UN Security Council Resolution 1325[45] recognized the important role women can and should be playing in pre-and post-conflict societies, as a means to prevent conflict and bring sustainable peace besides eliminating risk of violence in times of war.

5. Women in conflict, with its changing nature, are central victims but marginalized as agents in some cases. The hostile cultural environment places them in a more abusive position and makes conflict more on gender lines (physical, cultural and economic violence being rampant—even became institutionalized, such as in Taliban era). Neither do we see a realization emerging that keeps in consideration the nature and the type of violence and hostility that women face in these various conflict situations. Women also, unfortunately, have failed in generating any activism primarily due to two reasons: absence of a critical mass which requires a collective effort of thirty to thirty-five per cent of people, and the absence of any unitary action—which again is prevented by the division of society on ethnic lines. The two together have proven disadvantageous for women and made them more vulnerable to victimization. Any attempt to see their activity as non-political would jeopardize all chances of their effective role in formal politics. It is important that governments ensure the sanctity of international humanitarian law and norms by all segments of the societies involved in conflict. The active involvement of women in international humanitarian assistance programmes and in decision-making and implementation of all socio-economic-political programmes must be ensured. For security does not mean the end of war, it means the ability to go about your business safely, in a safe environment, to go to work, to go home and to travel outside your home knowing that your family is safe and will not be harmed. Security therefore requires civil society regaining faith and democratic control of all those organizations that have

authority to use or threaten to use force. This goal can't be achieved without building a security sector that protects and involves women.

NOTES

1. The very nature of the disequilibrium causes disillusionment and the sense of deprivation among masses.
2. Huma Baqai has extensively discussed the issue in her (unpublished) Ph.D dissertation on the *Non-Military Sources of Conflicts in South Asia 1971-2000.*
3. This is particularly true for the Taliban period for no initiative was taken to strengthen nation building. On the contrary, despite its negative connotations, all efforts were directed towards strengthening the obsolete state structure/s which contributed towards trampling the fundamental principles of the state–society equation. An equation that is essential for the development and progress of people living in a state irrespective of gender, class or creed.
4. Reference is made to the pre-partition socio-economic-political developments of United Kashmir. The intention is not to underestimate the repercussions of socio-political instabilities/upheavals in making societies vulnerable to conflicts at society level. They all lead to increased poverty—which (if) unattended intensifies issue of displacement and refugee-problem.
5. The concept of 'Social Exclusion' basically originated in France. It has been defined as a development which ruptures the social bonds in which individuals or groups belonging to communities are excluded from full participation in the society within which they live. For a detailed discussion of the concept see, Arjan de. Haan *'Social Exclusion': An Alternative Concept for the Study of Deprivation'.* The importance of social cohesion and its consequences for women are discussed in Courtney W. Holland ed. *Religious fundamentalism and Human Rights of women Macmillan.*
6. The term has been used to describe the increasing divide between civilizations by Akbar S. Ahmad in *Islam Under Siege.*
7. Different perceptions existed about the nature of the conflict that existed amongst and between the different groups in Afghanistan. The conflict, particularly during the rule of the Taliban was ideological. Islam as perceived by the Taliban was different from the common understanding of Islam. It relegated women to the lowest rung of the social structures causing immense damage to their security, self-esteem, dignity and human rights besides initiating a global debate on the radicalization of Islam. According to Foucault 'power is embedded in the social structures of the society that defines knowledge, identity and regimes of truth. These, in turn, manifest themselves into institutions and agents'. Quoted in *Gender, Peace and Conflict* edited by Inger Skelsback and Dan Smith, p-5.
8. In October 1996, after the Taliban took control, sixteen rules of conduct were decreed, one of which prohibited women from working anywhere other than in the medical profession. Even then, their work was subjected to numerous restrictions, for example, female nurses were discouraged from working alongside

male doctors and male doctors could not attend to female patients. Discussed in *Strengthening Protection in War,* ICRC, 2001, p-63.

9. Reference made to the changed social conditions of the Afghan women (both) inside and outside Afghanistan all in the name of religion.

10. The concept of legitimacy reminds us that a large part of social behaviour and social structures are determined not so much by interests and preferences as by rights and obligations. Quoted in *The Roots of Behaviour in War—A survey of Literature,* ICRC, 2004, ch. 11, p-93. In the case of Afghanistan it was the Islamization of Afghan Society that was used to exploit Afghan women.

11. Ibid., p. 108.

12. According to an estimate some 500,000 people fled Kabul when fighting broke out in 1992.

13. The new strategies that emerged out of the new thinking were designed to address the causes and consequences of forced displacement which brought attention to the circumstances that led to the making of the refugee or caused displacement. Mass population displacement, in this case, has not simply been a consequence of the armed conflict but an explicit objective of the warring parties. Further, the provisions of the Nairobi Forward-Looking Strategies under the Theme of Peace reflect the consideration of conflict related issues at the international level in the mid-eighties. The Copenhagen Conference (1980), Beijing Conference (1995) also helped tremendously in bringing forward women-related issues of contemporary times.

14. The nature of the sufferings of the Afghan women and their security-based needs demanded and required a proper and total understanding of the problems of female refugees.

15. The reproductive health of uprooted women is jeopardized by high birthrates, high incidence of teenage pregnancies, and sexually-transmitted disease. All these make it essential that the problems confronted by women can only be addressed in totality by targeting both men and women.

16. It may however be noted that since the impact of violence on women is gendered, the response should also be gendered. Discussed in Rita Manchanda's edited *Women, War and Peace,* Sage Publication, p-20.

17. The nature and volume of its impact changed during the different waves of conflict. According to Brocke-Unte 'Peace ought to be more than sheer absence of conflict or absence of fear' and has been described by her as 'negative peace'. A 'positive peace', she urges, is absence of all types of structured inequalities which lead to the irretrievable degradation of environment for particular sections of society. For further discussion of the issue see Rita Manchanda's 'Where are women in South Asia conflict' in *Women, War and Peace,* Sage Publication, 2001.

18. Women, by being marginalized, have also been used as agents of social transformation.

19. In-between the post-withdrawal period and prior to the 9/11 incident, the physical abuse of Afghan girls and women remained undocumented and unreported by the international media. In a patriarchal and tribal society women are socially and structurally disadvantaged. With the social order being to their

disadvantage, women, particularly during the Taliban rule, were forced into beggary or were forced to flee.

20. Huge numbers of civilians have been killed and maimed and forced to flee. In its spill-over effect the developments in Afghanistan had an intense negative affect on Pakistan's society, almost totally changing the social fabric of its society. Moreover, the tension between the two countries escalated, challenged the territorial integrity of the country, and created bitterness amongst the people. Within Afghanistan (after the Soviet withdrawal), the civilians were no longer victims of chance, for targeted killings based on ethnic loyalty made in-roads as a new phenomenon.

21. O'Kane (1997) on *WHO complicity with Taliban's* prescriptions against women health services, cited in, Susie Jacobs, Ruth Jacobs and Jennifer Marchbank *States of Conflict-Gender, Violence and Resistance,* on p-85. For the political impact of conflict on women see El-Bushra, J. and C. Mukarubuga (1995) *Women, War and Transition in Gender and Development,* Vol 3, no.3 Oxfam; also see proceedings of Majlis-e-Shoora convened under the transitory government. Vulnerability was not only a consequence of deprivation but of attacks. It was reported by Amnesty International in the mid-nineties that thousands of unarmed civilian women were killed by unexpected and deliberate rocket attacks on their homes mainly in Kabul.

22. According to M. Abbas, Secretary of Frontiers, refugee numbers reached the highest point in the 1990s with some 6.2 million sheltered in Pakistan and Iran. Out of the total some 3.2 million lived in Pakistan.

23. Reported in *Physicians for Human Rights,* 'The Taliban's War on Women', Boston 1998.

24. A large number of refugees during the 1980s and '90s moved out of the refugee camps and settled in different cities of Pakistan. Peshawar, Karachi, Quetta received a large number of them. There is a dearth of reliable statistics on the illegal migrants living in Pakistan. The report by Afzal Ali Shigri, Rtd. I.G. Sindh popularly known as the 'Shigri Report' in considered a major source.

25. Khattak Saba, *Violence and Home: Afghan women's experience of displacement,* Working paper series # 72, Islamabad, SDPI.

26. Lindsey, Charlotte, *Women Facing War.* ICRC Geneva.

27. Khattak, Saba, 'Militarization, Masculinity and Identity in Pakistan: Effects on Women' quoted in *Unveiling the issue*; eds. Nighat Saeed Khan and Afiya Zia. ASR Publications, 1995.

28. Khattak, Saba, 'Afghan women bombed to be liberated'?, *War Without Borders,* Middle East Report 222, Spring 2002.

29. Mehdi Sikander, 'Refugee Watch Issue' no. 10, July 2000, SAFAR (South Asia Forum For Human Rights).

30. Generally, violations against a civilian population are often considered non-gender-specific and are monitored and handled in a similar way. This is in spite of the fact, that men and women are treated differently during the conflict and their sufferings are different.

31. Nahla Valji, *Seeing Refugee Women as Refugees,* Track Two, Vol 9. No. 3, November 2000.

32. 'Women's Health and Human Rights in Afghanistan: A Population Based Assessment', *Physicians for Human Rights*, August 2001, PHR Washington D.C.
33. Quoted from *The Roots of Behavior in War—A Survey of the Literature*, IRCS, 2004, pp. 107-8.
34. Indicating the developments of the post 9/11 period in Afghanistan.
35. The violation of women in war attracted international attention in 1623–24 with the publication of Hugo Grotius's seminal work, *Dejure Belli a Pacis*. According to him the rights of non combatants should be protected and he urged that rape 'should not go unpunished any more in war than in peace'. Eventually, in the Middle Ages, war related violence against women was considered to be a crime and hence fell into the category of impermissible conduct.
36. U.S. State Department, 'U.S. International Strategy on HIV/AIDS', July 1995.
37. UN Security Resolution 1308 (17 July 2000), emphasizes the need for member states to develop effective, long-term strategies for HIV/AIDS education, prevention and treatment of their personnel.
38. In Pakistan there exists a conflict between bureaucracy and the feudal mindset.
39. The social engineering aims and works to transform society, which directly has its impact on women.
40. For instance, the role of women in the 90s; consolidating the peace constituency in South Asia or even in Somalia where the traditional role played by women in peace and reconciliation was that of peace delegate.
41. Reference made to participation in rallies taken out against the war on Iraq.
42. Security Council Resolution 1366 of 30 August 2001.
45. Resolution in 1325 adopted in October 2000.

Part II

Dynasties' Daughters or Asia's Roaring Tigresses?

6

A Spectacle of Masculine and Feminine Images of Political Leadership: A Feminist Reflection on the Current Crisis of Leadership in the Philippines

Lourdes Veneracion-Rallonza

Prologue: The Irony that is the Philippines

The Philippines is quite a land of ironies. In a region of Asian religions, the Philippines is predominantly Catholic, owing to its experience of 400 years under Spanish rule of the 'sword and the cross' with the 'natural flow' of Islam in the country was arrested with the coming of the Spaniards in the fifteenth century. What is left of the Muslim religion is generally concentrated in an administrative area known as the Autonomous Region of Muslim Mindanao (ARMM). During the 1970s and 80s, the Philippines was infamously labelled the 'sick man of Asia', but with the 20-year dictatorship ending in 1986 and the two succeeding governments' relative success in resuscitating the economy, the country earned the 'tiger cub' status in the 1990s. Sadly, by the year 2000, efforts to pole vault the country to a NIC (i.e. newly-industrialized country) status collapsed along with others in the region's debacle with the Asian Financial Crisis. However, as the other Asian countries were able to recover from this difficulty, the Philippines slid back to be the 'sick' one in the pack. In a report published by the Asian Development Bank (ADB), though the Philippines has posted a decrease in the *incidence of poverty* (i.e. poverty headcount) by 10.5 per cent from 1985 to 2000, the *magnitude of poverty* (i.e. actual number of poor Filipinos) increased by more than 4 million.[1]

As if the economic abyss is not enough, the political scene exacerbates the situation. In a country that continues to project itself to the world as democratic, political decisions and power configurations are negotiated at the top echelons of society. Behind the democracy rhetoric, a strong oligarchy runs the country because of the fact that only those who have the wealth can stand for elections and only the elite are able to direct national policies despite the rhetoric of equal power being in the hands of the 'sovereign Filipino people'. Intra-elite conflict is at its finest with the known phenomenon of 'political turn-coatism' and 'patronage politics'—political party affiliations are dictated not by ideology nor political stance but by mere need for political survival to perpetuate oneself in office. Elections (i.e. the basic requirement for a democracy) are held but have lost its meaning—with people forming the 'habit' of trooping to historic site of Epifanio Delos Santos Avenue (EDSA)— the site of two popular peoples uprising—to call for the removal of elected officials through 'people power'; elections are held but have lost its credibility—with election fraud charges flying all over the place and with the Commission on Elections (COMELEC) as one of the most inefficient government institution. Civil society does thrive but has not continually consolidated itself to form sustained contests with the government and may also be seen as deeply divided from within due to class differences and even interests. In effect, the country lives in suspended animation when faced with critical issues of its own survival as a state.

The current crisis in political leadership as sparked by the infamous 'Gloriagate' (or the scandal embroiling incumbent president Gloria Macapagal-Arroyo where she was supposedly 'caught' on tape with an election official) and opposition forces have inferred and have already concluded that these tapes showed the president's involvement in electoral cheating and fraud. This has brought into question (once again) the integrity of the country's political institutions and its leaders. As of October 2005, the melodrama that is Philippine politics continued to unfold with three women taking the centre-stage in the battle for political legitimacy.

With all this said, this study intends to look at the crisis in political leadership and legitimacy by focusing on the images projected by President Gloria Macapagal-Arroyo, former President Corazon Cojuangco-Aquino, and Susan Roces, a veteran actress who is the widow of a defeated presidential candidate, Fernando Poe, Jr. Their image projection will make simple references to Guy Debord's concept of *spectacle* or 'representations of the dominant model of life'[2] as manifested by news, propaganda, advertising and entertainment. More than this manifestation, the spectacle is related to the production and reproduction of realities—'a worldview that has actually been materialized, a view of the world that has become objective'[3]—and thus comes out as a political project where conjectures become realities when people begin to believe in its existence. In order to understand the masculine context of the spectacle, the study would first present the gender dimension of Philippine politics within the framework of its democracy project. It is within this context that the proposition is constructed as: the reproduction of feminine images of the three women is a mere reiteration of the masculinized character of Philippine politics. And with masculinized politics reigning, one can be assured that authentic societal transformation may too far-fetched for the land of ironies that is the Philippines.

The Gender Dimension of Philippine Politics

In the Philippines, electoral politics is seen as the primary mode of political participation. Since the time that Filipino women won the right to vote in 1937, women's voting turnout (for elections from 1947 to 2001) has been slightly higher than men. Hypothetically, if there are more women voters, then women are in the best position to effect changes in society. Of course, this is an over-simplified conjecture. For one thing, more women voters do not translate into more women in public office. In the election data from 1946 to 1987, the eleven instances that more women voted resulted only in a 4.98 per cent of women being elected[4]—an illustration that there is no consolidated 'women's vote' just yet in the Philippines. Interestingly, in the post-Marcos years when democracy supposedly had thrived, the gender dimension of the democratization project only saw a poor turnout of women elected in national and local elected positions:

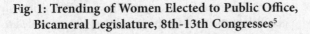

**Fig. 1: Trending of Women Elected to Public Office,
Bicameral Legislature, 8th-13th Congresses[5]**

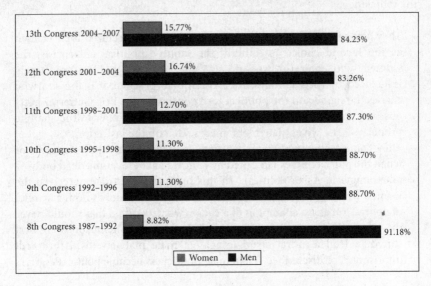

Fig. 2: Trending of Women Elected in Public Office, Executive and Legislative Positions at the Local Government Levels[6]

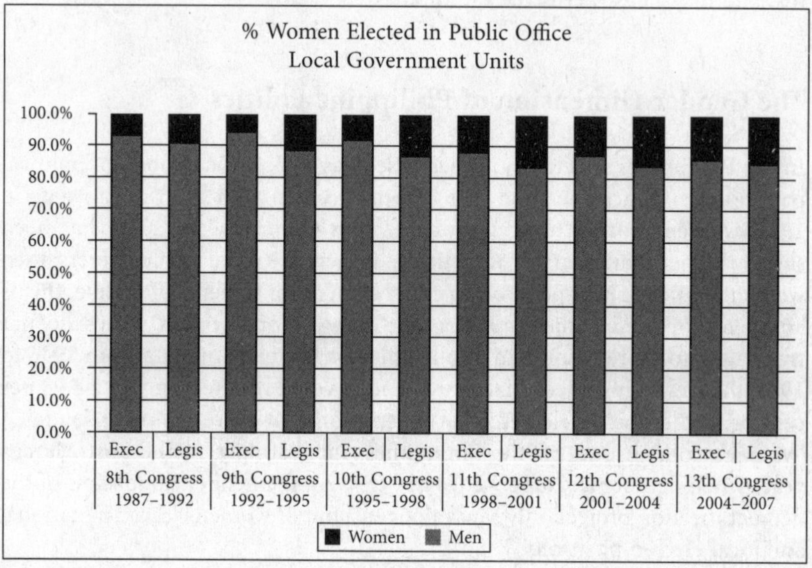

% Women Elected in Public Office
Local Government Units

	Exec	Legis	Exec	Legis	Exec	Legis	Exec	Legis	Exec	Legis	Exec	Legis
	8th Congress 1987–1992		9th Congress 1992–1995		10th Congress 1995–1998		11th Congress 1998–2001		12th Congress 2001–2004		13th Congress 2004–2007	

■ Women   ■ Men

Secondly, women elected into public office are not readily assumed to be bearers of women's issues and concerns. This is a fact primarily because women who occupy positions of (formal) political power tended to manifest the following:

- They come from (elite) political families that have socialized their women as the second choice to 'inherit' the family's political enterprise. The women who enter (or who do not enter) formal politics are largely influenced by their families. As a traditional practice, it is the son who carries the name and the political torch of the family. Eric Gutierrez aptly observes that 'political office is passed on from the father to the son like property.'[7] The wives, daughters, nieces, etc. are the last priority.
- They come from situations when they capitalize on a family 'tragedy' or when the patriarch dies (so called by Kincaid as the 'over my dead body'—phenomena in Asian politics).[8] In this light, the electorate perceived the women who have been left behind by the political leader as both a symbol of oppression and a champion of a cause (whatever it is) that should never die—thus, these women, according to Derichs and Thompson 'were best suited to lead a moral struggle against male machiavellis. Murdered, imprisoned, or discredited Asian male politicians became political martyrs

(at least for their supporters); their often ambivalent political backgrounds were conveniently overlooked as "their" cause was taken up by their female successors.[9] Likewise, women who come to power and who occupy the highest position in the country were able to do so because of the electorate's sympathy for a dead husband (who was actually the original political candidate).

- They come from negotiated spaces within the political machinery (i.e. political party) as part of a compromise to show the 'openness' to women running for public office reflective of what Drude Dahlerup referred to as some kind of 'tokenism' of women in politics.[10]

Simply put, women political leaders socialized in a system of patriarchy will manifest and propagate a male-mind set. As Farzana Bari aptly observes:

> It can be said that women's presence in formal politics will not bring a qualitative change by putting social issues on the national agenda. It can be argued that women, because of their gender alone will not place gender issues on the national agenda...women in the upper echelons of politics are more likely to become an elite group among women and develop their own vested interest.[11]

What is even more interesting in the case of the Philippines is that from the period of the 8th to 12th Congresses, there is a decline in pro-women bills filed in the legislature that saw a relative increase in women legislators.

Fig. 3: Women in National Legislature vis-à-vis Pro-Women Laws from 8th-12th Congresses[12]

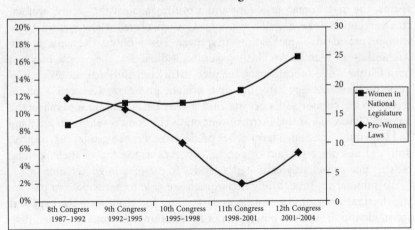

This essentially confirms the proposition that more women in office does not translate into more pro-women or gender-sensitive legislations. The upward trend posted in the 12th Congress may be attributed to the entry of grass-roots and progressive women politicians in the Party List mechanism of the country.[13] These women were part of a very active women's movement that tirelessly engages the state to advance women's empowerment. For example, Representative Etta Rosales, a member of the party-list *Akbayan*, was credited for the *Gender Balance in Political Participation and Representation Act* (House Bill 5708) while Representative Liza Maza (who was initially from *Bayan Muna* and then from the Gabriela women's party list) was credited for filing 15 out of 38 pro-women bills and resolutions.

In the executive branch, the story of two women who became Philippine presidents is likewise very interesting. Both came from essentially political families—one was an assassinated politician's (staunch opposition figure of a dictator) wife and the other was a politician's (former president) daughter. Both were educated in private and catholic schools—and their catholic education will always be a feature of their political actions; of course, one more pronounced than the other. Both came to the echelons of presidential power through a so called 'people power' revolt—although the first one installed as the president of a 'transitional government' and the other as the legitimate constitutional successor to finish the remaining term of an ousted president. In both instances of people power, military involvement was crucial in the changing of presidential leadership. This can be akin to the military image of the 'man in horseback' coming to an aid of a 'damsel in distress'—but in this case, the damsels may not have been distressed but more manifesting the image of 'ladies in waiting'. In this light, it is also very important to note that the military—probably because of its concerns not being addressed or its role in political changes not being recognized—launched several coups d'état against the first woman president and a mutiny against the second woman chief executive. Likewise, the Catholic Church played a key role in these women presidents' 'installation' in power. For without the calls of the Archbishop of Manila, Archbishop Jaime Cardinal Sin, the people may not have felt the sense of legitimacy for such extra-constitutional action such as 'people power'. At any rate, the first woman president, Corazon Aquino, retired to the comforts of a private citizen after her 6-year term of office; the second, Gloria Macapagal-Arroyo went on to run for a 6-year term after she had served the unfinished term of her predecessor. From a gender perspective, both did not place women or gender concerns at the top of their agenda. Neither one consciously exhibited a gender framework in governance.

To summarize, though Filipino women are able to participate in politics via electoral exercise (i.e. voting and standing for elections), the expected consolidation of 'women power' is not forthcoming. As voters, women may have the upper hand in numbers, but the expected manifestation of a 'women's vote' is more of a myth than a reality. Voting preference have not been significantly different from men—that is, of course, if the only parameter we are looking at is the election of more women in public office. As elected officials in the legislative and executive branches of government, women have not been able to push for more pro-women or gender-sensitive legislations and policies. More often than not, even the concept of feminism as a political line or principle has been pushed aside (for some, even demonized for fear of being negatively 'branded' as men-haters, anti-marriage, pro-abolition of the family, etc.). Thus, if women are not automatically pro-women, all the more that women political leaders will not be automatically feminists.

Feminism, in whatever strand, has its merits as a political line. Liberal feminists largely frame the struggle for women emancipation and empowerment by advancing institutional reforms; Marxist feminists see the impact of an oppressive capitalist system on women; radical feminists continuously contest the various manifestations of patriarchy; psychoanalytic and essentialist feminists target the gendered socialization in the family in connection with the shaping of one's identity; and post-modern and critical feminists contest dualist and hierarchical power relations as well as engage in deconstruction and reconstruction projects within multiple discourses. Though there is no such thing as a universal feminism, the common project is to improve the lives of womankind. A woman political leader who carries a feminist line has the edge of using gender as an analytical tool to guide policy-making—this would open to her more spaces to become a transformative leader who is cognizant of transversal politics. Women political leaders, by far, have not manifested this and thus, the perpetuation of a schema of masculinized politics.

Contextualizing the Spectacle: A Narrative of the Crisis in Political Leadership and Legitimacy from the Lens of a Feminist Spectator

Drawing from Debord's concept of *spectacle*, Philippine politics in general and women in politics in particular, depict a 'social relation between people mediated by images.'[14] Using a gender perspective, one will find an abundance of masculinized and feminized images of political leaders. For example, former President Ferdinand Marcos and his wife Imelda personified what Primitivo Mijares termed as a 'conjugal dictatorship'—a husband and wife team of authoritarian rule—in their 20-year-rule of the country. On the one hand, they depicted themselves as the mythical figures *Malakas* (the strong) and *Maganda* (the beautiful) in their desire to shape the 'New Society'. These images were meant to motivate the citizenry towards the transformation of the country. According to Debord, 'when the real world is transformed into mere images, mere images become real beings—dynamic figments that provide direct motivation for hypnotic behavior.'[15] Hidden from plain view was the country's poor—concrete edifices and walls with dainty colours and art works have put them behind the 'other side'. The primordial image of the good and the beautiful, as defined by the Marcoses, tried to make poverty and inequality as realities that could be dismissed as societal hallucinations. As Debord aptly observed:

> The spectacle presents itself as a vast inaccessible reality that can never be questioned. Its sole message is: 'What appears is good; what is good appears.' The passive acceptance it demands effectively imposed by its monopoly of appearances, its manner of appearing without allowing any reply.[16]

But of course, authoritarianism, despite its apparatus of fear, bred an equivalent force of discontent—coming from the opposing elite, the desperate masses and the discontented middle class. In a way, twenty years of authoritarianism, structural violence and misery paved the way for progressive social forces to generate the dissentious 'thought of history' that interrogated and contested the spectacle conjured by the ones in power. As the historical narrative went, Debord's prescription of translating historical thought to practical thought manifested itself in an organized dissent from the population. Contestations came in the form of organized struggles from various sectors of the society and reached its climax when the 'strong man' in Malacañang was no longer able to consolidate his power; particularly, his control of the military. Come 1986, after being challenged in the presidential elections by the widow of Ninoy Aquino and after a faction of the military broke away from his regime to launch a coup, a large segment of the metropolitan population (answering the call of the archbishop of Manila) trooped to EDSA to concretize the practical thought of the counter-hegemonic spectacle of 'people power'.

Fast forward almost twenty years later and another spectacle is manifesting itself. The context is not of dictatorship but a mad scramble for a president to maintain herself in power and the populace expected to repeat history. The crux of the contestation is the alleged illegitimacy of President Gloria Macapagal-Arroyo (PGMA), who because of being 'caught' in a phone conversation with COMELEC Chairperson Garcillano at the time of the 2004 presidential election canvassing, has been perceived to have cheated her way to the presidency. Her political opponents, particularly in the House of Representatives, wove an explosive spectacle generated by this infamous

'Hello Garci' tapes when they presented it as evidence in an impeachment move against her. At the height of the expose, ten government officials (known as the Hyatt 10) resigned from their respective posts, singing the same tune that they no longer wanted to be part of PGMA's administration. Civil society organizations—embodying varying shades of political colour—mobilized and called for her resignation. More radical groups, oddly converging with impatient political opponents of PGMA, organized to amass another (metropolitan-centred) popular revolt for her ouster. However, the tripartite moves for resignation, impeachment and ouster of the President did not generate the same counter-hegemonic spectacle of 'people power'—probably because it lacked two major ingredients: the legitimate call from the Catholic Church and the backing of the military. The death of Archbishop Jaime Cardinal Sin in June 2005 left the Catholic Church with no powerful figure that could undeniably move people to action. Thus, after the much awaited response from the Catholic Bishops Conference of the Philippines (CBCP), many people were surprised that the once politically critical collective now wanted to play it safe. In a pastoral statement entitled 'Restoring Trust: A Plea for Moral Values in Philippine Politics' released on 9 July 2005, the CBCP declared that:

> In the present situation we believe that no single concrete option regarding President Macapagal Arroyo can claim to be the only one demanded by the Gospel. Therefore, in a spirit of humility and truth, we declare our prayerfully discerned collective decision that we do not demand her resignation. Yet neither do we encourage her simply to dismiss such a call from others... In all these we remind ourselves that a just political and moral order is best promoted under the present circumstances by a clear and courageous preference for constitutional processes that flow from moral values and the natural law. Hence, we also appeal to the people, especially their representatives and leaders, to discern their decisions not in terms of political loyalties but in the light of the Gospel values of truth, justice, and the common good.[17]

The military likewise chose to be loyal to their Commander-in-Chief. Although coup rumours never really went away, the military tried to show that they were the men behind the President. Two days before the eve of the twentieth anniversary of the 'People Power Revolution', the Armed Forces of the Philippines (AFP) came out with a statement entitled 'The AFP Remains Apolitical and Non-Partisan' and it declared:

> In the light of emerging developments that may be causing confusion, anxiety and fear among our people and the general public, we wish to assure you that the Armed forces and its men and women, stands as one, strong and united behind the Chain of Command and the duly constituted authority...We also collectively

express our adherence and support to the present leadership as we remain loyal to our mandate as the protector of the people and defender of the state.[18]

Probably because of the circumstances that led to the second people power in 2001—the successful legal manoeuvring of then President Joseph Estrada's allies in the Senate of not opening the envelope that supposedly contained vital evidence to prove the 'guilt' of the President—there was an expectation that a similar expose against PGMA will again trigger spontaneous action by people in the street. This, of course, did not occur. In fact, probably driven by a misguided fear that the 'people power' habit will materialize against her, PGMA projected an image of an apologetic political leader in a 27 June 2005 address to the country:

> For the last several weeks, the issue of the tape recordings has spun out of control... You deserve an explanation from me, because you are the people I was elected to serve. As you recall, the election canvassing process was unnecessarily slow even after the election results were already in and the votes had been counted. I was anxious to protect my votes and during that time had conversations with many people, including a Comelec official. My intent was not to influence the outcome of the election, and it did not...I recognize that making any such call was a lapse in judgment. I am sorry. I also regret taking so long to speak before you on this matter. I take full responsibility for my actions...I want to assure you that I have redoubled my efforts to serve the nation and earn your trust.[19]

The image that the President projected was that of a very 'tame' individual—gone was the usual fiery lady and her widely recognized 'presidential temper'. But the widow of the defeated (and highly popular figure with the masses) presidential candidate created a counter-image of her own. In a 29 June 2005 speech in Club Filipino, Roces stated in response to PGMA:

> We Filipinos have a saying that a liar is the brother of a thief. I cannot accept your story, you betrayed the trust that the people gave you. You have no right to govern the country...You have embarrassed the Filipinos enough...Obviously, you have no love for your country. The gravest thing u have done is u have stolen the presidency, not once but twice! You start and I will finish it![20]

In contrast with PGMA, her image manifested that of an impassioned woman, who is very much willing to take on the leadership of the country. As former Senator Ernesto Herrera observed:

> If what the reality television GMA gave us was meant to elicit our sympathy then it was a disastrous episode because it elicited more anger and frustration from an already angry and frustrated citizenry, fed up as they are from the administration's seemingly egregious lies and falsehoods. In contrast, Susan Roces, the actress

looked like a genuine leader when she denounced GMA's 'I am sorry' speech last Wednesday...Even the most politically apathetic would have been unable to turn a deaf ear for she was speaking from the heart and expressing the thoughts in the minds of most Filipinos.[21]

Without a consolidated opposition force in the country, the coalition of (elite) politicians saw in Roces a symbol that can consolidate and push the people to go in the streets for another 'people power'—they called this the 'Susan factor'. In a sense, what the opposition was banking on was Roces to galvanize the unorganized masses, the same force who launched a people's revolt against PGMA in May 2004 but was never recognized as legitimate 'people power'—primarily because it was not able to oust PGMA from the position of the presidency. Though Roces herself has not considered herself as the leader of the opposition, it is the opposition themselves who wanted to project her as their 'moral force'.

I am here, just as I promised, that if you went to the streets, I would join you...We are united in aspiration and objective. Our aspiration that we may be heard....We know that if we are united, we will be heard...I take pride in you because you know that cheating is wrong, and should not be condoned. It's sad to know that you, the youth know this, but it seems the one's we should hope to be exemplars do not know or show this...Your future is what matters to us...bring back the honour of the Filipino![22]

This rally somehow tried to test if the 'Susan factor' will indeed deliver. By the opposition's estimates, the anti-PGMA protesters came up to 65,000; by the police estimates, the crowd only accounted for some 30,000 later reduced to 15,000 by police estimates.[23] There were other protests in various places in the country against PGMA but only a select few have been attended by Roces. To a certain extent, it is only the opposition composed of traditional politicians who would like to use the image of Roces. Definitely, the organized sectors of civil society can see through this; only the unorganized masses may be the ones who can be (mis)led to believe in the 'Susan factor'. As Debord intimated, they can be the ones that may be misguided by the spectacle: 'The more he identifies with dominant images of need, the less he understands his own life and his own desires...the function of (these) celebrities is to act out various lifestyles or sociopolitical viewpoints...(but) they offer no real choices'.[24]

With the failure of the 'Susan factor' to deliver a critical mass of people in the streets, another figure had to be supported if only to provide an anti-thesis to PGMA and the most logical option for middle class and business groups was former President Corazon Aquino. In a speech delivered on 30 June 2005, Aquino said:

People power has succeeded only if it is for others. It was so in 1986, when those who led the revolution led from the front; it was so in 2001. But People Power for oneself will never succeed. I, too, have been pressured to speak up. Excuse me but I had a good reason to keep my peace until I was ready. I was praying. Praying for light, for myself and our country...I believe that the Constitution contains all the ways by which one may safely effect even the most difficult political changes...To step outside the Constitution will only expose us to greater danger than the injustice we want to correct. I don't know how many people still believe in the power of prayer but I do. ...I repeat, without any embarrassment, my call for prayer and prayerful reflection so that, in the days and weeks ahead, the steps we take will be the right ones toward truth, justice, and peace.[25]

Responding to Aquino's message eight days later, PGMA confidently declared:

I was duly elected to uphold the Constitution and ensure that the institutions of the nation were strengthened not weakened. With all due respect to Former President Aquino and others, I say that their actions caused deep and grievous harm to the nation because they undermine our democratic principles and the very foundation of our constitution. Once again, we're subverting the rule of law and perpetuating a system that's broken and will remain broken until fundamental reforms are put in place...As former President Aquino is well aware, the president is charged by the nation to defend our hard won democracy at all costs. To those who've forgotten this, I say, take your grievances to Congress where I'm very willing to submit to due process as called for by our constitution.[26]

But Aquino has not retreated and continued to shop for public support in the only way she knows how—that of shrouding a moral movement with the force of faith and Catholic religion. As a strategy, Aquino makes the rounds in various Catholic schools and universities to deliver her message. In a speech during a church mass at the De La Salle University, Aquino said:

We pray for our leaders especially for the President and the Vice president and all who serve in government...At this juncture only two constitutional paths remain open for the peaceful and democratic resolution of the present crisis crippling the government and endangering the nation. The first and most expeditious is the President's voluntary resignation for a smooth transition to her constitutional successor, the vice president, and a swift return to normalcy for the country. This is the fastest and most orderly path to take. The second path is the long and inherently contentious process of a congressional impeachment that can only generate more divisions in society and cast more suspicions on the threatened institutions of our democracy. I ask the President to spare our country and herself from this second option and make the supreme sacrifice of resigning.[27]

When the impeachment move against PGMA was politically out-manoeuvred in the House of Representatives, Aquino became even more vigilant to be in public view—attending church masses that have been organized as prayerful gatherings for the 'truth'. In a 13 September mass celebrated at the Church of the Gesu at the Ateneo de Manila University, she outlined three key messages:

(1) that she believes in the truth
(2) that she believes in democracy
(3) that she believes that in 'any democracy a public office is a public trust, and none more so than the presidency'.[28]

Likewise, on the occasion of the 30 September 'Mass for Truth' held at Miriam College, Aquino reiterated her personal message 'clearly and equivocally' and drawing from that speech she noted: that her actions were befitting of a private citizen who has the right to speak her mind; that she was not anti-GMA but pro-truth; that she believed that more than a political and economic crisis, the country suffers from a moral one and thus goes on to profess that 'only moral clarity can lift us from uncertainty;' and that we must all come together in prayer, introspection and discernment.

But banking on divine intervention may not be enough to resurrect the so called 'Cory Magic'—that of mobilizing a critical mass of people in the streets, much like how it was done in 1986 and 2001. Such perceived failure have led some to observe that Aquino may have probably lost much of her political appeal.

Of course, both Roces and Aquino share the basic citizen-duty that frames their political call for PGMA to resign. But their status as private citizen is obscured by the fact that they are more than just ordinary citizens. Both exert vast influence—Aquino, being a former president and political icon of the first 'people power'; and Roces, being a veteran and award winning actress in the silver screen who just happens to be the widow of the closest presidential contender of PGMA in the 2004 elections. Both were also observed by Tony Lopez to be quite similar in several aspects:

> They are both widows. They are both deeply religious. Cory Aquino is a devotee of the Virgin Mary. Susan Roces is a devotee of the Black Nazarene and her patron saint is St. Jude, the hope of the hopeless. Both political neophytes, they have undergone practically the same political baptism...Cory and Susan are convent-bred and deeply religious. During their husbands' time, they were self-effacing, blending into the background.[29]

Given the shared images of a devout Catholic, morally upright, and dedicated wife, both Aquino and Roces reproduced the traditional household role of women transposed in the public sphere. And with such image, it was expected that they resurrect and recycle the perceived 'martyrdom' of their dead husbands and come out with an exact opposite of the image of PGMA.

As the narrative went, PGMA survived the critical first two weeks after the explosion of the 'Hello, Garci' tapes thanks to the much-awaited (but sorely disappointing) statement of the CBCP and to the non-partisanship pronouncement of the military. It created for her a breathing space to strategize particularly in the area of image building. By and large, PGMA suffers from a perceived 'lack of charisma' as she is continuously seen to have failed in being able to relate with the masses. Her campaign image of 'Gloria Labandera' (Gloria, the Laundry Woman) has failed to connect the idea that she identifies with the life of the majority of the Filipinos. In fact, a month before the wire-tapping expose broke out, the Social Weather Station (SWS) came out with its 14-23 May 2005 survey that reported 56 per cent of the Filipinos are dissatisfied with President Arroyo's performance compared to 26 per cent who were satisfied.[30] This same report stated that she had a net satisfaction rating of 33 per cent, a low net satisfaction rating of a president since 1986.

Although PGMA posted the highest votes for the Vice-President position she won in 1998, this same number of votes cannot be assumed and carried over to the elected position of the presidency. In fact, she took over the reigns of ousted President Estrada in 2001 because she was the constitutional successor for that position—a mandate that was upheld by the Supreme Court. From 2001-4, PGMA projected the persona of an 'Iron Lady' making very strong statements against groups that sought to destabilize her government or groups that threaten the stability of the state such as:

- 'Strike now so I can crush you...'—a statement she made against former President Estrada's supporters who stormed Malacañang in 1 May 2004.
- 'You'll fall with just one bullet'—a message she delivered strongly against the terrorist Abu Sayyaf Group (ASG).

PGMA also posed for pictures with suspected criminals captured by the police to project an image that she was on top of the country's anti-crime campaign. Even more telling was 2004 State of the Nation (SONA) address where she harped on the need for a 'strong republic', a rhetoric normally associated with male political leaders who tended towards authoritarianism. But the masculinist image did not work—the Machiavellian woman was seen as an ineffective way to connect with the people. Thus, there was a recognized need to recast a 'softer' image of the President. According to a featured report by the Philippine Centre for Investigative Journalism (PCIJ) in September 2005, a foreign firm was hired for two million US dollars to 're-engineer' the image of PGMA. To a certain extent, it may have paid off when she was named as the fourth 'Most Powerful Women in the World' by Forbes in 2005.

During the earlier period of the political crisis, PGMA first tried to project humility and approachableness to come out as the 'mother of the nation' calling for peace and reconciliation. She has even made reference to what her father, former President Diosdado Macapagal, has taught her and where she listened intently as a dutiful daughter; she has also unleashed the image of her own daughter, Luli, as a woman of ethic and substance—traits that would only come from her as a dutiful mother. PGMA tried to feminize herself. But when she was emboldened by the failure of the 'people power' to materialize against her, she morphed back to her 'Iron Lady' persona. She emasculated herself anew and as evidence, she came out with Executive Order (EO) 464 that was meant to restrain all public officials from attending investigations conducted by the legislative branch, unless they are allowed by the President herself. For the administration, EO 464 had basis in upholding national security (i.e. it is in the interest of our country's security that further destabilizing innuendoes should be done away with); but for Fr. Joaquin Bernas, S.J., dean emeritus of the Ateneo de Manila University and a known constitutional expert:

> It's a gag rule. She's obstructing the work of the legislature. She is blocking the checks and balances among co-equal branches of government. We are still a rule of democracy, not a rule of one woman.[31]

And so the spectacle goes on—woven by two feminine widows and an emasculated president at the centre of the political stage.

Epilogue: A Feminist Afterthought

Michael Genovese once observed that women emerge as national leaders:

(1) mostly in less developed countries
(2) in countries with some semblance of democracy
(3) with largely secular political regimes
(4) usually in times of political/social distress.[32]

As applied to the Philippines, the country is a struggling economy; it is a nominal democracy with election results always being contested and questioned; it has a secular political system despite the presence of a highly politicized Catholic Church; and the two women who became president were catapulted to power via 'people power'.

The images of the three women embroiled in the weaving of the spectacle that emerged during the dramaturgy of the crisis of political leadership and legitimacy manifested the masculine nature of Philippine politics. First, Roces portrayed herself as the impassioned widow of a (supposedly cheated) presidential candidate—Fernando Poe, Jr., a screen hero and popular movie icon idolized by the masses for his numerous movie portrayals as an underdog triumphing over villains. Being a movie figure, it would not have been a surprise if he won the 2004 presidential derby—just as his friend, former President Estrada, captured the presidency in 1998. The surprise came when he did not win. The death of Poe (by natural circumstances) and the expose exploding against PGMA several months after gave Roces the opportunity to fashion herself (though unintended) as a political figure who would dutifully carry the torch of her deceased husband. This has been the observation when she began attending press conferences and rallies to deliver impassioned and award-winning speeches. However, the 'Susan factor' did not deliver. Aquino, for her part, capitalized on her devoutly religious image and perceived moral ascendancy that is attached to it. Almost all her public speeches were delivered during church masses and prayer rallies. All her political messages were framed within the context of prayerful reflections. But this very trademark of the 'Cory magic' likewise fizzled out. As for PGMA, she initially tried the feminine formula but failed to overturn her more widely-known 'Iron Lady' persona and thus she eventually reclaimed and re-embodied it. In the context of the images projected by these women, Debord's observation that 'the admirable people who personify the system are well known for not being what they seem'[33] may be an appropriate response to the puzzle of why there has not been a third 'people power'. The Filipino people may not be really suffering from a 'people power' fatigue—it is possible that they are contemplating on how to transcend the spectacle.

Feminine images are meant to generate sympathy and fuel emotions while masculine images are utilised to emphasise power and authority. Feminine images thrive because they reify masculine ones. Thus, the masculine-feminine schema is not that of dichotomy but that of hierarchy. And this is the nature of the spectacle that the three women created through the images they projected. The Filipino people may not be fully conscious of the gendered dimension of the spectacle. Why did the 'Susan factor' fail to deliver? Why did the 'Cory magic' fizzle out? As of this writing, why has there been no consolidated movement to remove an already perceived illegitimate president from office—both by constitutional and extra-constitutional means? Does this mean that there is a possibility that people may actually prefer an emasculated woman president who can still conjure stability, false as it may be? These questions remain as puzzles and thus point to the fact that the society of spectacle is very much present on Philippine politics. Though there may be an 'awareness that some groups have vested interests in maintaining the status quo, forces to maintain it, and form false consciousness to reinforce it,'[34] the actualization of 'historical thought' that would generate a counter-hegemonic force to set in motion consolidated contestations and dissent may be an illusion in itself. For Debord,

> A critical theory of the spectacle cannot be true unless it unites with the practical current of negation in society; and that negation...can for its part only become conscious of itself by developing the critique of the spectacle, which is the theory of its real conditions—the concrete conditions of present day oppression—and which also reveals its hidden potential.[35]

Without the realization that the very masculine character of Philippine politics continue to fuel feminine images as both anti-thesis and synthesis of masculine images, people may not be able to transcend the spectacle. This may then naturalize them into apathy and inaction where they may falsely associate a manufactured stability (because of still functioning institutions) with the idea that change is no longer needed at this point in time. If this becomes the case, then the irony that is the Philippines be will perennially perpetuated....

NOTES

1. Schelzig, Karin. *Poverty in the Philippines: Income, Assets and Access.* Asian Development Bank Report, January 2005. [Online] Available: www.adb.org/Document/Book/Poverty-in-the-Philippines.pdf#search='ABD%20Report%20Poverty%20in%20the%20Philippines. [12 September 2005].
2. Guy Debord, *The Society of Spectacle*, translated by Ken Knabb. [Online] Available: www.bopsecrets.org/SI/debord/1.htm. [15 September 2005].
3. Debord, *The Society of Spectacle*.
4. Lourdes Veneracion-Rallonza, 'Women and the Democracy Project: A Feminist Take on Women's Political Participation in the Philippines,' in *Women's Political Participation and Representation in Asia: Obstacles and Challenges*, ed. Kazuki Iwanaga (Copenhagen: NIAS Press, *forthcoming in 2007*), p. 101.
5. Veneracion-Rallonza, 'Women and the Democracy Project,' p. 106.
6. Veneracion-Rallonza, 'Women and the Democracy Project,' p. 105.
7. Eric Gutierrez, *All in the Family: A Study of Elites and Power Relations in the Philippines* (Quezon City: Philippine Centre for Investigative Journalism, 1994).
8. Diane Kincaid, 'Over his Dead Body: A Positive Perspective on Widows in the US Conquers,' *Western Political Quarterly*, 31 March 1978.

9. Claudia Derichs and Mark Thompson, *Dynasties and Female Leadership in Asia*. A project proposal sponsored by the German Science Foundation, April 2003–2005. [Online] Available: www.hwwilson.com/print/cbinti_arroyo_ bibliography.htm. [10 September 2005].

10. Drude Dahlerup, 'The Effect of Electoral Gender Quotas: Are Quota Women Justified in Politics'. Paper presented at the 3rd International Conference on Women and Politics in Asia, Islamabad, Pakistan. 24-25 November 2005. [Online] Available: www.wpaf.org/b203.pdf. [5 October 2006].

11. Farzana Bari, 'Right of Women,' *The News* 15 May 1997.

12. Veneracion-Rallonza, 'Women and the Democracy Project,' 105.

13. Veneracion-Rallonza, 'Women and the Democracy Project,' 113.

14. Debord, *The Society of the Spectacle*.

15. Debord, *The Society of the Spectacle*.

16. Debord, *The Society of the Spectacle*.

17. www.cbcponline.net/documents/2000/html/restoringtrust.html, retrieved 5 October 2006.

18. www.afp.mil.ph/0/news/remains.php, retrieved 5 October 2006.

19. www.pcij.org/blog/?p=155, retrieved 5 October 2006.

20. http://pcij.og/blog/wp-docs/Susan_Roces_June29_Excerpts.pdf, retrieved 5 October 2006.

21. www.abs-cbsnews.com/storypage.aspx?StoryId=9528, retrieved 5 October 2006.

22. www.mb.com.ph/issues/2005/07/01/ENTR2005070138334.html, retrieved 5 October 2006.

23. www.pcij.org/blog/?p=244, retrieved 5 October 2006.

24. Debord, *The Society of the Spectacle*.

25. www.pcij.org/blog/?p=169, retrieved 5 October 2006.

26. www.ops.gov.ph/speeches2005/message-2005_jul08.htm, retrieved 5 October 2006.

27. http://gmapinoytv.com/article.php?articleid=1733, retrieved 5 October 2006.

28. www.newsflash.org/2004/02/hl/hl102820.htm, retrieved 5 October 2006.

29. www.manilatimes.net/national/2005/jun/22/yehey/business/20050622bus4.html, retrieved 5 October 2006.

30. www.sws.org.ph/pr050602b.htm, retrieved 5 October 2006.

31. Philippine Daily Inquirer (PDI), 30 September 2005, Volume 20, Number 294.

32. Michael A. Genovese, *Women as National Leaders* (London: SAGE Publications, 1993).

33. Debord, *The Society of the Spectacle*.

34. Debord, *The Society of the Spectacle*.

35. Debord, *The Society of the Spectacle*.

References

Bari, Farzana. 'Right of Women's Seats.' *The News* 15 May 1997.

Debord, Guy. *The Society of the Spectacle*, translated by Ken Knabb. Online. Available: www.bopsecrets.org/SI/debord/1.htm. 15 September 2005.

Dahlerup, Drude. *The Effect of Electoral Gender Quotas: Are Quota Women Justified in Politics.* Paper presented at the 3rd International Conference on Women and Politics in Asia, Islamabad, Pakistan. 24-25 November 2005. Online. Available: www.wpaf.org/b203.pdf. 5 October 2006.

Derichs, Claudia and Mark Thompson. 'Dynasties and Female Leadership in Asia.' A project proposal sponsored by the German Science Foundation, April 2003–2005. Online. Available: www.hwwilson.com/print/cbinti_arroyo_bibliography.htm. 10 September 2005.

Dolor, Beting Laygo. 'Philippines Fails to Make Cut as "Tiger". *Philippine News* (8 September 2004). Online. Available: www.philippinenews.com/news/view_article.html?article_id=abdcd01d333d7cd1c3db2eed7d99ceb0. 13 September 2005.

Genovese, Michael A. *Women as National Leaders.* London: SAGE Publications, 1993.

Gutierrez, Eric. *All in the Family: A Study of Elites and Power Relations in the Philippines.* Quezon City: Philippine Centre for Investigative Journalism, 1994.

Karam, Azza. 'Introduction: Gender and Democracy—Why?' In *Women in Parliament: Beyond Numbers,* ed. International Institute for Democracy and Electoral Assistance (IDEA), pp. 7-16. Stockholm: Institute for Democracy and Electoral Assistance, 1998.

Kincaid, Diane. 'Over his Dead Body: A Positive Perspective on Widows in the US Conquers.' *Western Political Quarterly 31* (March 1978).

Schelzig, Karin. *Poverty in the Philippines: Income, Assets and Access.* Asian Development Bank Report, January 2005. Online. Available: www.adb.org/Document/Book/Poverty-in-the-Philippines.pdf#search='ABD%20Report%20Poverty%20in%20the%20Philippines. 12 September 2005.

Tordesillas, Ellen. 'Presidential Makeover.' *Investigative Report Quarterly* (Issue 3 September 2005). Online. Available: http://pcij.org/i-report/3/makeover.html. 19 September 2005.

Veneracion-Rallonza, Lourdes. 'Engendering the State and Imaging Women Political Leaders: Corazon Cojuangco-Aquino and Gloria Macapagal-Arroyo as Cases to Point.' *In Quilted Sightings,* ed. Josefa S. Francisco and Cezar R. Tigno, pp. 67-83. Quezon City: Women and Gender Institute, 2001.

Veneracion-Rallonza, Lourdes. 'Women and the Democracy Project: A Feminist Take on Women's Political Participation in the Philippines.' In *Women's Political Participation and Representation in Asia: obstacles and challenges,* ed. Kazuki Iwanaga, 84-129. Copenhagen: NIAS Press, forthcoming in 2007.

http://gmapinoytv.com/article.php?articleid=1733, retrieved 5 October 2006.

http://pcij.og/blog/wp-docs/Susan_Roces_29June_Excerpts.pdf, retrieved 5 October 2006.

www.abs-cbsnews.com/storypage.aspx?StoryId=9528, retrieved 5 October 2006.

www.afp.mil.ph/0/news/remains.php, retrieved 5 October 2006.

www.cbcponline.net/documents/2000/html/restoringtrust.html, retrieved 5 October 2006.

www.manilatimes.net/national/2005/jun/22/yehey/business/20050622bus4.html, retrieved 5 October 2006.

www.mb.com.ph/issues/2005/07/01/ENTR2005070138334.html, retrieved 5 October 2006.

www.newsflash.org/2004/02/hl/hl102820.htm, retrieved 5 October 2006.

www.ops.gov.ph/speeches2005/message-2005_jul08.htm, retrieved 5 October 2006.

www.pcij.org/blog/?p=155, retrieved 5 October 2006.

www.pcij.org/blog/?p=169, retrieved 5 October 2006.

www.pcij.org/blog/?p=244, retrieved 5 October 2006.

www.sws.org.ph/pr050602b.htm, retrieved 5 October 2006.

7

Durga Amma and St. Sonia, the Redeemer—Images of Women Politicians in India[1]

Dagmar Hellmann-Rajanayagam

'When I grew up, I thought all Prime Ministers are women.' (Swarna Rajagopalan)

First Scenario

On 31 October 1984, 'an old woman taking a walk in her garden'[2] was shot by her own bodyguards. Indira Gandhi, Prime Minister of India from 1966 to 1977 and from 1980 to1984, died on the spot. The path she took and the place where she actually fell in 10 Janpath have now become a museum and a shrine which is regularly visited by hordes of visitors.

Second Scenario

On 18 May 2004, Congress President Sonia Gandhi stepped before the television cameras and her party members in New Delhi, and announced that an 'inner voice' had told her to renounce the position of Prime Minister for which her party had just nominated her: 'Friends, throughout these past six years that I have been in politics, one thing has been clear to me. And that is, as I have often stated, that the post of prime minister is not my aim.'[3] The country was stunned.

Indira Gandhi was the first Indian woman prime minister, (though the honour of being the first one world-wide belongs to Sirimavo Bandaranaike). Indira's government went down in flames in 1984 when she was assassinated, and she eventually became a martyr. Her daughter-in-law, Sonia, is today Congress president and very much the power behind the throne. She is also on her way to becoming a 'saint'.

Female success in politics still tends to be put down to dynastic succession, even-or particularly-in feminist writing.[4] While the dynasty certainly plays a role, it does not explain the continued selection of women as dynastic successors, even though men might be available for the position. How, then, do women reach the top and how does the public perceive and evaluate them? What are their agenda and priorities of policy-making?

Life Lines: Indira and Sonia Gandhi

Indira Gandhi was elected Prime Minister on 19 January 1966 after the sudden and unexpected death of Lal Bahadur Shastri, the second death in office of a Prime Minister within less than two years: Jawaharlal Nehru had died in 1964. Indira[5] was no political novice: she had been a member of the Congress for many years, had been elected its President in 1959,[6] and had been Minister for Broadcasting and Information.

She had been conscious of and active in politics practically from the time she could talk. Born in 1917 into a family of westernized, politically active lawyer Brahmins who engaged in the Indian National Congress (INC) and in the freedom struggle, she grew up with frequent absences of her parents and grandfather, due to their sojourns in prison. Her father's letters to her from jail have become famous.[7] While there is no doubt that her parents deeply loved her, her biographers point out the gender bias in the family: when she was born, the family actually expected a boy. Yet, being an only child, Indira according to her own statements never felt disadvantaged for being a girl;[8] she grew up with all the privileges of an upper-class child. Because she had never felt disadvantaged on account of her gender, she did not consider herself a feminist.[9] One might put it slightly differently: obviously Indira never saw the need to be a feminist since she was not treated badly enough. This view of feminism, though, seems to negate the necessity to enact laws or measures to help women at all. While empathizing with individual suffering, she remained detached from it because of her privileged position and therefore was never able to see women's disadvantages and suffering as a structural instead of a personal or religio-social defect.

In 1942 Indira married Feroze Gandhi, a truly revolutionary act, because Feroze was not a Hindu, but belonged to the tiny Parsi community and was socially and economically not on the same level as the proud, Brahmin, Nehrus.[10] The couple had two children, Rajiv and Sanjay. Feroze died suddenly of a heart attack in 1960.[11]

Indira did not attain the position of Prime Minister 'naturally': though asked to succeed Nehru in 1964, she declined the position and even voiced intentions to quit politics altogether. During the crisis of 1966, however, she accepted the nomination and was voted Prime Minister with the help of Congress President Kamaraj. He, together with a coterie of like-minded colleagues named the syndicate,[12] had only one aim: to prevent Morarji Desai from becoming Prime Minister.[13] Nehru's daughter seemed a suitable stopgap for the purpose. It was not really intended that she develop a mind and political aims of her own, though that was what in fact happened.

Sonia Gandhi was likewise offered the premiership after her husband Rajiv's assassination in 1991 and refused it for seven years. When she finally entered politics and the Congress won in 2004, she declined the position in the face of protests from her supporters.

Sonia Maino was born in 1946 in Orbassano in Tuscany and went to study English in Cambridge at the age of eighteen in 1965. There she met Rajiv Gandhi. They married in 1968[14] and had two children, Rahul and Priyanka. She became Indira's favourite daughter-in-law and took Indian citizenship in 1983. Sonia quickly adapted to conditions of life in India, yet tried very hard to keep politics out of family life,[15] though she was in the end unsuccessful.

When Rajiv was forced to enter politics as president of the Youth Congress after his brother Sanjay's death in 1980, Sonia fought against this decision, as she would against all further involvement in politics. She felt that it would lead to unhappiness and disaster.[16] As it turned out, she was right. Tragedy would strike twice in 1984 and 1991.

Rajiv was on his way back to power after a rather luckless period of government until 1989 when he was assassinated on 21 May 1991. Sonia withdrew from public life. Her silence earned her the epithet, 'The Sphinx of 10 Janpath'.

In the meantime, Congress' fortunes fell on increasingly bad times. Sonia at last acceded to the pleas of Congress leaders and became an official member of the Congress Party in 1997,[17] but was not able to turn its fortunes around. It seemed at the time that the Congress would sink into oblivion.[18]

Durga Amma

Indira took over the government at a critical political and economic time.[19] Both the syndicate and the old guard assumed that Indira would be pliable and easy to manipulate.[20] Her male colleagues called her unkindly *goongi gudiya*, the dumb doll, because she felt uncomfortable speaking publicly.[21] Many old Congress war horses saw her as a kind of niece whom they liked, but from whom they would not take orders.[22] But she refused to be just the rubber stamp for the decisions of the old men around her. She would follow her own policies, and these pleased neither faction.

Indira nationalized the banks,[23] and shortly after repealed the privy purses of the princes, both to great public acclaim.[24] Congress leaders from all ideological descriptions accused her of behaviour unseemly for a woman, especially because of her harsh treatment of opponents within the party.[25] But she always managed to elegantly marginalize those who opposed her or were ideologically not attuned to her.[26] When the old guard engineered her expulsion from the Congress by the CWC in 1969, she split the organization and gathered her supporters in the new Congress: Cong (R).[27] The remaining faction, the forces of the right, was known as Cong (O). Indira subsequently went to the voters directly with the reformed faction and won a two-thirds majority in March 1971, one year ahead of time, with the winning slogan *garibi hatao* (remove poverty).[28] The dumb doll had started to talk. Congress (O) very unadvisedly campaigned with *Indira hatao* (remove Indira). The voters duly punished them for this.

Then came Indira's finest hour: She had come into power indirectly through the war with Pakistan over Kashmir, which had—also indirectly—brought about Shastri's heart attack and death. She strengthened her rule by conducting another war with Pakistan, this time over the birth of Bangladesh. It was a tremendous victory, and Atal Bihari Vajpayee called Indira the Durga of India, a name that would stick to her ever after.[29] *The Economist* even portrayed her as 'Empress of India'.[30] During her rule, India had attained higher international standing than ever before.[31] President Nixon, however, not least because he was unable to browbeat her, detested Indira, and the feeling was entirely mutual.[32]

Some observers claim that Pakistan dared to initiate the war at all because she was a woman and they expected her to simply give up in the face of Pakistani aggression. Genovese goes even further: he says that had there been a male Prime Minister in Delhi at the time, Yahya Khan would not have dared to start a war.[33] This perception owes something to the impression spread after the negotiations in Simla. It was felt that Indira had gambled away all that India had gained during the war. It was alleged that she conceded too much to Zulfiqar Ali Bhutto without getting any commitments in writing in return.

Black Kali?[34]

Indira used to address the voters directly whenever she had a problem within the party. And often she addressed especially those groups of the population that would not necessarily contribute to an election success: her concern for children, who were not entitled to vote, is a case in point.[35] She also often specifically addressed women (who would vote for her because she showed concern for their children), the poor in general, Muslims and other minorities, people from the South who felt disadvantaged by the political and—at that time—economic dominance of the North, and Harijans (Dalits).[36] To all of them she presented herself as the 'mother of the nation' and the nation as her family and children.[37]

This tactics did not work forever, though. By 1974, the Bangladesh victory was forgotten, economic problems had increased exponentially, the second oil shock hit India hard, and her foes did not let it pass by. If she could not be dislodged politically, they reckoned there might be a way through the courts.[38] In June 1975, a judge in Allahabad declared her election victory in Amethi in 1971 invalid because she had used a government van to campaign. It was, as *The Guardian* remarked,[39] a mere technicality, comparable to a parking ticket, but it lost her her seat in the Lok Sabha, the Indian parliament. This court ruling came on top of a number of other grave problems: a railway strike and an ostensibly non-violent campaign against her government and its policies by the movement of Jayaprakash Narayan (JP) including calls for tax boycotts and an appeal to the security forces not to obey the orders of the government. In the face of these, she proclaimed Emergency on 25 June 1975.[40]

All biographers, even the most sympathetic ones, consider the Emergency Indira's greatest blunder.[41] But they grant that there might have been valid reasons initially: Dhar, for example states that JP had the—at least tacit and moral—support of the USA and that the most hard-core opponents of the Emergency came from the Rashtriya Swayamsevak Sangh (RSS) and the Jan Sangh, two strongly Hindu and right-wing organizations.[42] But the manner of implementation was considered disastrous universally. Many observers, however, overlook the fact that Indira withdrew the measure voluntarily in 1977 in order to hold elections even though some of her advisers recommended postponing these,[43] and accepted a disastrous defeat, which brought to power a cobbled government, held together only by one aim: to take revenge on Indira, both personally and politically. This single-mindedness of the Janata government backfired: people began to feel sympathy for her,[44] and in 1980 she overwhelmingly won the elections again. It was not least the Harijan vote that helped her.[45]

Enter St. Sonia

Sonia came into her own in 2004 when Congress won the elections against all expectations and predictions. The BJP indulged in an extremely nasty, even obscene, personalized campaign, the theme of which seemed to be to prevent Sonia Gandhi not only from becoming Prime Minister, but even from standing as a candidate for election altogether. It even announced plans to pass a law in the case of election victory that would prevent foreign-born citizens *and their offspring* from attaining the highest position in the land.[46] The points of attack were first and foremost her foreign origin, but also included, the Bofors affair.[47] Indian election campaigns are not noted for exaggerated reticence, but personalized attacks, especially on a woman candidate, never go down well with the electorate. Low caste women are especially said to favour women politicians who are perceived as being treated badly or unfairly on account of their gender: 'If she can be treated like this, what about us?'[48] And the BJP was duly punished. Sonia Gandhi was scheduled to be elected Prime Minister. But it was not to be.

In March 2004, in an unpublished piece, I formulated my thoughts on the forthcoming elections which in the meantime have turned out prophetic:

> Even if Congress can win to form a stable government, it is questionable whether Congress elders will allow Sonia to become Prime Minister. The foreign-born tag has a certain power even within Congress and would in any case make a useful stick to beat Sonia with, if other interests are at stake.

If the foreign-origin argument could not be used to prevent Sonia's candidacy and election victory, it might still come in useful to throw a spanner in the works regarding her aspirations to become prime minister.[49] And it worked. Congress did win, and the BJP watched developments in fascinated horror. It wanted revenge. Sonia probably knew[50] that the reproach of being a foreigner might always hold her back and prevent her from taking meaningful foreign policy decisions. And she stooped to conquer: she arranged for Manmohan Singh to become Prime Minister. Both moves led her prestige to rise sky-high: she was seen not only as a martyr, but simultaneously as an ascetic, a renouncer and as a forgiving saint, this last since she had made a member of a minority, from which the assassins of her mother-in-law had originated, the Prime Minister.[51] The BJP had cut its nose to spite its face. Recently, she has repeated the feat: when the opposition objected to her holding a position as MP while simultaneously acting as the chairperson of the NPC (National Policy Council) and the Rajiv Gandhi Foundation, because it is not permitted under the law to be an MP and act in a commercial enterprise at the same time, she resigned from all positions (though the latter two were unpaid) and went in for a bye-election in her constituency of Rae Bareilly. She won the contest overwhelmingly by a margin of over 400,000 votes.[52]

As chairperson of the United People's Alliance (UPA), Congress president and Head of the National Advisory Council, Sonia remains the final arbiter, who can influence and determine policies. Her prestige and reputation in the country rose to unprecedented heights: Saint Sonia, the renouncer. The BJP's fury was the measure of Sonia's success.

Perceptions and Evaluations

What is to be looked at are perceptions of the two women as politicians. Election analyses might give us some hints here, but for Indira this is difficult: the assumption that many women voted for Indira is exactly that, and is not supported by analytical evidence. For later elections, there is firmer ground and data to show how women and men voted.[53] The EPW (*Economic and Political Weekly*) election analysis 2004 starts off with the admission, that the outcome of the elections still remains a puzzle six months after the event![54]

Table 1: Election Results 2004

Party (combine)	Seats Contested	Seats Won
NDA (National Democratic Alliance)	543	189
BJP (Bharatiya Janata Party)	364	138
UPA (United People's Alliance)	535	222
INC (Indian National Congress)	414	145
Left Parties	112	61

Source: Compiled with information from EPW 18 December 2004, 5385.

What became clear was the fact that '... [t]he Congress is no longer the rainbow party that it used to be. It [is] a party that **depends excessively on support from women** [my emphasis D.H.R.], poor and the marginal communities....'[55] On the whole, more women do vote for the Congress than men, but the difference is marginal.[56] The upper and middle classes/castes and the urban population voted for the NDA, whereas the UPA was the combine of the low castes/classes and the rural electorate.[57] Congress thus is no longer the party of the middle class, that ground has now been occupied by the BJP and its allies. 36 per cent of women Congress voters would have chosen Sonia Gandhi for Prime Minister against 34 per cent of men.[58] The elections analysis even states that '..., the NDA lost this election despite Vajpayee and the Congress won it despite Sonia Gandhi.'[59]

On some issues women voted together,[60] while on others they might have voted as women, but fractured through the prism of caste/class/religion. On the whole, women candidates were frequently more successful in the elections than men since 1996, though these rates vary considerably across parties: '...both men and women voters are not apprehensive of women candidates. ..., the patterns of women's voting reveal a definite, focused understanding of the political choices they have.'[61]

The analysis cautions against treating gender as an independent variable, yet it also shows that there are indeed issues on which there exists a sort of consensus among women voters. Another question is, whether and why men vote for women? Tables and data cannot really inform us about the emotional motives.[62] However, these are more interesting than dry figures: While Sonia has become a saint, evaluations of Indira are more varied and more ambivalent: she was *personally and as a woman*, blamed for the excesses of the Emergency. Rajeswari Sunder Rajan describes some of the male authors' attacks which focus entirely on her gender: whether it is the black widow of *Midnight's Children* fame, where Salman Rushdie describes the castration by Doctor Death Sanjay on the instigation of the Black Widow, or gender-biased short stories where the distaste directed against the woman instead of the Emergency, is exemplified e.g. into a story about the misshapen fetus of a witch mother. The fetus is tormenting and spoiling the world which can only be healed by it being forced to crawl back into the womb of its mother, the black goddess Kali and who is then defeated by the white goddess Durga.[63] Castration *angst* supersedes political judgement. Sunder Rajan's account gives the impression (subsequently confirmed in various conversations the author had with Indian colleagues and interview partners) that vasectomy was the one 'crime' Indira is being blamed for until today, while all other measures of the Emergency are long forgotten.[64]

The difference between Kali and Durga bears repetition: Durga is powerful, but not really autonomous, always under male control. The appellation Durga was complimentary. Kali, however, is the only goddess who is not under male control and therefore ambivalent and controversial. The comparison to Kali meant that she acted autonomously, not according to male wishes; consequently she took the wrong decisions for which she was duly criticized and rejected.[65] Academic writing follows not far behind the political: Indira is blamed for the Emergency on account *of being a woman*.[66] While use and abuse of power is normal for men, for women it is utterly reproachable when done autonomously. Credit for the lifting of emergency is never granted.[67] And yet both before and after becoming Prime Minister, she was called the only man in the cabinet.[68] The appellation is betraying: if the only man in the cabinet is a woman, this is a perception that does not augur well for female power or female virtues.

While at the beginning of her career, Indira was blamed for not being religious enough, though given a religious appellation after the Bangladesh war, in later life, and after the emergency, she was blamed for being excessively religious. Morarji Desai, though even more excessively religious and decidedly quirkier, was never on this account doubted to be able to fulfil his political obligations. Nor, for that matter, was the self-admitted fundamentalist Vajpayee. Moreover, men found it difficult to communicate with her because she could listen quietly and often used silence as a weapon against verbal pressure.[69] Also, her ability of multi-tasking confused and irritated more one-track-minded men.[70] Sonia, in contrast, is said to operate in an exemplary democratic and consensual fashion, which makes her style of functioning quite different from that of her mother-in-law.[71] But like Indira Gandhi, Sonia also addresses the disadvantaged, the lower castes, women, and minorities. Whatever the comments of her rivals, acting as the *wiedergänger* of Indira Gandhi went down well with the voters.

Indira rejected the above appellation as she did others that referred to gender in politics: in one famous quotation, she said she wanted to be seen not as a man or woman, but as a human being.[72] She refused to be judged on her gender.[73]

Indira the Great?

But of course she was. In the Bangladesh war, Indira's gender was of supreme significance, both in a positive and negative way: Durga is the goddess called upon by the male gods in crises where all other means fail. That she was victorious was important. Much more important, however, was that she fulfilled male expectations. Conversely, when she seemingly conceded too much in Simla, again it was her gender that was seen as responsible: women are weak.[74] And the Emergency only came about because women cannot be trusted with power: she became Kali. Till today, Indira is still compared to her father, Jawaharlal Nehru, and the comparison invariably turns out unflattering for her, since she is accused of having betrayed his legacy. To him, all male and political virtues are attributed whereas Indira is ascribed all vices of the female and the power hungry. Nehru is considered secular, a democrat, opposed to dynastic succession, incorruptible, mild and suave, Indira, a surface democrat (whatever that may be), religious bigot, autocratic, attached to power, corrupt, and attempting to found a dynasty (which had incidentally existed for decades). The point is that these political vices are attributed to her gender, whereas her father is seen in a pink halo of blamelessness. That he was criticized precisely for weakness and indetermination is conveniently forgotten.[75] Dhar remarks that Indira herself considered her father weak,[76] an evaluation shared by a number of commentators of the time, but conveniently overlooked later.[77]

But in spite of all that, Indira is on the way to become Indira the Great.[78] Without doubt, she counts as one of the great Prime Ministers of India. The twentieth anniversary of her demise in 2004 was celebrated and remembered with pomp and with heartfelt participation by the population.[79] Even those among her biographers—and they are increasing—who deride and condemn her cannot deny her grudging respect.[80] The former German Chancellor

Helmut Schmidt put it succinctly: in an appreciation after her assassination, he called her a *zoon politicon*.[81]

Founding a Dynasty?

Congress held on to the dynasty and its women seemingly against all odds: for seven years it pressured Sonia to take the reins, until she gave in. Why did the party do this? One answer is the *'goongi gudiya'* argument: women are merely a symbol: A doll by definition cannot speak, cannot act, or is at most manipulated by those who hold the strings.[82] As such, she stands on the same level as a flag or a tune, like a national anthem, something intrinsically without value, empty of content, but therefore open to all manner of projections. In this reading, the choice of Sonia would be a thoroughly male chauvinistic act.

The argument has a certain seductive plausibility, except it has not worked. It might have been convincing when Indira Gandhi was first appointed Prime Minister. She had no vassals behind her, was not tied down by caste, region, class, religion, language or faction.[83] Like Sirimavo Bandaranaike of Sri Lanka, she was a compromise candidate, not, as is so often the case nowadays, candidate of first choice. She was not so much seen as a better, kinder sort of man, but as the only choice possible under the circumstances of Indian politics at the time and firmly under male control. In other words, even at that time she was chosen *because* she was a woman and was expected to act as a woman in politics as well.[84] Female leaders are supposed to guard the dead leaders' legacy, not act for themselves.[85] The symbol should portray the virtues of the deceased leader without being active itself. It failed spectacularly with Indira. And it failed with Sonia. To refuse political pressure for seven years points to a steadfastness which does not indicate that the person is weak. While some feminists might argue that there is no limit to male stupidity, one wonders whether Congress leaders would really be dense enough to commit the same error over and over again: choose a symbol and get a Kali?

In returning to the vexed question of dynasties: Why would Congress leadership be so eager to continue the dynasty? Was the memory of Indira the Great still so powerful that it was believed that only a Nehru/Gandhi *woman* could turn the tide? Had the name itself become a mere symbol, or was it something more—a guarantee of competence and efficiency? The Gandhi family can be said to be perceived as pan-Indian, in some way as the heart of the Congress.[86] There seems to exist a nearly automatic assumption, that by necessity a Nehru/Gandhi descendant will eventually have to take over Congress leadership, regardless of political inclination, qualification, or gender. The only way for the BJP to attack Sonia was to show that she was not a legitimate member of the dynasty.

That is not, however, how the argument is put in many discussions. Instead, both Indira and Sonia have been accused of harbouring desires to found a dynasty of their own, or more precisely, to push their children into positions of power. Many authors attributed to Indira an intention to establish a dynasty for her son(s), especially Sanjay, out of misplaced and distorted motherly love.[87] Similarly, Sonia is now often reviled for allegedly wishing to continue dynastic rule and acting as a place marker for her children in the Congress Party.[88] There is a certain paradox here: Indira was accused of betraying the Nehru heritage, in other words, of betraying the same dynasty she was supposed to be desirous of establishing.[89] Against this line of argument, it is salutary to read what Malhotra has to say about dynasties in India and in South Asia in general. He points out that these are not a one-time or one-dynasty phenomenon, but are wide-spread in South Asia and are obviously loved by the people. It is, therefore, misplaced to criticize Indira or Sonia for harbouring dark desires of dynasties when in reality they are just following a general trend.[90] It would be much more pertinent to enquire into the role of the party in all this.

There seems to be a determination to be blind to the facts. In Indira's case, the electorate endorsed a decision not taken by her but by the Congress syndicate. Sonia had to be pushed for seven years to enter politics by the party seniors. So, is it not rather the old men of the Congress who have decided to keep the dynasty going at all costs and regardless of individual inclinations of the persons concerned?[91] Women and men rise to the top on the dynastic principle, but only women are harshly criticized when they themselves try to follow it up. Men may push sons into positions of power without a murmur being heard about misplaced fatherly love, e.g about the son of Morarji Desai or the antics of the sons of the Dravidian leaders in South India, especially Karunanidhi.[92] Equally, while greed for power is perceived as normal for men, when exercised by a woman, it is seen as not unsuccessful or politically inopportune or a bad political decision, but as the outcome of her dark and evil female nature. Aggressive male politicians are seldom reduced to their male hormones or organs.

Conclusion: Answers searching for a question?

The costs of being a female political leader were excessively high for the dead and are not getting less for the living: Indira was termed sexually frigid and a bad wife to her husband long before becoming the black widow of short story fame. Sonia was fiercely attacked both before and after the elections with the fiercest attackers being BJP women: 'she is not one of us'. No sign of female solidarity here. One might wonder why any woman would want to consent to enter politics at all under these circumstances. And yet they do!

In India—and Sri Lanka—there is already a second generation of female leaders coming to the fore. Despite appearances, once in power, different women are endorsed or rejected for different and individual character traits and policies, features that are difficult to predict. Gender does play a large role, but we still have to ask what role: personality and individuality must not be neglected. And here women go beyond the emptiness of the symbol: they become political players in their own right who can succeed and fail.

Female leaders have to prove themselves in the litmus test of general elections as men must, and prove they did. Indira might not have *hataoed* the *garibi* (beaten poverty), but she was seen as at least trying, and she won a major war against great odds. Sonia was seen as doing something no male politician would do: she renounced office voluntarily. India has no fear of strong women as long as they are not in the house, but safely removed to a higher sphere, whether politician or goddess (and where they may still be perceived as somehow controlled by men).

The electorate obviously favour dynasty over gender and (national) origin. Indeed, right after Sonia announced her decision to renounce the position, protest from Congress members and members of the public were fast and fierce.[93] Again and again the people voted for the tried and tested name, the continuation of the ruling family, for the *children of power*. The magic of the name in those cases works for the women as well as for men, maybe even better for women. Indira, who specifically addressed female voters, also gave women a sense of their own, albeit latent, potential: if she can do it, we might, though we do not (yet). A woman with the magic name may be expected to achieve something that men cannot.

The argument of course works both ways as the punishment can be swift as well. When the dynastic successor is not up to scratch, s/he is often voted out without ceremony, at least in India. Indira lost the elections in 1977. And Sonia only managed to win elections after trying unsuccessfully twice, in 1998 and 2000. She, more than anybody, has demonstrated the limits of dynastic and female succession. Yet, myths of black widows and castration fears of the middle class notwithstanding, these fantasies did not prevent the people from voting for Indira. The black widow really seems to have been a figment of fevered male imagination.

Contrary to what the clamour of the chattering classes would have you believe,[94] Indian elections are not decided in the cities and by handphone-wielding, Maruti-driving, IT-employed whiz-kids, but by the poor peasants and labourers in remote villages, accessible only on dusty roads, on foot or on bullock carts, where even a television constitutes major progress, and where people think more about their defective pump sets, the cost of electricity, the loans they have to repay, and a failing monsoon.[95] Opinion pollsters shied away from the dusty roads and middle-of-nowhere villages. They did not take the trouble to talk to the poor—as, incidentally, Sonia Gandhi did—and they got all the wrong answers.[96] The poor who voted for Indira and the Congress, who voted for Rajiv and for Sonia, were the people who believed in the charisma of the Nehru/Gandhi name. The Indian village still puts its trust in the dynasty. And if it is Durga Amma or St. Sonia who helps them with their problems, so be it.

NOTES

1. This is a slightly extended version of a paper presented at the WPA-Conference in Islamabad in November 2005. It arose from research work done during three years in a project 'Dynasties and female political leaders in Asia'. I thank the University of Erlangen and WPA for providing the funding for the conference and the publication. Durga is one of many names for the fighting aspect of the goddess in Hinduism; Amma is Tamil for 'Mother'. Indira Gandhi was known as *Durga Amma* not only in the South, but throughout India.

2. Pranay Gupte, *Mother India. A political biography of Indira Gandhi* (New York: Scribner et al. 1992), p. 111.

3. Sonia Gandhi, *My own inner voice* [Online] 18 May 2004. Available: http://www.outlookindia.com.

4. Rajeswari Sunder Rajan, *Real and Imagined Women. Gender, culture and postcolonialism,* (London and New York: Routledge 1993), p. 119.

5. As is usual in India, politicians are often referred to just by their first, not their last or family names. This actually indicates both familiarity and respect, not, as in the West, disrespect. This paper sometimes follows this Indian habit.

6. Sonia Gandhi ed., *Two alone, two together: letters between Indira Gandhi and Jawaharlal Nehru, 1940–1964* (London: Hodder & Stoughton 1992), p. 627.

7. Jawaharlal Nehru, *Letters from a father to his daughter: being a brief account of the early days of the world written for children* (Calcutta: Oxford University Press, 1945).

8. Indira Gandhi, *My Truth Presented by Emmanuel Pouchpadass* (New Delhi et al.: Vision Books 1980), p. 22.

9. Ibid., p. 99.

10. Pupul Jayakar, *Indira Gandhi: a Biography* (London et al.: Penguin 1992), 90/97 and 106/112; Katherine Frank, *The Life of Indira Gandhi,* (New York: Harper Collins 2001), p. 244.

11. Jayakar, *Indira Gandhi,* p. 114.

12. Inder Malhotra, *Dynasties of India and Beyond* (New Delhi: Harper Collins 2003), p. 55.

13. Ibid.

14. Rupa Chatterjee, *Sonia Gandhi. The Lady in Shadow* (Delhi: Butala Publications 1998), p. 10.

15. Ibid., 19-26; Sonia Gandhi, *Rajiv*, (New Delhi: Viking 1992), p. 1.

16. P.C. Alexander, *My Years with Indira Gandhi* (New Delhi: Vision Books 1996), pp. 154–5.

17. Chatterjee, *Sonia Gandhi*, p. 207.

18. '*On the Move*' [Online] 1 September 2000. Available: http://www.outlookindia.com; '*The Intangible Ayes*' [Online] 22 August 2003. Available: http://www.outlookindia.com.

19. *Cf.* Prithvi N. Dhar, *Indira Gandhi, the "Emergency", and Indian Democracy* (Oxford: Oxford Univ. Press 2000), p. 369.

20. Malhotra, *Dynasties*, p. 67.

21. Jayarkar, *Indira Gandhi*, 137; Alexander, *My Years*, 47; Malhotra, *Dynasties*, p. 46.

22. Gupte, *Mother India*, 259. Even Aung San Suu Kyi considers both the members of the military junta and those in her party as 'uncles' whom she had known from childhood. In neither case did it prevent these women from asserting and realising a will and decisions of their own.

23. Malhotra, *Dynasties*, p. 72.

24. Jayakar, *Indira Gandhi*, p. 153.

25. Gupte, *Mother India*, p. 374.

26. Ibid., p. 378.

27. Jayakar, *Indira Gandhi*, p. 157.

28. Inder Malhotra, *Indira Gandhi: a personal and political biography* (London et al.: Hodder & Stoughton 1989), p. 129.

29. Jayarkar, *Indira Gandhi*, p. 175.

30. Malhotra, *Indira Gandhi*, p. 77.

31. Gupte, *Mother India*, p. 299.

32. Jayarkar, *Indira Gandhi*, p. 169. Katherine Frank even claims that Nixon was afraid of her: Frank, *Life of Indira Gandhi*, 335; similarly Henry Kissinger, *White House Years* (Boston et al.: Little, Brown 1979) 864 and 879: 'He considered her [....] a cold-blooded practitioner of power politics.' This from a power politician of the purest water is praise indeed! 'Mrs Gandhi [...] was as formidable as she was condescending,...' Nixon called her an 'old witch' and complained that India did not listen to the USA as Pakistan did: Gandhi, *My Truth*, p. 150.

33. Michael A. Genovese, ed., *Women as national leaders* (Newbury Park et al.: Sage 1993), 8. The statement sounds seductive, yet considering that Pakistan did start a war in 1999 when a decidedly male Prime Minister was ruling, it might be taken with a grain of salt.

34. Kali is the fearsome, wild and ferocious aspect or manifestation of the goddess Durga. Kali is said to drink blood and dance on corpses. She is normally portrayed as black, with a skirt of human arms, a necklace of skulls and foetuses as earrings. Not even her husband Siva can control her; in fact, she just walks over him—literally.

35. Gupte, *Mother India*, p. 453.

36. Harijans (literally: children of God) is a name Mahatma Gandhi coined as a somewhat more respectable name for the, former, untouchable castes. Meanwhile, these castes have rejected the term as condescending and prefer to refer to themselves as Dalits (the broken or crushed ones).

37. Jayakar, *Indira Gandhi*, p. 365, says she behaved like the typical Indian mother; Gupte, *Mother India*, p. 334, calls her *Bharat Mata* (Mother India, precisely the title of his book).

38. Dhar, *Emergency*, p. 233.

39. Malhotra, *Indira Gandhi*, p. 84.

40. Dhar, *Emergency*, pp. 257-60.

41. Ibid., p. 259; similar Jayakar, *Indira Gandhi*, 235f.; Malhotra, *Dynasties*, 85f.

42. Dhar, *Emergency*, 264. Which is patently untrue: the hard left opposed Emergency equally.

43. Ibid., pp. 312, 351; see also Jayakar, *Indira Gandhi*, p. 237. Malhotra and Dhar even speculate that she called elections because she became impatient with Sanjay's excesses (Dhar, *Emergency*, 336 and Malhotra, *Dynasties*, 94), which, if true, would invalidate the dynastic argument.

44. Malhotra, *Dynasties*, 198; Dom F. Moraes, *Mrs Gandhi*, (London: Cape 1980), p. 198, relates the anecdote of his serving maid who lamented the treatment of Indira after her election defeat. A similar reaction was found towards Jayalalitha after she was sent to prison.

45. Jayakar, *Indira Gandhi*, 279. Malhotra, *Dynasties*, p. 112, points out that the Harijans never suffered more than under the Janata government that succeeded Indira in 1977.

46. *Cf*. Prem Shankar Jha, '*Who is an Indian?*' [Online] Rev. 3 November 2003. Available: http://www.outlookindia.com; 'Sonia can't be Mayor of Ahmedabad', [Online] Rev. 13 November 2003. Available: http://www.indianexpress.com.

47. The Bofors gun had been purchased from Sweden. Very soon after the deal was concluded, allegations surfaced that the seller had paid illegal commissions and bonuses (kickbacks) to people involved in the deal on the Indian side up to and including then Prime Minister Rajiv Gandhi. An Italian businessman, Quattrocchi, was rumoured to be involved in these shenanigans as well. Though it seems certain that bribes of some sort have been paid to various people, Rajiv was posthumously cleared of blame in the affair. The Bofors gun is said to have contributed decisively to the victory over Pakistan in the short Kargil war in 1999. *cf*: Sukumar Muralidharan, '*A Verdict under Scrutiny*'; [Online] Rev. 14-27 February 2005. Available: http://www.flonnet.com. Sukumar Muralidharan, '*The Lindstrom disclosures*' [Online] Rev. 24 April–7 May 2005. Available: http://www.flonnet.com.

48. Personal information by Dr S. Sumathi, Dept. of Anthropology, University of Madras. This was said with regard to the way former Chief Minister Jayalalitha of Tamilnadu was treated in the Assembly when she lost the elections in 1996: Members of the DMK (Dravida Munnetra Kalakam) pushed her around and even tried to pull her sari off.

49. Janak Raj Jai and Rajiv Jai, *Sonia's foreign origin—A non-issue* (New Delhi: Regency Publications 2004), 48 and 53. '*Sushma to lead life of Sanyasin*'. [Online] 18 May 2004. Available: http://www.sify.com/news. '*BJP, Allies to Boycott Sonia's Swearing-in Ceremony*' [Online] 17 May 2004. Available: http://www.hindu.com.

50. In an interview given to the *New Sunday Express* she claimed that she considered the issue of her foreign origin a pretext because the BJP lacked a programme,

because she herself felt completely Indian and had never encountered any resentment on account of her originating from Italy. (*The New Sunday Express*, 7 March 2004, p. 6).

51. P. Jayaram, '*Manmohan Singh: Emerging from shadows of Sonia (100 days of Manmohan government)*', [Online] 26 August 2004. Available: http://www.yahoo.com/news/india news. Krittivas Mukherjee, '*Sonia Gandhi among The Guardian's Women of the Year*' [Online] 21 December 2004. Available: http://www.yahoo.com/news/india news.

52. '*Communist boost in Indian polls*' [Online] Rev. 13 October 2006. Available: http://news.bbc.co.uk/2/hi/south_asia/4760423.stm [11 May 2006].

53. Yogendra Yadav, 'The elusive Mandate of 2004', Economic and Political Weekly National Election Study 2004 pp. 39, 51, 18 December 2004, pp. 5383-96.

54. Ibid., 5383—this one continues to escape our analytical grasp.

55. Ibid., p. 5391.

56. Ibid.,pp. 5392-3.

57. Ibid., pp. 5394-5.

58. In Tamilnadu, this figure was 46 per cent for the whole electorate compared to 27 per cent countrywide. Ibid., p. 5490. The corresponding figures for Vajpayee were 33 per cent and 39 per cent.

59. Ibid., p. 5396.

60. Rajeshwari Deshpande, 'How gendered was women's participation in Election 2004?' Economic and Political Weekly National Election Study 2004 pp. 39, 51, 18 December 2004: pp. 5431-6. Unless otherwise indicated, the remarks in this paragraph follow this article.

61. Ibid., p. 5433.

62. Brahma Chellaney, though, thinks he has the answer: the men vote for the mother goddess, a concept, he says, central to Indian thinking: Brahma Chellaney, 'Why India accepts a foreign-born leader,' The Japan Times, 19 May 2004, p. 17. Dipankar Gupta has a less flattering explanation: according to him, men vote for the symbol: Dipankar Gupta, 'Sonia, the Ideal Symbol,' *Newsweek*, 10 May 1999, p. 41.

63. Sunder Rajan, *Real and Imagined Women*, p. 111; also Jayakar, *Indira Gandhi*, p. 231.

64. Sunder Rajan, *Real and Imagined Women*, p. 110.

65. *Cf.* Neluka Silva, *The Gendered Nation. Contemporary Writing from South Asia* (New Delhi et al.: Sage 2004), pp. 57-58.

66. Chandrika, however, was harshly criticized for proclaiming emergency in 2003 and had to revoke it after one day.

67. Frank, *Life of Indira Gandhi*, p. 322. See e.g. her claim that Sanjay blackmailed his mother into declaring emergency etc.

68. Dhar, *Emergency*, 122; Gupte, *Mother India*, p. 374; Indira Gandhi, *My Truth*, p. 77. Alexander, *My Years*, p. 36, mentions that she disliked this description intensely.

69. Alexander, *My Years*, p. 63.

70. Dhar, *Emergency*, p. 120.

71. Venkitesh Ramakrishnan, '*Mixed Record, Frontline 22*' [Online], 9 June 2005. Available: http://www.flonnet.com.

72. Indira Gandhi, *My Truth*, p. 99.
73. Malhotra, *Indira Gandhi*, p. 191.
74. Dhar, *Emergency*, p. 223.
75. Judith Brown, *Nehru, A Political Life* (New Haven and London: Yale University Press 2003), pp. 276-77, 279; see also chapter 16 therein.
76. Dhar, *Emergency*, p. 123.
77. Brown, *Nehru*, p. 331.
78. Malhotra, *Dynasties*, p. 99.
79. '*Tributes Paid to Indira Gandhi*' [Online] Rev. 13 October 2006. Available: http://www.hindu.com/2004/11/01/stories/2004110104581100.htm [1 November 2004].
80. *Cf.* Frank, *Life of Indira Gandhi*, p. 347.
81. Malhotra, *Indira Gandhi*, p. 191.
82. Dipankar Gupta, 'Sonia, the Ideal Symbol,' Newsweek, 10 May 1999, p. 41.
83. Frank, *Life of Indira Gandhi*, p. 289.
84. *Cf.* Alexander, *My Years*, pp. 34-35.
85. Sunder Rajan, *Real and Imagined Women*, p. 107.
86. Chatterjee, *Sonia Gandhi*, p. 251.
87. *Cf.* Chatterjee, *Sonia Gandhi*, pp. 42-43 and idem, *The Sonia Mystique* (New Delhi: Virgo Publications 2000), p. 36; also Malhotra, *Dynasties,* p. 95.
88. For a nuanced discussion of this assumption, *cf.* Malhotra, *Dynasties,* p. 200.
89. Gupte, *Mother India*, p. 111.
90. Malhotra, *Dynasties*, pp. 25-26. He is, however, also of the opinion that Indira did want to build a dynasty for Sanjay to follow her: *ibid*, p. 67.
91. *Cf.* Indira Gandhi, *My Truth*, 89, where Indira herself relates that Shastri offered a minister's post because '...he must have a Nehru in the Cabinet to maintain stability'.
92. For the case of Morarji Desai, cf. Malhotra, *Dynasties*, p. 106.
93. 'Why did Sonia change her mind? And: Sonia Gandhi turns down PM post.' [Online] 19 May 2004. Available: http://news.bbc.co.uk/2/hi/south_asia/.
94. *Cf.* Gupte, *Mother India*, 111: he claims she was not mourned in India, though this statement was belied by the immense popularity with which the 20th anniversary of her death was celebrated in India.
95. *Personal communication,* by Nitin Gokhale, Deputy Editor, Tehelka.
96. *Personal communication,* by Nitin Gokhale. Another voice questioning the accuracy of the polls was V. Venkateshan, 'Unfounded optimism' [Online] Frontline 10-23 April 2004. Available: http://www.flonnet.com. The article questioned the basis for the BJP's optimism and showed the flaws in the election programme.

References

Brown, Judith. *Nehru, A Political Life*, New Haven and London: Yale University Press, 2003.

Chatterjee, Rupa. *Sonia Gandhi. The Lady in Shadow*, Delhi: Butala Publications, 1998.

Chellaney, Brahma 'Why India accepts a foreign-born leader.' *The Japan Times* (19 May 2004).

Deshpande, Rajeswari. 'How gendered was women's participation in Election 2004?' Economic and Political Weekly, National Election Study 2004 pp. 39, 51 (18 December 2004), pp. 5431-6.

Dhar, Prithvi N. *Indira Gandhi, the "Emergency", and Indian Democracy*, Oxford: Oxford University Press, 2000.

Frank, Katherine. *The Life of Indira Gandhi*, New York: Harper Collins, 2001.

Gandhi, Indira. *My Truth*, Presented by Emmanuel Pouchpadass, New Delhi et al.: Vision Books, 1980.

Gandhi, Sonia ed. *Two Alone, Two Together: letters between Indira Gandhi and Jawaharlal Nehru, 1940-1964*, London: Hodder & Stoughton, 1992.

Gandhi, Sonia. *Rajiv,* New Delhi: Viking, 1992.

Genovese, Michael A., ed. *Women as National Leaders*, Newbury Park et al: Sage Publications, 1993.

Gupta, Dipankar 'Sonia, the Ideal Symbol,' Newsweek (10 May 1999): 41.

Gupte, Pranay. *Mother India. A political biography of Indira Gandhi*, New York: Scribner et al., 1992.

Jai, Janak Raja and Rajiv Jai. *Sonia's foreign origin—A non-issue*, New Delhi: Regency Publications, 2004.

Jayakar, Pupul. *Indira Gandhi: a Biography*, London et al: Penguin, 1992

Kissinger, Henry Alfred. *White House Years*, Boston and Toronto: Little, Brown, 1979.

Malhotra, Inder, *Dynasties of India and Beyond*, New Delhi: Harper Collins 2003.

Malhotra, Inder. *Indira Gandhi: a personal and political biography*, London et al.: Hodder & Stoughton, 1989.

Moraes, Dom F. *Mrs Gandhi*, London: Cape 1980.

Nehru, Jawaharlal. *Letters from a father to his daughter: being a brief account of the early days of the world written for children*, Calcutta: Oxford University Press, 1945.

Silva, Neluka. *The Gendered Nation. Contemporary Writing from South Asia*, New Delhi et al: Sage Publications, 2004.

Sunder Rajan, Rajeswari. *Real and Imagined Women. Gender, culture and postcolonialism*, London and New York: Routledge, 1993.

The New Sunday Express (7 March 2004): 6.

Yadav, Yogendra. 'The elusive Mandate of 2004.' *Economic and Political Weekly*, National Election Study 2004 pp. 39, 51, (18-24 December 2004): pp. 5383-96.

Electronic Resources (as of 5 October 2006)

'BJP, Allies to Boycott Sonia's Swearing-in Ceremony', 17 May 2004, online. Available: http://www.hindu.com.

'Communist boost in Indian polls' [Online] Rev. 13 October 2006, available: http://news.bbc.co.uk/2/hi/south_asia/4760423.stm [11 May 2006].

Jayaram, P. Manmohan Singh: 'Emerging from shadows of Sonia' *100 days of Manmohan government*, [online] 26 August 2004., available: http://www.yahoo.com/news/indianews.

Jha, Prem Shankar. 'Who is an Indian'? 3 November 2003. online, available: http://www.outlookindia.com.

Mukherjee, Krittivas. 'Sonia Gandhi among The Guardian's Women of the Year', [online] 21 December 2004, available: http://www.yahoo.com/news/indianews.

Muralidharan, Sukumar. 'A Verdict under Scrutiny', 14-27 February 2004, online, available: http://www.flonnet.com.

Muralidharan, Sukumar. 'The Lindstrom disclosures', online. 24 April–7 May 2004, available: http://www.flonnet.com.

'On the Move', online. 1 September 2003, available: http://www.outlookindia.com.

Ramakrishnan, Venkitesh. 'Mixed Record, *Frontline*' 22, online. 9 June 2005, available: http://www.flonnet.com.

'Sonia can't be mayor of Ahmedabad', online. 13 November 2003, available: http://www.indianexpress.com.

'Sonia Gandhi turns down PM post', online. 19 May 2004, available: http://news.bbc.co.uk/2/hi/south_asia/.

'Sushma to lead life of Sanyasin', online. 18 May 2004, available: http://www.sify.com/news.

'The intangible ayes', online. 22 August 2003, available: http://www.outlookindia.com.

'Tributes Paid to Indira Gandhi', [online] Rev. 13 October 2006, available: http://www.hindu.com/2004/11/01/stories/2004110104581100.htm [1 November 2004].

Venkateshan, V. 'Unfounded optimism'. *Frontline* online. 10-23 April 2004, available: http://www.flonnet.com.

'Why did Sonia change her mind?' online. 19 May 2004, available: http://news.bbc.co.uk/2/hi/south_asia/.

8

A Leader-in-waiting—Female Political Leadership in Burma[1]

Andrea Fleschenberg

Nobel prize winner Aung San Suu Kyi is, since 1990, Burma's (now Myanmar's) democratically legitimized leader-in-waiting. She remains popular among common Burmese, ethnic nationalities and exiled groups spread all over the world—despite her long house arrest imposed by one of Asia's most enduring and parochial military dictatorships, the State Peace and Development Council (SPDC, till 1997 named State Law and Order Council, SLORC).

Although an accidental political leader, she always perceived herself somehow destined by her father's political legacy (which remained unfinished due to his assassination shortly before the country's independence in 1947)—a view widely shared by the population and even partly by the ruling Burmese military, the *Tatmadaw*. Like her father Aung San, the country's most revered independence hero, she remains untested in her performance, her leadership capacity and skills in conventional, institutionalized politics. She therefore falls under the category of female political leadership against intact authoritarian regimes which determines to a significant extent her status, motivation and means of political agency—comparable, to a certain extent, to Wan Azizah Wan Ismail and, in earlier career stages, Corazon Aquino, Benazir Bhutto, Khaleda Zia, Sheikh Hasina Wajid as well as Megawati Sukarnoputri. Her political leadership corresponds to the type of a *transforming leader* as defined by Burns,[2] meaning that she intends and tries to alter the present status quo of an oppressive authoritarian military regime through a democratic transition and through the establishment of a new political culture which follows universal democratic principles and Buddhist values. Even though she achieved an important political victory by winning a landslide victory with her party, the National League for Democracy (NLD), in the elections held on 27 May 1990, a successive power transfer by the military power-holders never took place, leaving Aung San Suu Kyi in a nonpositional[3] leadership situation.

But such formal details remain irrelevant to the population and to the political reality of Burmese power politics and negotiations. She is perceived to be 'the virtual leader-in-waiting of her nation'[4] by most of the population and, until recently, the undisputed authority of a democratic Burma, of national transformation and national reconciliation by opposition actors.[5] The main question of this analysis is therefore: What are the key features of a political leadership (style) and agenda of a female politician who stands with Mahatma Gandhi and Václav Havel denouncing violence as a means of oppositional struggle?

The Gender and Socio-Political Environment

Burma is the last remaining praetorian regime of Asia besides Pakistan which, being male-oriented and dominated, creates a challenging power setup for female political leadership in general. Post-colonial Burma is a country with a rather fragmented populace[6] due to its parochial praetorian dictators. It has a short record of parliamentary democracy and a decades-long one of continuous inter-ethnic secessionist fighting from the periphery against the central, Burmese-led military regime.[7] Its isolatory authoritarianism has both structural and strategic sources—until 1988 a socialist, and since 1962 a nationalist ideology which justifies total state command and control by military appointees over large sectors of society and the economy.[8] The military regime (SPDC) is ranked as one of the world's most repressive societies.[9]

In current Burma, there are three major players who all draw the terminology of their political values and traditions primarily from Burmese culture, mostly from Theravada Buddhism: (a) the military junta including its extensive vertical crony system across the territory,[10] (b) the *sangha* (Buddhist clergy),[11] and (c) the pro-democracy movement under the leadership of Aung San Suu Kyi which is the less visible one in terms of physical and institutional presence under authoritarian rule. Thus, the latter rather represents a symbolic power and counter-weight based on a mixed set of universal and Buddhist democratic values.[12]

The *Tatmadaw*-based regime is framed within a pre-colonial setting of quasi-sacred absolutist dynastic rule to prove that its own patrimonial authoritarianism is actually a legitimate as well as historically continuous state and power pattern within Burmese political culture.[13] This notion is strongly and, one can say, successfully challenged by Aung San Suu Kyi and the opposition movement given her continuous popularity and the perceived illegitimacy of the military regime, viewed as non-Buddhist in its performance, since the events of 1988 (a bloody military takeover) and 1990 (an electoral defeat), respectively.[14] Aung San Suu Kyi 'reappeared like an avenging nemesis to haunt U Ne Win and his cronies with the memory of Aung San, the only truly unifying name in Burmese politics today.'[15]

When one travels throughout Burma, women's overall presence in public life, especially in the economic sector of everyday commodities, is striking in a country where the society's life and fate is exclusively dominated by male decision-makers in the form of the military in the political field (with the key exception of *The Lady*) and Buddhist authorities (the *sangha*) in the spiritual field.

> Traditionally political power was a male preserve and membership of the Buddhist monk-hood an exclusively male privilege. Cultural concepts ensured official power gravitated to the male while Buddhist ideologies reaffirmed men's superior status in the hierarchy of rebirth. Despite this, women played critical roles in society, the economy and the household and in many areas enjoyed equality with men.[16]

The exclusively male military regimes[17] of nearly half a century severely impacted on the status of Burmese women: the state was profoundly militarized and became more masculine which had a 'detrimental impact on women's lives as their customary independence and status was eroded.'[18] Given this context, the exceptional challenge to the regime and its legitimacy through Aung San Suu Kyi's alternative leadership and societal vision becomes even more evident and significant. 'As the space ascribed for women in Burma was reduced, it was a woman leader who demanded an equal space not only for women but for all members of the community that is modern Burma.'[19] As one of Aung San Suu Kyi advisors put it: 'Although women have equal rights, there are nearly no important women in politics. The only important woman is under arrest.'[20]

What gendered picture can be painted of Burma's current socio-political environment? As official statistics are biased, contradictory or key data is missing—hence reliable data scarce, only trends of female participation and leadership posts can be outlined. Women participate in high numbers in different parts of the economy with a female economic activity rate in the year 2002 of 65.8 per cent although no specific sub-data of employment sectors and income ratio are available.[21] Women received their active voting rights under British colonial rule in 1935 and passive rights in 1946 shortly before the country's independence with women being elected straight into Burma's first democratic parliament in 1947.[22]

**Table 1: Number of Elected Female Members to *Pyithu Hluttaw*
(1947-1990)[23]**

Election Year[24]	*Pyithu Hluttaw* (Parliament)	
	No. of Seats/Women	% of Women
1947[CA25]	n.a./7	n.a.
1952[CE]	n.a./2	n.a.
1956[CE]	n.a./5	n.a.
1960[CE]	n.a./3	n.a.
1974[NCE]	452/9	1,99
1978[NCE]	465/13	2,79[26]
1981[NCE]	475/13	2,74
1985[NCE]	489/15	3,07
1990[CE]	485/14[27] (all from NLD)	2,88

So far, very few women have entered the male domain of politics throughout the country's modern history. Interestingly, like in most of South and South-East Asian countries, there appears to be a pattern of dynastic pathways to female political involvement. In 1947, for instance, after the assassination of the post-independence shadow cabinet under Aung San, the wives of the deceased independence leaders were appointed as temporary members of parliament.[28] Such a co-option of women into politics via familial ties existed already during British colonialism and continues still, under various military regimes since 1962 where the generals' wives occupy important posts as brokers in the political patron-client wickerwork/pyramid and in their leadership of corporatist or social organizations.[29] In the current political set up, only those women can be successful who are 'politically correct' (for the regime) and hence do have the right connections at their disposal, which means women from privileged descent—this applies to the economy, to government service as well as to social organizations.

An apolitical daughter turns into a leader in her own right

Like all female Asian and four out of five Latin-American top politicians, Aung San Suu Kyi's political biography is characterized by a particular family background—her descent from a political family with nationwide fame and charisma. Subsequently, even as an *accidental politician*, the beginning of her political career was eased by her inherited family legacy, thus her leadership was hardly questioned 'because she is the daughter of the god-like, most revered national hero and his qualities are projected on her in an unpondered manner'.[30] Interestingly, Aung San Suu Kyi could draw back on two political role models and reference points in her own family—her father, the national hero and independence leader, and her mother, Daw Khin Kyi, appointed director of social welfare in the cabinet of U Nu and the country's first female ambassador.[31] One of her close aides explained that Aung San Suu Kyi herself confirmed her mother had been a vivid example in her values and deeds while she only knows her father through books and narratives of other persons.[32] Brought up by her mother to live by traditional social and moral values and the Buddhist faith, she is regarded as 'an exemplar of what we Burmese regard as seemly, in matters of dress, comportment, conduct and bearing, in public and private'.[33]

Aung San Suu Kyi was born on 19 June 1945 in Rangoon (now Yangon), Burma, two years before her father, Bogyoke (General) Aung San, was assassinated alongside his cabinet colleagues on 19 July 1947 shortly before the country's independence from British colonialism. Aung San Suu Kyi's privileged educational career at renowned schools and colleges in Burma, India and Great Britain resembles that of other female career politicians who were also socialized in a prominent political family and in renowned national and international elite networks, apart from tertiary education at an international elite university. Moreover, Aung San Suu Kyi received her education from gender-segregated institutions—in India as well as in Great Britain. During her studies at Oxford University she met her husband, Michael Aris, a British scholar on Tibetan Studies, with whom she has two sons. This marriage opened the field to much criticism, in particular from the regime rather than the population, as inter-ethnic marriages are not widely considered acceptable in Burma, especially with someone originating from the former colonial power.

As the royal advisor in international and UN affairs, she followed her husband for two years to Bhutan before she dedicated subsequent years as housewife and mother to her young family. Although Aung San Suu Kyi's life was very much determined by her academic and family life, she certainly felt she was a *politician-in-waiting* as she reminded her husband before their marriage.[34] However, at the time of her return to Burma in March 1988 to care for her ailing mother who died in December of the same year, Aung San Suu Kyi's only 'intention regarding politics was to start several libraries in my father's memory'.[35] Swept away by the events of the popular mass rising in 1988[36], her entrance into politics has been one of an *accidental politician*—like she admitted in her first political speech at the Shwedagon Pagoda in Rangoon on 26 August 1988 in the presence of more than half a million people with a portrait of her father looking on.

The present crisis is the concern of the entire nation. I could not as my father's daughter remain indifferent to all what was going on. This national crisis could in fact be called the second struggle for national independence.[37]

In the beginning of her political career, Aung San Suu Kyi can be characterized as an 'invested symbol'[38] when she portrayed herself as 'my father's daughter', standing in for his political legacy and continuing his political work.[39]

Following the establishment of the NLD Aung San Suu Kyi soon became the leader of the national pro-democracy movement which she legitimized with her landslide victory in the parliamentary elections held on 27 May 1990. In these elections, considered relatively free, the NLD secured 80 per cent of the seats while the pro-regime party National Unity Party (NUP) had to content itself with an unexpectedly poor record of 2 per cent.[40] Outstanding in this electoral victory is the fact that Aung San Suu Kyi could not actively participate in the campaign. Given her long years abroad and the supposed influence on her of anti-government (read communist and ethnic insurgents) and foreign powers, but not before hundreds of successful NLD election rallies across the country, the military junta disqualified crowd-pulling Aung San Suu Kyi as a potential candidate and set her under house arrest from 20 July 1989 onwards.[41]

During the past years, Aung San Suu Kyi has received several human rights awards for her political activism, with the Nobel Peace Prize in 1991 being the most prestigious. Despite widespread international attention and support, the Nobel laureate remains under house arrest in more or less complete isolation since 1989. Only in 1995 and 2002 her isolation was interrupted by short periods, although her freedom of movement and space for political agency remained highly constrained.

Aung San Suu Kyi has become *the* opposition leader in Burma. However, her political future remains uncertain and there is a need to question whether she would be accepted as a national leader or head of state by the populace and main political actors after centuries of exclusively male dominance in social and political life. There are some conflicting opinion patterns regarding this acceptance. Two main opinion clusters emerged in the interviews conducted inside Burma. On the one hand, Aung San Suu Kyi is perceived as the undisputed and legitimate leader of her people, including, presumably, elected parliamentarians and ethnic groups who would trust her decision-making and follow her.[42] Her popularity and hence leadership acceptance is said to be rooted in her charisma, her familial descent as her father's daughter[43] and her commitment to her principles and her words which are followed by actions. It is assumed that there will be no gender-based discrimination in case of her coming to power, mainly because of her descent and her capabilities.[44]

On the other hand, the opinion is prevalent among members of Burma's social elite (journalists, academics, NGO activists) that it will be difficult for her to be accepted as a national leader given the projected support, derived from her father's and not her own political standing, by the older generation and her supportive inner-party group (the 'old uncles') to which younger people are not as much obliged to. The 'old uncles' especially encounter a very critical reception among the Burmese who still see them as former generals and former Ne Win associates, not adept enough in their political and intellectual skills and hence not genuinely committed to her cause.[45] From a gender perspective, Aung San Suu Kyi represents the ideal version of a Burmese woman—soft, assertive, cautious/prudent and respectful enough to give men in the party their space—without granting pre-eminence to men she would not have been accepted by them.[46] Regarding inner-party criticism and challenges of leadership, Aung San Suu Kyi herself runs a unitary stance and defends her leadership team.[47]

Another critical point lies in the fact that some ethnic leaders might not follow her if she fails to acknowledge their interests. Although otherwise stated in declarations on the tripartite dialogue and negotiations with the regime, several ethnic representatives said in private that their support for Aung San Suu Kyi depends mainly on her compliance of ethnic interests as defined by their leaders—a support which can be withdrawn at any time despite her popularity among the different ethnic communities.[48] Nevertheless, ethnic coalition partners in the pro-democracy movement as well as armed groups continue to back the concept of a tripartite dialogue with Aung San Suu Kyi as prime transition agent and indispensable negotiator for democratization.

In summary, similar to exceptional opposition politicians or freedom fighters such as Nelson Mandela, Václav Havel, Mahatma Gandhi and Xanana Gusmão, during the last one and a half decades, all efforts on behalf of the regime to make of Aung San Suu Kyi a *persona non grata* could not change her position as *the* most widely and broadly admired and respected pro-democracy leader in and outside Burma.

Min Laung *or* Fighting Peacock?—Leadership Performance and Agenda[49]

To assess Aung San Suu Kyi's style of political leadership, her policy-making, agenda-setting and strategies, (public) perceptions prevalent among the Burmese inside their country and within the exiled movement must be evaluated. Aung San Suu Kyi appears to have achieved an iconic status as leader of the Burmese pro-democracy movement soon after her entrance into political life which remained unquestioned and without public criticism for nearly one and a half decades. As shown above, her public portrayal is one of an honest, popular, sacrificing and courageous leader for democracy.—the only person who can bring democracy, freedom and prosperity to Burma and save its people.[50] In recent years, the emergence of dissenting single voices in her own political camp increased and broke the taboo not to question her agenda for change, her decisions and strategies in interaction with the military regime.[51] Especially among the exiled movement based in Thailand and in the USA, a certain public bashing of Aung San Suu Kyi's strategies, which failed to achieve a power takeover or a power sharing, (the now preferred option by her critics), became popular during the last few years.

> She is truly Burma's democracy icon and will remain so for many decades more. The Burmese are proud to have a Nobel Peace Prize winner, but they also yearn for an astute political figure able to confront tough-minded generals, hoping then that they can aspire to lives of freedom, prosperity and human dignity. (…) Military leaders and Suu Kyi must be aware that the two sides they represent are going in different directions. It really takes two to tango. While dancing out of step, they can bring nothing but disorder and disunity to the country they all claim to love. I believe they have missed great, great opportunities.[52]

But such criticisms, including the charge that she is not politically informed, are rejected by many people with diverse backgrounds inside Burma (e.g. diplomats, close aides, party members and the populace) as pro-regime or deriving from people who do not know her personally. As one diplomat put it, Aung San Suu Kyi is perceived in a dual way: feared as well as esteemed for her intellect, she is the undisputed and genuinely admired figurehead of her people, known in the last shack of the country.[53] Moreover, political analyst Aung Naing Oo cautioned that one can only criticize her in a democracy because nowadays criticism is a sacrilege.[54] For instance, one of the most well known Thailand-based opposition newspapers in Burma, *The Irrawaddy*, follows the editorial line of portraying Aung San Suu Kyi not in a critical but a supportive way—in order not to weaken her political agency and bargaining position—as a politician who has not been able to do much but possesses high popularity even if she is criticised in private for running a one-woman-show and for missing opportunities due to her idealism and stubbornness.[55]

In contrast, the public image of Aung San Suu Kyi in the Burmese state media is determined by a full censorship on the NLD and related activities, on the one hand, and the instrumentalization of dialogues among her and the regime and its outcomes by the SPDC for its own 'public relations' purposes. The rule of the military and Ne Win was based on the legacy of (General) Aung San. Facing thus a legitimacy crisis through the daughter of Aung San, the Myanmarification policy was thought to introduce new legitimacy patterns for the regime by inventing its own tradition.[56] The distorted revival of anti-colonial nationalism and pre-colonial royal rule was well suited with regard to the regime's main challenge, Aung San Suu Kyi and her biography.[57] From 1988 onwards, she was presented as wife of an ex-colonialist, with rude words suggesting abnormal sexual behaviour on her part, and strong nationalist undertones, claiming that she is anti-Buddhist and working for foreign nations, and thus ready to sell out the country once in power.[58]

Moreover, 'the SLORC blamed Aung San Suu Kyi for obstructing the process of maturing change in Burma and for her failure to acquiesce in the SLORC's control of Burma'.[59] After the end of her first house arrest in July 1995, Aung San Suu Kyi recommended to demand a dialogue for the power transfer which was met by fierce verbal attacks from the junta claiming that Aung San Suu Kyi is not a Burmese citizen and hence a threat to internal security.[60] In 1998, an official campaign charged her once again with links to foreign powers and demanded her expulsion from Burma, manifested several times in 'spontaneous' public gatherings where she was charged with consorting with criminal, dissident or terrorist organizations.[61] After 2000, the media policy slightly changed with an announced 'change' towards 'disciplined democracy' and regular secret talks from November onwards which softened the tone towards her and admitted negotiations with the opposition leader.[62] After being titled as Mrs Michael Aris during the 1990s in the state-sponsored press, then No. 2, Khin Nyint referred to her as Ma Suu Kyi (little sister Suu Kyi) which signifies in the Burmese context a degradation in status (thus political standing) rather than familiarity in Western terms.[63]

In contrast, her own fellow pro-democracy activists and sympathizers emphasize her indigenousness and hence her popularity.[64] An insider-outsider cognitive pattern in the perceptions related to Aung San Suu Kyi of the military regime and its supporters, on the one hand, and the pro-democracy movement and its supporters, on the other, can be identified. This perceived dichotomy manifests itself in charges of collaboration with foreign powers, the questioning of her being truly Burmese to challenge the legitimacy of her cause while the opposition emphasizes her ideal type appearance and behaviour for Burmese sociocultural standards, evidenced in her undoubtful popularity among ordinary people who inform themselves via alternative sources such as British Broadcasting Company (BBC) and Voice of America (VOA) radio broadcasting (English and Burmese service).

The question emerges, what are the leadership tools and the political agenda which allow Aung San Suu Kyi to maintain her largely undisputed leadership claim? According to Thailand-based representatives of the democratic shadow government, an exchange of policy-agenda and policy-consultation takes place among her and the NCGUB although for safety reasons they could not specify the *modus operandi*. Exiled political activist

Bo Kyi explained that on the one hand, the Thailand-based movement has secret exchange channels with her, and that they also read her speeches, messages and videotapes, which are regularly smuggled out of the country, to understand her policy imperatives. Such exchange might follow indirect paths, for example, when journalists were asked to raise certain questions, formulated by activists, in their radio interviews to Aung San Suu Kyi which she would then answer knowing their original source.[65] But coordinating and joining efforts with an isolated leader might prove difficult for some activists in exile who are dissatisfied that Aung San Suu Kyi did not issue a statement about her position on the Bangkok Process and the proclaimed Roadmap.

Given the lack of information, and her tightly constrained political agency amounting to complete isolation since 2003, it remains merely speculative and difficult to figure out what kind of leader Aung San Suu Kyi would be once elected or appointed in office as head of state or government or even in a political set up with somewhat free agency. Several people interviewed inside Burma fear that she is too idealistic and not down to earth enough for 'bread and butter' issues, while others have no doubts about her ability to govern the country as one could tell from her exemplary actions and sacrifices so far.[66]

Perceptions of Aung San Suu Kyi's leadership style are divergent within her close circle inside Burma and rather uniform within the exiled movement. Some describe her interpersonal skills, communicative and intellectual capabilities as 'perfect'—eulogizing her as charismatic, eloquent, very straightforward, clever, true to her principles, sacrificing, considerate and polite towards others, participatory, humorous, open, flexible down to the last detail, down to earth, honest as well as conscious that leading in such a process implies making mistakes.[67] Exiled political analysts highlight the contextual conditions (repressive regime vs. democracy struggle) which frame Aung San Suu Kyi's leadership features, apart from her own NLD organizational constraints.[68]

Her emancipatory-participatory politics approach materialized in concrete terms with weekly 'People Forums' through the public gate speeches[69] or in her country-wide tours. Those unconventional democratic practices, in particular the gate speeches, attract huge crowds of diverse social backgrounds:

> [the public gate speeches]...were an attempt by the NLD leadership to communicate their ideas to the people and to inspire them to take part in the political movement. Daw Aung San Suu Kyi had a mailbox attached to the front of her gate so that people could drop off questions during the week. Her staff selected the most pressing questions for her to address. The reading and answering of the letters gave the talks a give-and-take feeling, and the audience frequently chimed in with laughter and applause.[70]

In addition, after each of her releases she quickly proceeded to tour the country to garner popular support and to reorganize the party country-wide when most of the members were politically inactive or imprisoned. Apart from regular central executive committee meetings, those of different party branches, study groups, festivities, commemorations and press conferences took place whenever possible.[71]

In contrast, internal Burmese critics from her circle of (former) close aides and advisors claim that she is quick-tempered, changeable, and not stringent in her plans and decisions and cannot stand criticism.[72] Critics claim that she annoyed several good, capable and pragmatic party members. Internal party critics, including elected members of parliament, were declared to be traitors and to have switched sides.[73] There is also direct criticism related to her leadership behaviour from some international journalists and diplomats who claim that she does not separate her personal identity from her political image and, furthermore, has a reputation for haughtiness as she 'retreats behind an academic snobbism that tends to intimidate and discourage people from approaching her.'[74] Critics also claim that her party is not run in a democratic way as she does not, for instance, tolerate competition to breed a possible successor or to admit other capable and efficient women to the party council or its executive council.[75]

So is democracy 'the only game in town' for Aung San Suu Kyi's political agency and leadership?[76] What are her credentials in terms of democratization efforts and a pro-democracy political agenda? Once again, evaluating the space for political agency and for the implementation of her agenda (in general terms) is rather complicated in Burma's political power context and relies mainly on perceptions gathered. Even for long-term country analysts it is difficult to assess the intentions and positions of the main political actors as their agenda remains highly intransparent and sealed off/insular.[77] Opinions gathered in NLD statements, literature and interviews clearly evidenced that Aung San Suu Kyi's political agenda is mainly determined by the democratization struggle of the NLD and its opposition allies.[78] There are only few detailed indications about concrete agenda components or plans in the available primary sources—the election programme of 1990,[79] her speeches and books.[80] In the current political set-up, achieving democracy seems 'the only game in her political camp'.

> Due to the revolutionary situation its main focus lies on democratization. If she gets the chance to express her views, we can prove her leadership credibility, but till now she wasn't able to show her political ideas which are based on democratic procedures, civil society, good governance, rule of law and human rights, but no defined political programme so far.[81]

In addition, the chairman of the NLD-LA (Liberated Areas) confirmed '[t]he party agenda has no detailed programme. The main aim is democratic change and special attention is needed to our ethnic brothers in order to set up a Federal Union' because the 'major policy principle is unity of diversity, no centralised state economy' and with education as another major concern 'to break with ignorance, enlighten people.'[82]

According to the 1990 election manifesto, the economic objectives of the NLD can be characterized as those of a free market economy, stable fiscal and monetary policies to allow stability in prices and employment, foreign investments, diversification of export goods, reduction of foreign debts, resumption of aid and assistance from abroad, a reviewed tax system encouraging speedy development of private enterprise and sound economic development on the basis of a 'political system firmly rooted in the rule of law.'[83] Interviewees inside Burma agreed that detailed political programmes can be developed and formulated later, giving Aung San Suu Kyi the benefit of doubt about her agenda-setting which was often justified with morality-based assessments such as 'she is unique and has sacrificed so much for the country.'[84]

Thus, most Burmese inside the country could neither define the main components of her political programme, which led to some uncertainty about the future political system and its impact on the nationalities question, as well as the sustainability of the transition, in particular among interviewees of non-Burmese origin inside and outside the country.[85]

On the other hand, frequent criticism is raised in relation to her morality-based political leadership qualifying her agenda-setting and political agency too idealistic, too unrealistic and highly moralized in terms of content leading to failed strategies and political stagnation after fifteen years of struggle.

> The question is not the government, but how she can manoeuvre politically and if she is smart. She acts as a hero—stand on your ideas, don't care about success or failure—and not as a leader—interest-driven, willing to compromise, with supporters.[86]

US-based exiled Burmese political activists Zarni and May Oo criticize the iconic status and focus on Aung San Suu Kyi as a main catalyst for change. In their view, this international and national perspective, avoids 'diversity of ideas and approaches', is hostile towards other possible windows of opportunities.[87] Without proposing alternative strategies for internal activists, both authors even question the democratic commitment of Aung San Suu Kyi and dissident organizations which, in their view, 'have done little to encourage or foster democratic thinking and civic norms. Citizens have been isolated with old habits and traditions, without exposure to democratic ideas.'[88]

Apart from her leadership style and agenda, when women politicians are evaluated, their commitment to overcome the gender-related democracy deficit quickly comes into focus. Is Aung San Suu Kyi thus 'only' a national leader or also a pro-women leader? Like in the case of her general political agenda, almost no information is available regarding her commitment to women's issues and what space, if any, it occupies on her political agenda. The gender issue and a feminist perspective were clearly not infused into the Burmese pro-democracy movement[89] or the NLD itself. According to her Thailand-based spokesperson Win Khet, she does not think of women's issues as a special matter of concern.[90] Nevertheless, she encourages female members of the NLD to participate in meetings although the party itself, as well as the executive body, is male-dominated.[91] In addition, she frames the gender issue as part of the democracy struggle when, in her statements on Women's Day, she focuses on empowerment and unity among women from different Burmese ethnicities.[92] Committed to the 'universal benefits of the growing emancipation of women', she wants to promote the acknowledgement and the inclusion of women on the basis of equality in political life and freedom struggles.[93]

In reports on the situation of women in Burma and their narratives of social life and pro-democracy struggle, issued by the support group Alternative ASEAN Network on Burma (ALTSEAN), Aung San Suu Kyi often managed to smuggle out solidarity statements or one of her speeches was edited from a videotape and published as a foreword.[94] In those statements she refers to the plight of women under dictatorship. Evoking traditional images and role models of women as 'home makers, tenders of the hearth around which the family gathers, weavers of the gentle ties that bind faster than the strongest iron chains', she nonetheless points on possible female contributions 'towards the building of a nation that is a safe and happy home for its peoples.'[95] In the context of a male-biased society and political life, she frames women's participation within traditional acceptable gender roles and applies it to different policy issues, e.g. national reconciliation.

Most of the Burmese inside and outside the country, especially the female populace, have little doubt that Aung San Suu Kyi is a role model for them and, once in power, will be active on behalf of women and their political and social empowerment.[96] To counter her powerful leadership and role model, the regime moved to establish a sort of a state-guided feminism spearheaded by organizations like the Women's Affairs Committee and the Myanmar Women's Entrepreneurs Association.[97]

The Way Out?

What kind of political future might await Aung San Suu Kyi? With the events taking place since autumn 2004, all those hoping for a liberalization, a breakthrough of perceived 'soft-liners' or a roadmap towards a hybrid democratic regime were proven wrong.[98] After the subsequent purges of Khin Nyunt's power network and of local and regional commanders thereafter, the SPDC's No. 1, parochial 'hard-liner' General Than Shwe, managed to occupy, countrywide, all key positions with his own allies and to receive the US-label of 'outpost of tyranny'.[99]

> So there is a real risk that, instead of the long-awaited political breakthrough, the clock has simply been turned back a decade and the stage set for a replay with the same actors, the same script and, quite possibly, the same ending. (...) The pro-democracy movement, symbolised bravely by Aung San Suu Kyi, remains alive in the hearts and minds of millions, but under the existing depressed political, social and economic conditions, it does not have the strength to produce political change.[100]

Aggravatingly, Burma lacks a record of constitutional change of power and a solid consensus over the basis of legitimate political power—both impact on the precarious means of interaction between the military regime and the opposition.[101] Moreover, the long duration of the political impasse and stagnation undermines the leadership claim and its legitimacy of both sides, leaving only a margin for a power-sharing compromise.[102]

Alongside Thailand-based Burmese women activists from various ethnic origins, her own circle of close aides and friends foresee that Aung San Suu Kyi will not be released any time soon,[103] given the incident of 30 May 2003 which destroyed the relationship between both political actors and given the delegitimizing symbolism and strength of a released and political active leader endangering the generals power.[104] Few trusted the roadmap process to be a genuine proposition and rather believed it to be once again a step of the regime marked by empty promises, long discussions and a military version of 'disciplined democracy', the Chinese way, as a final goal.[105]

There are conflicting opinions about her leadership options—a non-positional leader-in-waiting, a social activist or a political-administrative functionary as future head of state or government, ambassador or minister. Some believe that she will never come to power, given the geopolitical position and proximity to influential (semi-)authoritarian regimes which could be challenged by their own people through a powerful symbol of a prime minister or president named Aung San Suu Kyi. But few question that any successful and legitimate democratic transition will take place without Aung San Suu Kyi as one of the leading figures who will surely serve in a post-military or caretaker government.[106] Among the exiled community and the international solidarity movement, there is consensus that Aung San Suu Kyi will and must be released, will be the country's crucial transition agent and will become the overall popularly accepted prime minister or president after a transition take place.[107]

But given the continuous firm grip of the SPDC under General Than Shwe (despite reports of internal power quarrels), it seems unlikely for Aung San Suu Kyi to be able to determine her political fate by herself in the near future unless an unpredictable window of opportunity opens up quite often as it does in the history of democratization.

NOTES

1. This case study is a preliminary version of a larger study conducted for the research project 'Dynasties and female political leaders in Asia', supported by the German Science Foundation (DFG) whose publications are available at www.uni-duisburg.de/Institute/OAWISS/institut/mitarbeiter/Dynasties/index.htm.
2. Jean Blondel, *Political Leadership* (London: Sage, 1987), pp. 20, 24.
3. The difference between *positional*, or institutional, and *nonpositional* refers to the fact whether the politician or leader holds an official, institutionalized office, usually in the field of conventional politics such as in the executive or legislature.
4. John Kane, *The politics of moral capital* (Cambridge: Cambridge University Press, 2001), p. 160.
5. See commemorative editorials for her 60th birthday on 19 June 2005 in: *The Irrawaddy*, 'Salute to The Lady', 17.06.2005; *The Irrawaddy*, Aung Naing Oo, 'Time to Break the Deadlock', 17.06.2005.
6. The ethnic group of Burmese represents 68 per cent of the population with other ethnic nationalities, highly fragmented, living mainly at the border areas: Shan (9 per cent), Karen (7 per cent), Rakhine (4 per cent), Chinese (3 per cent), Mon (2 per cent), Indian (2 per cent) and others (5 per cent). The outstanding majority is Buddhist (89 per cent) and only 4 per cent follow Christianity, primarily among the ethnic minorities like the Kachin and Karen or the mother of Aung San Suu Kyi, Daw Khin Kyi. (www.freedomhouse.org, retrieved 15 July 2006).
7. In 1997, Peter Carey characterized the military junta as a 'narco-military dictatorship' (*From Burma to Myanmar: Military Rule and the Struggle for Democracy* (London: RISCT 1997), p. 13.
8. Jalal Alamgir, 'Against the Current: The Survival of Authoritarianism in Burma,' *Pacific Affairs*, 70, Fall 1997): pp. 333-50, 334, 340. Major investments are made in collaboration with military-led or –owned companies—a major reason of Aung San Suu Kyi's call for no foreign investments. Despite an investment stop from Western countries, ASEAN economies and neighbouring countries stepped in as economic benefactors (ibid., 347f).

9. Freedom House, 'The Worst of the Worst', [Online] Rev. 2005, pp. 9-10. Available: www.freedomhouseorg/research/mrr2005.pdf. [15 July 2006].
10. Matthews suggests that probably ten per cent of the population, apart from an emerging urban middle class, materially benefit from the military's crony system and patronage-driven economy—a number certainly on the rise, as is the size of the Tatmadaw (Bruce Matthews, 'The Present Fortune of tradition-bound Authoritarianism in Myanmar', *Pacific Affairs* 71 1/1998): 7-23, 14-15).
11. The *sangha*, with approximately 150,000 members country-wide (excluding novices), has played a significant role in the organization of the opposition (Alamgir, 'Against the Current', 343). During the 1988 events, monks, alongside students, actively supported the pro-democracy movement and engaged as moral authorities in tasks usually performed by police, e.g. to secure calm and order during mass rallies (René Hingst, *Burma im Wandel. Hindernisse und Chancen einer Demokratisierung in Burma/Myanmar* (Berlin: Logos Verlag), 187-188).
12. Sheila Nair identifies 'a concern for "indigenizing" her political struggle and locating it within a Burmese cultural and spiritual milieu' ('Human Rights and Postcoloniality. Representing Burma', in *Power, Postcolonialism and international relations*, ed. Geeta Chowdhry and Sheila Nair (London et.al.: Routledge, 2004), 254-284, 276).
13. See discussion in: Matthews, 'The Present Fortune', 11; Mya Maung, 'The Burma Road from the Union of Burma to Myanmar', *Asian Survey* (30 June 1990): 602-624, 603-607. But others object, as '[t]he traditional concept of dynastic rule and legitimate authority goes back much further in time and was influenced by Buddhist and Hindu concepts of leadership. Despite personalized rule, a tradition of righteous kingship guided by moral and ethical codes of conduct served as a counterbalance to despotic tendencies of absolutist rule' (Tin Maung Maung Than, 'Myanmar. Military in charge', in *Government and Politics in Southeast Asia*, ed. John Funston (London/New York: Zed Books 2001), 203).
14. Oliver Wagener, 'Pagoden, weiße Elefanten und die Generäle', Südostasien 4/2003): 30-33, 32-33; Chao-Tzang Yawnghwe, 'Burma. The Depolitization of the Political', in *Political Legitimacy in Southeast Asia*, ed. Muthiah Alagappa (Stanford: Stanford University Press, 1995), pp. 170-92, 170.
15. Win Kanbawza, *A Burmese perspective. Daw Aung San Suu Kyi. The Nobel Laureate* (Bangkok: n.a., 1992), p. 168.
16. Jane Mills, 'Militarism, civil war and women's status: a Burma case study', in *Women in Asia. Tradition, modernity, and globalisation*, ed. Louise Edwards and Mina Roces (Ann Arbor: The University of Michigan Press, 2000), pp. 265-90, 265.
17. According to Mills, women constitute less than 1 per cent of military members, largely in medical and clerical duties and no combat roles (ibid., 274).
18. Mills, *Militarism, civil war, and women's status*, p. 266.
19. Ibid.
20. Interview conducted in Rangoon, March 2004.
21. http://hdr.undp.org/statistics/data/countries.cfm?c=MMR [15 July 2006].
22. http://hdr.undp.org/statistics/data/countries.cfm?c=MMR [15 July 2006].

23. Mills, 'Militarism, civil war, and women's status,' 283; Yi Yi Myint, Myanmar Gender Profile (n.a., 2000), pp. 42-43; Josef Silverstein, 'Aung San Suu Kyi. Is she Burma's Woman of Destiny?' Asian Survey 30 10/1990): 1007-19, 1009-10.

24. CA=Constituent Assembly, CE=competitive elections, NCE=non-competitive elections, na=not available.

25. In the 1974 Constitutional Assembly three out of 97 members were female (Mills, Militarism, civil war, and women's status, 275), confirming the pattern of female political representation of the post-independence period of under 5 per cent.

26. Yi Yi Myint lists only twelve female parliamentarians (2,58 per cent) who won seats in the 1978 elections (Yi Yi Myint, Myanmar Gender Profile, 43) although— given her background as President of the pro-regime Myanmar Women Entrepreneur's Association (which operates under the umbrella of the regime's mass organization Union Solidarity and Development Association USDA)—she is rather selective with data indication which only covers the years 1974–1985 under the rule of Ne Win or the military-controlled National Convention which had in 1993, according to her figures, 3.99 per cent of female members.

27. Out of 2296 candidates in the first free elections since 1960, 84 were women (3.65 per cent) (Mills, Militarism, civil war, and women's status, 283).

28. Overall, four women replaced their assassinated husbands and three women were elected to the post-independence Constituent Assembly in 1947 (Silverstein, 'Aung San Suu Kyi,' 1009; Mi Mi Khaing, The world of Burmese women (London: Zed Books, 1984), 159).

29. According to Yi Yi Myint's report on Burma's gender profile few women head government departments in the position of Director General or Managing Director (the highest rank available to a woman as several interview partners confirmed), but there are no current or long-time official statistics available (Yi Yi Myint, Myanmar Gender Profile, 38). In the country report to the 1995 Beijing Conference, it is stated that although women hold 40 per cent of public service posts in state organs and ministries, a meagre 0.4 per cent hold high level posts resulting in 0.11 per cent of public employees (ibid., 39).

30. Interview with former close aide of Aung San Suu Kyi in Rangoon, March 2004.

31. Later, she worked as chairperson of the Social Planning Commission and the Council of Social Services and travelled extensively worldwide. See: Ma Than E, 'A Flowering of the Spirit: Memories of Suu and Her Family,' in Freedom from Fear, ed. Aung San Suu Kyi and Michael Aris (London: Penguin Books, 2. revised edition, 1995), 275-291, 279f; Bertil Lintner, Aung San Suu Kyi and Burma's unfinished renaissance, Working Paper 64, Centre of Southeast Asian Studies: Monash University Australia): 12.

32. According to this close aide, Aung San Suu Kyi promised her mother not to leave the country until democracy is restored (interviewed in Rangoon, March 2004; similar opinion gathered in an interview with Bo Kyi, head of AAPPB, Maesot, April 2004).

33. Ma Than E, A Flowering of the Spirit, p. 280.

34. Aung San Suu Kyi and Michael Aris, eds., Freedom from Fear (London: Penguin Books, 2. revised edition, 1995), p. xix.

35. Barbara Victor, *The Lady. Aung San Suu Kyi Nobel Laureate and Burma's Prisoner* (New York: Faber & Faber, 1998), p. 32.

36. For a detailed account of the 1988 events onwards see: Lintner, *Aung San Suu Kyi and Burma's unfinished renaissance*; Christina Fink, *Living Silence. Burma under military rule* (London/New York: Zed Books, 2001), 50ff.

37. Aung San Suu Kyi quoted in: Bertil Lintner, *Outrage. Burma's struggle for democracy* (London/Bangkok: White Lotus, 1990), 115f.

38. Kane, *The politics of moral capital*, p. 149.

39. John Parenteau, *Prisoner for Peace. Aung San Suu Kyi and Burma's struggle for democracy* (Greensboro: Morgan Reynolds, 1994), p. 103.

40. Voter turnout was at 72.59 per cent of which 59.87 per cent voted for the NLD securing the party 392 out of 485 mandates—compared to 21.16 per cent of the votes for the pro-regime NUP (Maria Widmann, 'Megawati Sukarnoputri und Aung San Suu Kyi. Umstände und Bedingungen ihres politischen Aufstieges' (Diploma thesis, University of Passau, 2001), 45).

41. 'Unfortunately, she is not leading the life of a normal citizen today because she is trying to cause political confusion and instability and unrest when we finally have peace and tranquillity in the country. Although we love and respect her father, it is very difficult for us to have the same feelings for her because of her actions. Frankly, if Aung San Suu Kyi had come back and worked for the country and married a Myanmar citizen, she might have been able to become a national leader' (former PM Khin Nyint quoted in: Victor, *The Lady*, 32).

42. Opinion gathered in interviews conducted in Rangoon and Mandalay 2004.

43. Interviewees, regardless of their class and professional background, always referred to Aung San as Burma's most important and most loved martyr and national hero. As one businessman put it, Aung San Suu Kyi would not have the standing and would not be tolerated by the ruling government if it would not be for her father—a central figure and rallying point of the military and its self-understanding. (Interviews conducted in Rangoon, March 2004).

44. Interview with an academic, Rangoon, March 2004.

45. NLD party chairperson Tin Oo had been chief of staff and defence minister under Ne Win from 1974–1976, but was jailed for an alleged coup attempt while NLD spokesperson U Lwin (before 1988 Colonel Maung Lwin) was vice prime minister under Ne Win (Chee Soon Juan, *To be free. Stories from Asia's Struggle against oppression* (Clayton: Monash Asia Institute, 1998), 72; Hans-Bernd Zöllner, 'Vom Ende einer Illusion. Zur aktuellen Lage in Myanmar,' in *Internationales Asienforum* 34 3/4/2003): 251-270, 254). Initially there were three groups and some factions inside the NLD which she personally managed to unify: (a) the Aung San Suu Kyi group composed mainly of intellectuals and nearly all arrested with U Win Thin as the most important and well known one, (b) the Tin Oo group of former military men and (c) Aung Gyi who already left the NLD before the 1990 elections (interview with Bo Kyi, Maesot, April 2004).

46. Interview with a female professor, Rangoon, March 2004.

47. Interview with Aung San Suu Kyi in 2002, in *The Irrawaddy Online*, 'Two Interviews with Aung San Suu Kyi'. [Online] no date. Available: http://www. irrawaddy.org/aviewer.asp?a=218&z=6. [15 July 2006] Furthermore, she

emphasizes her dependency on the support of the younger generation and their crucial participation in the pro-democracy struggle, like during her country-wide tours in 2003 (see: ALTSEAN, 'On the Road to Depayin: Speeches by Daw Aung San Suu Kyi'. [Online] no date. Available: http://www.altsean.org/ontheroad.html. [15 July 2006].

48. Interviews conducted in Rangoon (March 2004), Maesot (April 2004), Lisbon (August 2004); see also: Amitav Gosh, 'A reporter at large. Burma,' *The New Yorker*, 12.08.1996): 49.

49. Min Laung, the king-to-be, is primarily related to Aung San but also by some to Aung San Suu Kyi (Gustaaf Houtman, 'The Culture of Burmese Politics,' in *The Irrawaddy*, January 2004): 20-21; Hans-Bernd Zöllner, 'Dialog im verminten Gelände. Die Gespräche zwischen der Militärjunta und der Opposition in Myanmar,' in *Internationales Asienforum* 3-4-2001): 291-318, 302). The *Fighting Peacock* is nowadays the symbol of the opposition party; a symbol banned since Ne Win's military coup in 1962 as it was formerly used on student union flags referring to the powerful legacy of Aung San (Fink, *Living Silence*, 56).

50. Opinion gathered in interviews conducted in March and April 2004 among the Thailand-based opposition movement and political activists; see opinions of women activists and writers in: ALTSEAN, *Burma—Women's Voices for Change* (Bangkok: n.a., 2002), 44ff, 70; idem, *Burma: Voices of Women in the Struggle* (Bangkok: n.a., 1998), 30ff, idem, *Burma. More Women's Voices* (Bangkok: n.a., 2000), pp. 7, 47.

51. The best known and most recent case came from the US-based Free Burma Coalition in 2004 led by Zarni and May Oo (Zarni and May Oo, 'Common problems, shared responsibilities: Citizen's quest for national reconciliation in Burma/Myanmar, Report of a Citizen Exiles Group.' (Washington: The Free Burma Coalition, 2004).

52. Aung Zaw, 'Regrets—the residue of the 1990 Election,' in *The Irrawaddy* 27 May 2005.

53. Interview conducted in Rangoon, March 2004. Military representatives largely derive from rural or urban lower classes with a rather low educational record and thus face a political counterpart with high educational qualifications— especially for Burmese standards, a sharp intellect and a descent from one of the most significant Burmese political families, hence an elite background.

54. Aung Naing Oo, political analyst and journalist, interviewed in Chiangmai, March 2004.

55. Opinion gathered in interviews with Shawn L. Nance, journalist with *The Irrawaddy*, interviewed in Chiangmai, March 2004). Christina Fink, a scholar on Burmese politics, explained that Aung San Suu Kyi, a woman of steel with incredible determination, is invaluable for the transition incorporating the idea to institutionalize democracy (interviewed in Chiangmai, April 2004).

56. Hingst, *Burma im Wandel*, p. 213.

57. Hingst, *Burma im Wandel*, pp. 230-31.

58. Silverstein, 'Aung San Suu Kyi,' 1014. In the state media she was even compared to a famous Burmese traitor, Maung Ba Than, who helped British troops to conquer Burma (Janelle M. Diller, 'The National Convention: An Impediment

to the Restoration of Democracy,' in *The Challenge of Change in a Divided Society*, ed. Peter Carey (London/New York: Macmillan), 27-54, 30).

59. Robert I. Rothenberg, ed., *Burma. Prospect for a democratic future* (Washington: Brooking Institution Press, 1998), p. 2.

60. Hingst, *Burma im Wandel*, p. 246.

61. Buhrer and Levenson, *Aung San Suu Kyi, demain la Birmanie* (Arles: Editions Philippe Picquier, 2000), p. 47.

62. Yeni, former co-editor of *ABSDF-magazine* and journalist with *The Irrawaddy* nowadays, interviewed in Maesot, April 2004.

63. Hingst, *Burma im Wandel*, p. 301.

64. The foreign media uses a different imagery. Some foreign observers very much fancy the image of *Beauty and the Beast* when writing about Aung San Suu Kyi, e.g. Chee Soon Juan writings: 'Here was a diminutive lady—Gandhi-like in her tenacity with moral fibre to match, intellectual hostage to none, an archetype of Asian comeliness—fighting a hideous monster of a military regime' (Juan, To be free, 59; see, among others: Cathy Scott-Clark and Adrian Levy, 'Aung San Suu Kyi.' [Online] Rev. July 2001. Available: http://www.prospect-magazine.co.uk/article_details.php?id=3525 [15 July 2006].

65. Interview conducted in Maesot, April 2004. According to Zin Linn and Dr Sann Aung (elected parliamentarian in 1990), usually inside leaders are the main force and strategizers while exiled forces are in supportive roles as they cannot be dialogue partners (interviewed in Bangkok, April 2004).

66. Interviews conducted in Rangoon and Mandalay, March 2004. A typical opinion gathered was the following: 'I do not know her personally. I have never seen her at a rally and cannot judge how she is and what kind of leader she will be. But I think she has a good character and she is very intelligent and qualified. She is popular as she is her father's daughter, but she is also respected and recognized due to her own political standing. She will be accepted but it will be difficult for her as a woman. She will be hard in her decisions if needed'.

67. Interviews conducted in Rangoon, Burma, March 2004; Chiangmai and Mae Sot, Thailand, April 2004.

68. Interviews conducted in Chiangmai, March and April 2004.

69. Finke, *Living in Silence*, p. 88.

70. Ibid.

71. Finke, *Living in Silence*, p. 87.

72. Bertil Lintner (in a telephone interview, Chiangmai, April 2004) questioned the assessment that Aung San Suu Kyi is authoritarian because the NLD is not a political party in Western terms but an expression of change for the Burmese people thus never a 'properly' organized party.

73. Interviews conducted in Rangoon, March 2004.

74. Victor, *The Lady*, 222, see also: Scott-Clark and Levy, *Aung San Suu Kyi*.

75. Interview conducted in Rangoon, March 2004.

76. 'I've always told you, she said, 'that we will win…that we will establish a democracy in Burma, and I stand by that. But as to when, I cannot predict.' (quoted in: Amitav Gosh, *Dancing in Cambodia, at large in Burma* (Delhi: Ravi Dayal Publishers, 1998), 114).

77. While before 2003 several scholars and journalists favoured a theory of 'hardliners' (Than Shwe) and 'soft liners' (Khin Nyunt), the extensive purge and persecution of the latter, his allies and cronies in the wake of Burma's chairmanship of ASEAN (2006) came as sort of a surprise to most of the watchdogs and left no clear indications about the political fate of Aung San Suu Kyi.

78. 'Due to her isolation and house arrest, as well of her supportive surroundings, a policy-making and cooperation is impossible. (…) She's willing to sacrifice her life for the struggle which is the price to pay for being in Burmese politics' (Bo Kyi, head of AAPPB, interviewed in Maesot, April 2004).

79. The NLD manifesto of November 1989 is a broad and all-inclusive document with ambiguities in which popular sovereignty, human rights and democratic procedures along the lines of the United Nations Charter are strongly emphasized while the question of federalism and ethnic nationalities remains open until after parliamentary elections (Silverstein, 'Aung San Suu Kyi,' 1017).

80. Her books date back to the years 1991, 1995 and 1996 and contain collections of essays, interviews and reports on the socio-political and economic situation inside Burma or deal with her political thought as a concept to achieve transition to democracy (see: Aung San Suu Kyi, *Freedom from Fear*; idem, *Letters from Burma* (London et.al.: Penguin Books, 1997); idem, *Der Weg zur Freiheit. Die Friedensnobelpreisträgerin aus Birma im Gespräch mit Alan Clements* (Bergisch Gladbach: Bastei Lübbe, 1997) [English title: *The Voice of Defiance*].

81. Interview with Myint Thein, Joint Secretary NLD-LA, Maesot, April 2004.

82. Interview with Win Khet, Maesot, March 2004. Zin Linn and Dr Sann Aung, representatives of the exiled shadow government NCGUB, confirmed that the two major topics on the agenda are human rights/democracy and the ethnic issue with dialogue as agency framework for the exiled movement (interview conducted in Bangkok, April 2004; for Aung San Suu Kyi's statement on the main priority to establish democracy see: Buhrer and Levenson, Aung San Suu Kyi, 27).

83. Aung San Suu Kyi, *Letters from Burma*, pp. 43-44.

84. Interview with one of her close aides, conducted in Rangoon, March 2004.

85. Interviews conducted in Rangoon, Chiang Mai and Maesot, March 2004.

86. Interview with a NGO activist, conducted in Rangoon, March 2004. He further elaborated that her agency does not impress Burmese intellectuals.

87. Zarni and May Oo, *Common problems, shared responsibilities*, 11f, p. 8.

88. Zarni and May Oo, *Common problems, shared responsibilities*, p. 13.

89. Mills, *Militarism, civil war and women's status*, p. 284.

90. Interview conducted in Maesot, April 2004.

91. Anelyn de Luna (ALTSEAN), interviewed in Bangkok, April 2004.

92. Anelyn de Luna (ALTSEAN), interviewed in Bangkok, April 2004.

93. Opening Keynote Address by Aung San Suu Kyi to the NGO Forum on Women, Beijing, 31.08.1995, quoted in: ALTSEAN, ed., *Burma and the role of women* (Bangkok: n.a., 1997), p. 58.

94. See ALTSEAN, *Burma. Women's voices together* (Bangkok: n.a., 2003); idem, Burma. *More women's voices*; idem, Burma. *Voices of women in the struggle*, Foreword.

95. ALTSEAN, Burma. *Voices of women in the struggle*, pp. 3-4.
96. Interviews with former government servants, academics, NGO activists and teachers, conducted in Rangoon, March 2004, and exiled women activists in Chiangmai and Mae Sot, Thailand, March-April 2004.
97. Mills, *Militarism, civil war and women's status,* 285.
98. Many regarded the seemingly positive gestures of the SPDC in the Bangkok Process and Roadmap Process under Khin Nyunt as a public relations ploy, and therefore subject to reversal once the military junta would attain its objectives in the form of resumed foreign assistance and a better international image (Ardeth Maung Thawnghmung, 'Preconditions and prospects for democratic transition in Burma/Myanmar,' in *Asian Survey* 43 3/2003): 443-460, 443). Some academics like Nemoto and Thawnghmung predicted a transitional coalition government or a hybrid regime after a power-sharing deal and the drop of the NLD demand for a parliament based on the 1990s election results when many of the parliamentarians have died or are in exile (ibid., 458).
99. André and Luise Boucaud, 'Birmas Generäle streiten sich und suchen Freunde,' in *Le Monde Diplomatique* (German edition), June 2005: 14-15.
100. International Crisis Group, 'Burma: Sanctions, Engagement or Another Way Forward?' Asia Report 78. [Online] Rev. 24 April 2004. Available: http://www.crisisgroup.org/home/index.cfm?id=2677&l=1. [15 July 2006].
101. Zöllner, *'Dialog im verminten Gelände,'* p. 299.
102. Zöllner, *'Dialog im verminten Gelände,'* p. 293.
103. Interviews conducted in Rangoon and Mandalay, March 2004.
104. 'They are afraid of her, because they could make mistakes before she does, even though it is she who was and is always flexible, ready to talk and to negotiate', said one of her friends during our interview in Rangoon, March 2004.
105. Interviews conducted in Rangoon, March 2004.
106. Several interviewees suggested that for a successful transition both actors are needed: Aung San Suu Kyi because she creates a legitimate and internationally acceptable image and because she can communicate policies to the outside world, for instance as a foreign minister, which would be unacceptable if presented by the regime. (Interviews conducted in Rangoon, March 2004).
107. This consensus extends to different types of pro-democracy activists who have been in exile for a few months or for several years according to interviews conducted in Maesot, Chiangmai and Bangkok in March and April 2004.

References

Alamgir, Jalal. 'Against the Current: The Survival of Authoritarianism in Burma,' *Pacific Affairs* 70 (3/1997): 333-50.
ALTSEAN. *Burma. Women's voices together*. Bangkok: n.a., 2003.
ALTSEAN. *Burma. Women's Voices for Change*. Bangkok: n.a., 2002.
ALTSEAN. *Burma. More women's voices*. Bangkok: n.a., 2000.
ALTSEAN. *Burma. Voices of women in the struggle*. Bangkok: n.a., 1998.
ALTSEAN, ed. *Burma and the role of women*. Bangkok: n.a., 1997.

ALTSEAN. *On the Road to Depayin: Speeches by Daw Aung San Suu Kyi*. No date. Online. Available: http://www.altsean.org/ontheroad.html. 15 July 2006.

Aung San Suu Kyi. *Der Weg zur Freiheit. Die Friedensnobelpreisträgerin aus Birma im Gespräch mit Alan Clements*. Bergisch Gladbach: Bastei Lübbe, 1997 [English title: *The Voice of Defiance*].

Aung San Suu Kyi. *Letters from Burma*. London/New York: Penguin Books, 1997.

Aung San Suu Kyi and Michael Aris, eds. *Freedom from fear*. London: Penguin Books, 1995 [2. revised edition].

Aung Zaw. 'Regrets—the residue of the 1990 Election.' *The Irrawaddy* (27 May 2005).

Blondel, Jean. *Political leadership. Towards a General Analysis*. London: Sage Publications, 1987.

Boucaud, André and Luise. 'Birmas Generäle streiten sich und suchen Freunde.' *Le Monde Diplomatique* [German edition] (June 2005): 14-15.

Buhrer/Levenson. *Aung San Suu Kyi, demain la Birmanie*. Arles: Editions Philippe Picquier, 2000.

Carey, Peter, ed. *The challenge of change in a divided society*. London/New York: Macmillan, 1997.

Carey, Peter. *From Burma to Myanmar: Military rule and the struggle for democracy*. RISCT Conflict Studies No. 304, London: RISCT, 1997.

Diller, Janelle M. 'The National Convention: An Impediment to the Restoration of Democracy,' In *The Challenge of Change in a Divided Society*, ed. Peter Carey, pp. 27-54. London/New York: Macmillan, 1997.

Fink, Christina. '*Living Silence. Burma under military rule*'. London/New York: Zed Books, 2001.

Freedom House. '*The Worst of the Worst. The World's Most Repressive Societies*.' Rev. 2005. Online. Available: www.freedomhouse.org/research/mrr2005.pdf. 15 July 2006.

Gosh, Amitav. *Dancing in Cambodia, at large in Burma*. Delhi: Ravi Dayal Publishers, 1998.

Gosh, Amitav. 'A reporter at large. Burma,' The New Yorker (12.08.1996): 39-54.

Hingst, René. *Burma im Wandel. Hindernisse und Chancen einer Demokratisierung in Burma/Myanmar*. Berlin: Logos Verlag, 2003.

Houtman, Gustaaf. 'The Culture of Burmese Politics.' *The Irrawaddy* (January 2004): 20-21.

International Crisis Group. 'Burma. Sanctions, Engagement or another way forward'? Asia Report N. 78. Rev. 26 April 2004. Online. Available: http://www.crisisgroup.org/home/index.cfm?id=2677&l=1. 15 July 2006.

Juan, Chee Soon. *To be free. Stories from Asia's Struggle against oppression*, Clayton: Monash Asia Institute, 1998.

Kanbawza, Win. *A Burmese perspective. Daw Aung San Suu Kyi. The Nobel Laureate*, Bangkok: n.a., 1992.

Kane, John. *The politics of moral capital*, Cambridge: Cambridge University Press, 2001.

Lintner, Bertil. 'Aung San Suu Kyi and Burma's unfinished renaissance,' Working Paper 64, Centre of Southeast Asian Studies, Monash University Australia, 1990.

Lintner, Bertil. *Outrage. Burma's struggle for democracy*, London/Bangkok: White Lotus, 1990.

Ma Than E. 'A Flowering of the Spirit: Memories of Suu and Her Family,' in *Freedom from Fear*, ed. Aung San Suu Kyi and Michael Aris, 275-291, London: Penguin Books, 1995 [2. revised edition].

Matthews, Bruce. 'The Present Fortune of tradition-bound Authoritarianism in Myanmar,' *Pacific Affairs* 71 (1/1998): 7-23.

Maung Thawnghmung, Ardeth. 'Preconditions and prospects for democratic transition in Burma/Myanmar,' *Asian Survey* 43 (3/2003): 443-460.

Mi Mi Khaing. *The world of Burmese women*, London: Zed Books, 1984.

Mills, Jane. 'Militarism, civil war and women's status: a Burma case study.' in *Women in Asia. Tradition, modernity and globalization*, ed. Louise Edwards and Mina Roces, pp. 265-90, Ann Arbor: The University of Michigan Press, 2000.

Mya Maung. 'The Burma Road from the Union of Burma to Myanmar,' Asian Survey 30 (6/1990): 602-24.

Nair, Sheila. 'Human Rights and Postcoloniality. Representing Burma.' in *Power, Postcolonialism and international relations*, ed. Geeta Chowdhry and Sheila Nair, pp. 254-84. London/New York: Routledge, 2004.

Parenteau, John. *Prisoner for Peace. Aung San Suu Kyi and Burma's struggle for democracy*, Greensboro: Morgan Reynolds, 1994.

Rothberg, Robert I., ed. *Burma. Prospects for a democratic future*, Washington: Brookings Institution Press, 1998.

Scott-Clark, Cathy and Levy, Adrian. '*Aung San Suu Kyi*'. Rev. July, 2001, online, available: http://www.prospect-magazine.co.uk/article_details.php?id=3525. July 15, 2006.

Silverstein, Josef. 'Aung San Suu Kyi. Is she Burma's Woman of Destiny?' Asian Survey 30 (10/1990): 1007-19.

The Irrawaddy Online. 'Two Interviews with Aung San Suu Kyi,' no date. Online, available: http://www.irrawaddy.org/aviewer.asp?a=218&z=6. 15 July 2006.

Tin Maung Maung Than. 'Myanmar. Military in charge,' In *Government and Politics in Southeast Asia*, ed. John Funston, pp. 203-51, London/New York: Zed Books 2001.

Victor, Barbara. *The Lady. Aung San Suu Kyi. Nobel Laureate and Burma's Prisoner*, Faber & Faber: New York, 1998.

Wagener, Oliver. 'Pagoden, weiße Elefanten und die Generäle. Politische Ideologie und Religion in Burma,' *Südostasien* (4/2003): 30-33.

Widmann, Maria. 'Megawati Sukarnoputri und Aung San Suu Kyi. Umstände und Bedingungen ihres politischen Aufstieges,' Diploma thesis, University of Passau, 2001.

Yawnghwe, Chao-Tzang. 'Burma. The Depolitization of the Political,' in *Political Legitimacy in Southeast Asia*, ed. Muthiah Alagappa, pp. 170-92. Stanford: Stanford University Press, 1995.

Yi Yi Myint. *Myanmar Gender Profiles*. n.a.: 2000.

Zarni and May Oo. 'Common problems, shared responsibilities: Citizen's quest for national reconciliation in Burma/Myanmar, Report of a Citizen Exiles Group,' *The Free Burma Coalition* (October 2004).

Zöllner, Hans-Bernd. 'Vom Ende einer Illusion. Zur aktuellen Lage in Myanmar,' Internationales Asienforum 34 (3-4/2003): 251-270.

Zöllner, Hans-Bernd. 'Dialog im verminten Gelände. Die Gespräche zwischen der Militärjunta und der Opposition in Myanmar,' Internationales Asienforum 32 (3/4/2001): 291-318.

Part III

Beyond Numbers—From the Grassroots towards Top Political Power

9

The Private Roots of Public Participation: Women's Engagement in Democratic Politics in Pakistan

Marion R. Müller

Introduction

> In the dust and strife of life in Parliament I often longed for the peace and leisure of the days in *purdah*. But there could be no turning back, no return to the secluded and sheltered existence of the past. I had to continue on this new road on which the women of my country had set out (…). And who can deny that this is a richer, fuller and more rewarding way of life?[1]
>
> Our society is a male-dominated society and not interested in women's issues and we [women] are very uneasy in these surroundings. But at the same time we are very confident. If the law remains and we do not have to get out of the assembly, we will not go back without any reason. Everyone says that you should resign and go back to your home (…) but we will in all walks of life resist this attitude.[2]

After a military putsch in 1999, the Pakistan government under General Musharraf announced its intention to bring the country back to democracy following a plan to devolve power to the grassroots. Under this plan, significant legal and administrative reforms were introduced and elections were held accordingly. In the local government elections in 2000/2001, around 40,000 women were elected on the local government level. Moreover, since the general elections in 2002, women hold 21.6 per cent of seats in the National Assembly and 17 per cent in the Senate.[3] Pakistan now has one of the highest percentages of representation of women in national governance in South Asia ahead of Bhutan with 9.33 and India with 8.84 per cent.[4] What, however, does this mean for a country that is known for its rigid patriarchal structure and as one of the most restrictive contexts for women's rights?

Examples from other countries show that within a process of democratization to bring about the development of democratic politics, it is not enough to set up democratic institutions. Likewise, an increase of women's representation in political office, for example through affirmative action, does not necessarily translate into policy outcomes that include women's interests.[5] The quotations of Shaista Suhrawardy Ikramullah (1948) and Samia Rahel Qazi (2004), show how the highly gendered and patriarchal structures of society and of state systems in Pakistan obstruct women's political voice and agency. This is the case despite the period of fifty-six years that lies between the two statements. However, even if the two women's interests might differ considerably, the quotations also reflect the fact that both women are inspired by their opportunity to access political office and, in their very own way, claim, the project of representing women's issues in politics. By asserting this claim, they start to resist existing gendered norms and likewise initiate a first step towards a process of change from within these norms. It is this contradictory linkage between women's voice, women's political presence and their opportunities for influencing the establishment of a gender equity agenda that is the concern of this paper. With the intention of contributing towards the discussion on women's involvement in political decision-making, it will analyse *what conditions are necessary to promote the involvement of women in democratic processes and to open up spaces for the translation of women's voice into political influence.*

Taking the introduction of affirmative action in Pakistan as a starting point will show that it is a variety of factors that have to be taken into account for the definition and analysis of women's political effectiveness. Mechanisms and structures within the political system and the state that have to be supportive towards a gender equity agenda will be pointed out. The analysis will show that it is only if these factors are in place, that women's interests can successfully be translated into political influence.

The specific socio-cultural context of Pakistan and the long years of resistance towards women's political participation make the introduction of affirmative action in 2000 very interesting for the study of women's political participation. The local government system will be taken as an entry point for looking at women's access, presence and influence in the latest democratic project of Pakistan. Composed of four provinces—Punjab, Sindh, Balochistan and the North West Frontier Province (NWFP)—the country exemplifies considerable cultural and ethnic diversity. Additionally, geographic, demographic and economic differences lead to broad political inequalities. For a better illustration of socio-cultural and region-specific circumstances (e.g. tribal culture) the North West Frontier Province (NWFP) has been selected as an example in parts of this paper.

Locating women's engagement in democratization

Generally, the political empowerment of women has been on the international agenda for decades. Supported through the Beijing and Beijing plus 5 conferences, the Convention on the Elimination of All Forms of Discrimination Against Women (CEDAW) as well as the International Covenant on Civil and Political Rights (ICCPR), there has been a concerted effort by feminists around the world to increase women's representation in political institutions and the overall political process. It is hoped that the establishment of democratic mechanisms providing women access to public office will create not only the space for women to become legitimate political actors and confirm the right of women to belong to the public sphere but moreover will lead to an effective representation of women's interests. Effective political representation is understood as the capacity of women political representatives to engage with a feminist agenda and consequently to influence an engendered decision-making within political institutions and the community.[6]

Recent research on democratization and decentralization extensively reviews the different contexts for the success or failure of democratic processes and focuses on the impact of decentralization on poverty reduction, service delivery or even local accountability.[7] Yet the discussion of democratization rarely includes a focus on the institutionalized barriers that prevent a true engagement of women's voice and agency as part of a pro-poor policy agenda.[8] Waylen accordingly observes that 'institutional democratization does not necessarily entail a democratization of power relations in society at large, particularly between men and women'.[9] To put it in other words: it is often overlooked that women's access to democratic institutions does not automatically lead to women's influence in decision-making. Due to cultural reasons women might, for example, not be able to participate in decision-making, let alone voice their demands. Yet, where access to political office is guaranteed but not supplemented with the opportunity to exercise the right of participation, it means only little in practice. It therefore can be assumed that a systematic engagement with political institutions is needed to dissolve traditional institutionalized patterns and prevailing patriarchal structures in a transformative process towards the recognition of gender equity concerns in policy making and implementation.

Such a process of the engendering of governance institutions consequently implies several steps: First, it means a re-structuring of those institutions at every level to introduce accountability to women as citizens. Such a process needs to imply the recognition of concerns of choice, but also control and autonomy to an extent where women are enabled to voice opposition.[10] Through the acknowledgement of women's opportunity for influencing political processes and decision-making, women's participation is getting valued as political activity. Secondly, it means critically assessing and effectively challenging rules, procedures and priorities that exclude women from participation in decision-making and that also exclude the incorporation of women's interests into the development agenda. Changes in patterns of exclusion are a necessary prerequisite for the facilitation of women's voice in civil society and the organization of women's citizenship agency.[11] Finally, it is important to define women's interests as based on various influential factors, like race, class, age, ethnicity. Women's interests, at different times or phases of their lives, might conflict with each other and be subjected to constant re-negotiation within a specific socio-cultural and historical context.[12] Likewise it cannot be assumed that women would unanimously agree on or support gender issues and it is possible that state policies, attempting to reflect women's interests, do benefit one group of women while harming another. Molyneux identifies this dilemma as 'conditionality of women's unity'[13] while Jeffery summarizes the diversity in women's voice and agency:

> In brief, the question is not whether women are victims or agents but, rather, what sorts of agents women can be despite their subordination. We need to explore the distinctive ways and diverse arenas in which women deploy their agency, the different people over whom they may exercise it, and the agendas that orient and direct it. Only then can we determine what is key to feminist agency and imagine how women's agency might translate into feminist political activism.[14]

Goetz outlines a framework for analysing the determinants of women's political effectiveness through a 'voice-to-representation-to-accountability' relationship.[15] This framework enables us to analyse the capacity of institutions located within the arenas of civil society, the political system, the state, and of the global political economy to put gender equity interests on their agenda. According to Goetz, it is essential to measure to what extent these institutions influence women's chances to assert their voices and how far such institutions provide accountability to women.[16] Hence, derived from this framework, women's political participation can be seen as an interrelated process between access to political office, political presence and claiming of citizenship agency, and an engendering of governance institutions through political influence.[17] This definition of women's political participation as *acting out of agency towards political influence* will provide the starting point for the assessment undertaken in this paper.

Institutional arenas such as the state, the political system and civil society are predominantly organized along patriarchal structures and are reproducers of gender differences and inequalities.[18] In a discussion on women's political representation, it therefore becomes necessary to single out the gendered dimensions of political contestation in all these arenas. This paper attempts to do so while looking at the institutional arenas of the state and the political system. It is important to understand that the process leading from women's access to political institutions to their acting out of agency towards political influence is not linear and is intrinsically linked with the socio-cultural conditions in which women live. This also means that the analysis undertaken in this paper and located within a specific socio-cultural context can only in part be derived from a blueprint of an existing conceptual framework for women's political effectiveness. Additionally, in any religiously or culturally conservative context, the attempt to change long prevailing, patriarchal structures is most likely to provoke resistance on the part of the defenders of traditional norms and values. The scope of such resistance prescribes women's actual room for manoeuvre on gender issues and can demobilize women's voice and agency. Any attempt to discover the private roots of public participation consequently needs to *personalize the political* in considering 'the inner workings of social and political life'[19] and needs to carefully listen to the voices of those who are the actors within the political project of democratization: the women themselves. Or, as Rai states, '[d]emocratization (…) has an exciting potential for the lives of women. Whether this potential is realized or not will in large part depend upon whether and how issues arising from women's experiences in both the private and the public spheres are addressed.'[20]

Imagining the political: women and the nature of the state

The framework of the state

In fifty-seven years of existence Pakistan has experienced twenty-five years of military rule and dictatorship. Frequently interrupted attempts to restore the country to democracy have so far only resulted in no elected prime minister being able to stay in office long enough to hand over power to an elected successor.[21] Because of this turbulent history, the overall framework of the state in Pakistan, according to Shaheed, is articulated through 'the development of a centralized state structure and the denial of co-cultural leadership; the instrumental use of Islam as a legitimizing ideology by the elites; the continuation of the feudal structure and its attendant attitudes that permeate society; the concept of modernization and functional inequality adopted by the state; and the militarization of society.'[22]

Additionally, corruption and autocracy on the part of the country's leadership, as well as a state of indebtedness, have led to a lack of effective public institutions and a civic life dominated by a small elite population that contributes to an absence of a culture of democracy and public accountability.[23]

Some scholars see these as the factors that have diminished people's general trust in democratic governance.[24]

Defining access: affirmative action policies in Pakistan

Women have always been present in the formal political history of post-independence Pakistan, though their presence has always been restricted by the traditional and patriarchal structures of the society. As a result, the number of women taking political office has been persistently low and dependent on affirmative action measures and on patronage by the political leadership. The constitution of Pakistan guarantees the equality of all citizens before the law including the equality of political rights for women and men.[25] Pakistan, since 1995, has been a signatory to the CEDAW convention which was ratified in 1996. In 1983, the first Commission on the Status of Women was set up[26] and made a permanent statutory body in 2000.[27] The first Ministry for Women's Development was initiated in 1989.[28] The allocation of resources to the Ministry and the influence and decision-making power of both institutions varied with different governments but were generally very limited in scope. In 2002 the Ministry for Women's Development brought out a national policy for development and empowerment of women. The document, however, does not mention issues related to women's rights and women's political participation.[29]

The limited affirmative action methods that were introduced between 1947 and 1999 to a large extent failed to achieve valuable political participation of women at decision-making levels. Even though the number of women in parliament at times increased, for example due to a reservation of twenty seats in 1985 over the period of the seventh and eighth legislatures, or the fact that the prime minister was a woman herself, this did not produce an effective

Fig. 1: Percentage of women in Pakistan's Legislatures (1947-2002)[30]

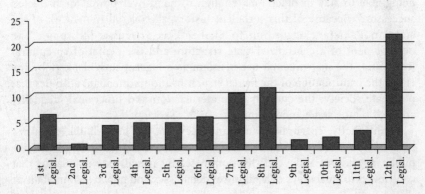

improvement in women's status on any level of the Pakistani society. Quotas for women in government services had been introduced at times (e.g. under Benazir Bhutto) but did not exceed 5 per cent.[31] Moreover, affirmative action measures introduced on the national level rarely included measures to improve women's participation at the level of local government. The reservation of additional seats for women served only to fill these seats but did not encourage a general increase in the numbers of women competing for them. It can largely be said that constitutional guarantees as well as Pakistan's commitments to international laws were not being successfully realized by the respective state governments. This was the situation until 1999, when General Pervez Musharraf assumed power in the country.

Devolving power to the grassroots

Shortly after the coup, the Supreme Court of Pakistan legitimized the military action under the 'doctrine of state necessity', provided that elections were held within the following three years.[32] With the intention of bringing the country back to democracy, General Musharraf announced his commitment to devolve power to the grassroots under a 'Devolution of Power Plan'. This included the devolution of political power, decentralization of administrative authority, deconcentration of management functions, and distribution of resources to the district level and diffusion of the power-authority nexus.[33] The new system introduced on the local level was a three tiered system ranging from the union over the *tehsil*/town to the district level.[34] Under the Local Government Ordinances 2001 and the Legal Framework Order of 2002, a 33 per cent seat reservation for women on all levels of local government and 15 per cent of seats in the Provincial Assemblies and the Parliament were introduced. Launching a historical momentum for the participation of women in Pakistan's politics,[35] the local government elections in 2000/2001 increased the number of women representatives on the local level to 36,105.[36] In the general elections held in 2002, a further seventy-four women took office in the National Assembly,[37] seventeen women in the Senate and a total of 128 women in the four provincial assemblies.[38] A countrywide survey conducted after the elections in 2002 shows that there was great optimism regarding women's representation in politics and expectations among the people that this would have a positive impact on the democratic development of the country. Such expectations were found to be especially high among women.[39]

In Pakistan, most forms of decentralization have so far been introduced through military governments. Civilian governments, meanwhile, have not shown much interest in establishing devolved democratic support mechanisms. Including the elections in 2000/2001, there were five local government elections held under military rule and two under civilian rule. A constitutional protection of local government has never been established[40] and no government has shown relevant political will towards local level democracy. Instead, matters of local governance have always been perceived as provincial matters, and this has led to huge structural differences between the four provinces. This is especially noticeable in the case of women's participation. Except for the elections of 1998, where in one of the provinces (Balochistan), women's representation rose to over 25 per cent, the percentage of women representatives has remained at 5 to 12 per cent, which is minimal.[41] In the North West Frontier Province and in Sindh, no local government elections were held between 1987 and 2000/2001.[42] Overall, no attempt of decentralization in Pakistan has promoted any significant change or a true shift in power relations on any level, neither between the ruling elite and the poor, nor between men and women. Also since the elections of 2000/2001 have taken place, there are relentless problems reported in the functioning of the latest local government system which lead many women councillors to conclude that they are not able to respond adequately to the demands of their communities. Lack of resources and problems experienced in the delivery of services—according to 50 per cent of the councillors—led to frustration with their role as public representatives.[43] Many among them simply feel overburdened and some have decided not to run again for the next elections.[44]

Personalizing the political: the presence of women councillors

Samina Naz shows in her review of the Local Government Ordinance in the North West Frontier Province that it is the present structure of the law that places serious impediments on women councillors. First of all, it completely omits a definition of women's roles and responsibilities. In practice, this leads to women being automatically assigned to issues concerning women or social welfare. This shows a feminization of women's needs and interests.[45] In Graff's interviews, some councillors even state that they believe they have been elected to look after the concerns of women due to the traditional *purdah* (seclusion) system.[46] Another assumption made is that women only use social welfare services[47] but are not interested in, for example, infrastructure development or transportation issues. A second obstacle is that the law does not ensure the presence of women councillors in council or committee meetings, which leads to women simply not getting involved in important processes like the budget planning. Another, rather paradoxical result is that due to the lack of official support for women's participation, male councillors think they can launch a legal complaint against women who do actively participate in the meetings of their councils.[48]

Complaining that she is the only woman attending the union council meetings, Samina Naz describes another set of problems that hold back women's participation in local level decision-making:

> We are actually six women in our council, but none of the others are attending the sessions. One of them got married after the election and her in-laws do not allow her to come. One died. A third lives too far away to attend the sessions and she has three children as well. The fourth was initially from the support panel of the Nazim (Mayor), and when she found out that he was acting illegally she started to advocate against him. He threatened her so she now is afraid to come. The fifth has a beauty parlour in her house and she is earning good money with it. She does not want to lose this way of income.[49]

Such conditions, together with the gendered structure of the local government system, are common impediments to women's participation on all levels of the system, all over Pakistan.[50] Definitely the public participation of women has been visibly increasing at all levels of local and national governance. But, as Samina Naz's statement shows, women still face tough resistance in asserting their voice within what is possibly the most critical social institution: the family or the family clan. In fact—and this will be seen in the following chapters—women's mere presence in public office actually leads them into a confrontation with the highly political project of challenging the patriarchal structures of Pakistan's society. The women councillors are expected to effectively contribute towards the development of their area; however, their performance depends on conditions like their personal economic or educational background or the encouragement they get from their families, especially in combining political responsibilities with their reproductive role. If, however, the democratization process is to have any significance for women's demands and be inclusive of women's interests, women's political participation has to be acknowledged as a permanent crossing of boundaries between the private and the public spheres. It is only then that both the private and the public sphere will experience a process of transformation.

Yet, according to the framework used here, the responsibility for including of women's interests into policy agendas has to go far beyond a sole state responsibility. The next chapter consequently will take a look at the political system and political parties as its major representatives. Despite the fact that the local government elections were actually supposed to be on a non-party basis in the latest elections in Pakistan, an open competition among political parties about women candidates and voters was taking place on all levels.[51]

Institutionalizing the political: political parties and women's involvement in the political system

One of the assumptions that goes along with introducing affirmative action is that political parties will automatically cultivate women candidates as the reservation of seats for women in governance institutions will provide an incentive to increase women's party membership. But *de facto*, women meet stiff resistance from political parties. They do not get access to or influence in decision-making procedures and they are rarely fielded as candidates for non-reserved positions. In Pakistan, only a limited number of women have been able to enter this arena with the aim of improving women's position from within the party structures.[52]

At present, more than seventy political parties are registered in Pakistan. One third of them are religiously oriented, two thirds regionally based, and the majority of them do not have any representation in the country's national or provincial Legislative Assemblies.[53] Overall, there is not only a great absence of formal professional political leadership (male and female), but the structures of the major political parties of the country are inefficient and poorly institutionalized.[54] The number of political parties that have women in their Central Executive Councils is said to be only two or three with not more than two women members each.[55] Even despite the fact that a recent survey shows that, with few exceptions, the political parties in Pakistan support the reservation of seats for women,[56] none of them has worked out any concrete support structure which would provide on-the-job training, financial assistance or proper access to (male dominated) party networks and structures. How far such a restricted attitude is internalized, especially in conservative religious party structures, becomes clear in the statement that Samia Rahel Qazi, herself a party representative and member of the National Assembly, makes against reservation of seats for women:

> The Jamaat-e-Islami[57] is strongly opposing this large number of women in the parliament because, according to our opinion, a nomination through a quota is against basic democratic rules. We think this is totally a military ruled democracy. Additionally, many women who are now in office have no political background or training and because we do not have strong political institutions, it is not possible to bridge this gap. We think that a few properly trained women should go to parliament; there is no rule in Islam or in the constitution against this. But, it is the basic duty of women to make their home more peaceful and more prosperous and train the human being as the basic unit of the society, within their homes. Women took the decision to go for politics in such a large number only because it was introduced by law and we are very much law obeying people. However, I do not think that it is true that when women come into politics there will be a change in women's condition.[58]

The statement indicates the paradox situation many women party members have to face when trying to balance the highly gendered agendas of their parties with their own commitment and their sense of their own value as women politicians.

Party membership structures

Political parties in Pakistan include different categories of women members, of which the most prominent category is made up of those who are relatives of prominent or active male members of political parties. A second category comprises those women who came in through mainstream politics. Many of them belong to more affluent political families and keep a distance from their fellow women party members on the worker level or in the party's women's wing. A third category comprises women active at the community or professional level. They are invited by the parties to join as they are able to mobilize more support among women on the local level and are active during election campaigns or at political rallies.[59] Women, who participate in party politics out of their own interest and choice, are low in numbers. Because of a lack of membership structures, many women do not define themselves as affiliated with any specific party. Instead, they support parties that their families are affiliated with[60] or that offer them the most interesting incentives. Shahin Akter's statement reveals the confusion that exists among many women:

> I myself have contested elections on behalf of the Jamaat-i-Islami, they asked me for it and I got my votes from them. However, myself, I gave my vote for the Pakistan People's Party because my brother is involved with them. Now they have asked me to found a women's wing for them in my union. But how can I do so now as my husband, who is a member of Awami National Party, is coming back from abroad.[61]

Women's wings and party manifestos

On national and provincial levels, all the major political parties except the Awami National Party have introduced women's wings, which usually have a separate hierarchy and structure. It is mostly the party leaders who nominate women for relevant positions and by and large none of the women's wings have any relevant decision-making power or autonomy.[62] Women's wings do not take any initiative in enhancing women's understanding of the political process or of politics more generally. They likewise cannot be seen as providing support to their members in asserting their interests or in pushing forward a women's equity agenda. Party manifestos show a similar picture. Whereas in the elections of 1988 and 1993, the political parties had promised concrete steps towards women's inclusion in the national development process, the manifestos of 1997 were much more vague and only the Pakistan People's Party had included a section that solely dealt with women rights and development.[63] The same is true of the manifestos of 2002, where women, under the section of political reforms, are encouraged to take part in all walks of life (Pakistan Muslim League-Q manifesto). More generally, the reservation of seats for women is supported (Pakistan People's Party manifesto), and even more generally, under the section for fundamental rights, women are guaranteed equal rights with men in the political field (Awami National Party manifesto). All manifestos mention women in relation to health, education or economic empowerment.[64] To overcome the poor performance of political parties in terms of women's participation, the foundation of a separate women's party in which women would have sole decision-making power was discussed among feminists at the end of the 1990s.[65]

Caucusing across party lines

In the elections of 1993 and 1997, a cross party caucus mobilization of women was initiated by a national level NGO with the aim of educating women party members and women voters about the political process and the importance of their contribution. This initiative promptly led to political parties addressing women's issues and while some of them integrated a women's agenda into their manifestos, others chose at least to address women as a vote bank or for election rallies. For some more progressive parties like the socialist Pakistan People's Party, the inclusion of women in rallies at that time was not unusual. For the conservative and right-wing oriented Jamaat-e-Islami, however, it meant setting a new trend; it was the first time the daughter of its leader (Samia Rahel Qazi) appeared in public, appealing to women to actively participate in political affairs through their representation in the National Assembly.[66]

In 1997, the political education programme started to mobilize women of different political parties to participate in various seminars, workshops and discussions. Reports of experiences with the programme show that whereas it is easy to find an entry for discussion across party lines on general gender issues such as problems women face in their parties, differences rapidly surface between the representatives if it comes to issues of women's rights and traditional laws in Pakistan.[67] The Jamaat-e-Islami, for example, has supported civil society activities and taken up the issue of violence against women in their election campaigns but still strongly opposes any amendments to the Hudood Ordinances. Women representatives of the party, like Noor Marjan then, have to distinguish women's interests from the interests of their parties:

The women members of the Provincial and National Assembly are just defending the party interests because they want to advocate against the military government. I also try to advocate for women's interests in my party, for example on the Hudood Ordinances. You know some people in Jamaat-e-Islami, they just start shouting if it comes to this topic, but in fact they are just defending a decision taken by another military dictator. And, if I say that I will not talk on the Hudood Ordinances because I am from the Jamaat-e-Islami, it is not the solution of this problem. I am trying to advocate to the provincial level representatives of the party that they will talk to the party leadership. There is a big gap between the grassroots and the leadership of the party on those issues.[68]

Such examples show how malleable, even though resistant, notions of 'tradition' and religion are. Political parties in Pakistan have at times found it expedient to claim feminist ground by showing that they can and do have active women members and front women candidates. On other occasions, and mainly influenced by conservative elites of the local level, they block policies that would support women's mobility and decision-making power. It is political institutions frequently undertaking these opportunistic shifts in their priorities that contribute to the persistent lack of legitimacy of political leadership.

Personalizing the political: the presence of policy making

Many women activists feel that party politics do not matter much or at least less than local level politics and that it is actually the reign of family clans and traditional leaders that is reflected within the party structures.[69] Indeed after the last elections, 76 per cent of women members of legislative assemblies and about 82 per cent of Nazims (Mayors) were found to be close relatives of members of the National or Provincial Assemblies.[70] A closer examination of the situation in the North West Frontier Province also shows that the *jirga* system, introduced about six hundred years ago through the Pashtun tribes, has grown into a strong political institution. Composed of tribal elders and other influential leaders, the *jirga* committees watch over the enactment of rules and regulations on all levels of society in accordance with traditions and customs.[71] *Jirgas* are exclusively male institutions that neither allow women's participation nor acknowledge women's interests.[72] The *jirga* system also prevails among settled urban Pashtun populations in other geographical regions, e.g. Karachi. According to Shaheed,[73] male-dominated tribal and feudal structures exert a strong influence on the political system and on women's political participation. Because of their strong institutionalization within society, they can actually be seen as an important factor in determining Pakistan's political leadership.

Reports from the 1997 and 2000/2001 elections and the 2004 by-elections show that conservative factions of society, represented through *jirgas*, together with political parties, tried to stop women from voting or standing for elections.[74] Initiated by traditional leaders, in the districts of Swabi, Dir and Mardan, in 2000/2001 written agreements were made across party lines whereby party activists worked to stop women from putting themselves up for office. Religious authorities issued *fatwas* or imposed threats (for example, the annulment of marriage certificates or the refusal of proper burial ceremonies) on those women and their families who were found to be casting their vote or standing for elections.[75] Examples like these show the extent to which women's attempts at political participation were challenging traditional power-configurations. Tripp accordingly observes that 'as new contenders for power and resources, women face serious limitations that have to do with the way in which deeply ingrained ideologies, pre-existing patterns of authority, and long-standing interests seek to maintain the status quo and keep political power in the hands of male elders.'[76]

These examples also indicate that even if influential people and political parties on the national level are committed to women's participation in politics, they do not necessarily exert influence on traditional institutions at the local level.

The political system, exemplified through political parties, resembles a large and interwoven network of patriarchal and traditional structures. To untie it, is a long-term and extremely difficult project which, if at all, can only be managed by a gender advocacy lobby based within the system itself and on the levels of state and civil society.

Conclusion

This chapter has laid out the assumption that women's political influence and effectiveness does not automatically arise through the setting up of democratic institutions. Following a framework developed to assess women's political effectiveness, for the context of Pakistan, it has been illustrated that there are a range of factors that determine women's access, presence and influence in political decision-making. It has been described how, in the specific context of Pakistan, these factors are located within the arenas of the state and the political system. Moreover, it has been argued that it is the arena of 'the personal of the political' and of social life that has to be taken into account to understand fully the way that women choose to act out towards political influence. The analysis shows that at present, in the case of Pakistan, the support available to women's political effectiveness within these arenas is very limited. Instead, it is their very patriarchal structures and conservative nature that creates impediments to an establishment of a gender equity agenda.

If the state is serious about claiming affirmative action policies as a step towards gender equality, policy makers at the same time have to understand that recognition of women's political rights needs to be accompanied by measures setting in place mechanisms that support women in demanding these rights. Instead, as the examples show, the devolution of power to the grassroots has mainly strengthened the longstanding, unequal power-relations between feudal/tribal leaders and the poor as well as between women and men. Policy decisions have led to a truly tremendous increase in women's presence, however, if women's political participation is not to remain symbolic only, the state's political will to facilitate linkages throughout the arenas of the political system and the civil society, and its ability to guide the devolution of power process, are inevitable. Yet, it is still to be seen in what ways these requirements will be realized and it is probably too early to come to a final conclusion about these developments.

At the centre of the political system, the political parties have so far not felt any necessity to advocate policies that would bring them anywhere near a commitment towards a gender equity constituency. Strongly influenced by traditional power holders and following their own patriarchal structures, they prefer to ghettoize women's issues through separate women's wings, their manifestos also do not state a progressive agenda along issues of gender equity. Most political parties prefer to see women as their voters or as signatories to their policy decisions but they do not intend to include women in the process of policy-making. Yet in the prospect of the next government elections that might be held on a party basis, political parties need to come up with strategies and policies addressing women's concerns. This also means to link up with civil society activists and get their support for the development of a joint strategy.

What could not be analysed here but still is of utmost interest towards the establishment of women's political effectiveness is the capacity of civil society in Pakistan to support the establishment of a gender equity agenda. It would be important to see the extent to which the women's movement and other forms of associations as representatives of the gender advocacy lobby enable women to assert their voice and challenge gendered structures within the state and the political system as well as within the parameters of state policies, religion and traditions. Negotiation of women's interests here, in turn, immediately challenges the patriarchal structures of the society and the state.

Civil society activists in Pakistan state that affirmative action provoked a tremendous change in the complexion of societal structures as well as a serious challenge to traditional gender relations. And, statements of women councillors show how women exercise agency and attempt reform even within relatively hostile institutional environments. They represent a number of women in local government who are joining hands with women's activist groups and have, through being 'elected activists', created for themselves the space to take up the extremely difficult task of lobbying the structures of the political system *and* the civil society from within. On the other hand, it is civil society groups that in parallel need to lobby for changes in formal institutional structures. This clearly is a new and great challenge for women's activist groups in Pakistan. By actively including local women representatives and their opinions in further planning and advocacy strategies, they get the opportunity to review their own internal accountability structures. It also means demanding that the state show responsibility towards constitutional and international commitments to improve women's participation in political decision-making processes. Progress in these attempts within the area of civil society will at the same time be driving factors towards the establishment of a democratic society in Pakistan.

Despite this highly critical assessment of the present situation for women's political effectiveness, the comments by women, quoted above, show that some change has come about, if not in the lives of all women but still in the lives of quite a few. It is often small steps such as the attempts of women councillors to advocate for change from within their conservative environment that indicate the beginning of a slow but steady process of translation of women's voice into a transformation of the social and political culture of Pakistan. Farooq Sultan Azam enthusiastically recounts that after her time in office as a district councillor, in the next provincial elections, she will run for a seat in the Provincial Assembly. She says that now she feels empowered to do this:

> You know, everything involves political manoeuvring in a woman's life, from start till her death. All the roles of women, as a mother, daughter, grandmother, is politics. This political role however is denied in our society (...) The society is suppressing women and poor people but if they stand up and decide to face all the problems, with the passage of time the problems will subside and no longer be important.[77]

NOTES

1. Shaista Ikramullah Suhrawardy, *From Purdah to Parliament* (Karachi: Oxford University Press, 2000), p. 168; Shaista Suhrawardy Ikramullah was one of the two women members of the first constitutional assembly of Pakistan in 1948.
2. Interview with Samia Rahel Qazi (Jamaat-i-Islami (JI) Office, Islamabad, 19.07.04); Samia Rahel Qazi is a member of the National Assembly of Pakistan,

leader of the JI Women's Wing and vice president of the JI Political Cell for Women in 2004.

3. Bilal Gulmina, *Women Parliamentarians: Swimming against the Tide* (Islamabad: Freedom Publishers, 2004), p. 17.

4. Bilal, *Women Parliamentarians*, 17.

5. See for example: Goetz Anne-Marie, 'Women's Political Effectiveness: a Conceptual Framework' in *No Shortcuts to Power—African Women in Politics and Policy Making*, ed. Goetz Anne-Marie and Hassan Shirin (London: Zed Books, 2003), pp. 29-81; Molyneux Maxine and Razavi Shahra 2002, 'Introduction' In *Gender Justice, Development and Rights*, ed. Molyneux Maxine and Razavi Shahra, *Oxford Studies in Democratization* (New York: Oxford University Press, 2002), pp. 1-43; Rai Shirin M., 'Gender and Democratization: Ambiguity and Opportunity.' In *Democratization in the South—the Jagged Wave*, eds. Robin Luckham and Gordon White (Manchester University Press, 1996), pp. 220-42.

6. Goetz, *Women's Political Effectiveness*.

7. See for example: Robinson Mark, 'Participation, Local Governance and Decentralized Service Delivery,' paper prepared for a Ford Foundation workshop in Santiago on New Approaches to Decentralized Service Delivery (Institute of Development Studies, 2003); Crook Richard and Manor James, *Democracy and Decentralization in South Asia and West Africa—Participation, Accountability and Performance* (Cambridge: Cambridge University Press, 1998).

8. See for example: Norris Pippa, *Electoral Engineering—Voting Rules and Political Behaviour* (Cambridge: Cambridge University Press, 2004).

9. Waylen Georgina, 'Women and Democratization—Conceptualizing Gender Relations in Transition Politics', *World Politics* 46:3:1994, 327-54: 329.

10. Rai, *Gender and Democratization*; Molyneux and Razavi, Introduction.

11. Mukhopadhyay Matrayee, 'Introduction: Gender, Citizenship and Governance' In *Gender Citizenship and Governance—A Global Source Book*, ed. Minke Valk, Sarah Cummings and Henk van Dam, Gender Society and Development Series, KIT Royal Tropical Institute Amsterdam (London: Oxfam Educational, 2004), pp. 13-29.

12. Wieringa Saskia, 'Women's Interests and Empowerment: Gender Planning Reconsidered', *Development and Change* 25/1994, pp. 829-48.

13. Molyneux Maxine, 'Mobilization without Emancipation? Women's Interests, the State and Revolution in Nicaragua', *Feminist Studies*. 11, 12:1985, 227-54: 234.

14. Jeffrey Patricia, 'Agency, Activism, and Agendas' In *Appropriating Gender— Women's Activism and Politicized Religion in South Asia*, ed. Patricia Jeffrey and Amrita Basu (New York: Routledge, 1998), 221-43: 223.

15. Goetz, *Women's Political Effectiveness*, p. 29.

16. Goetz, *Women's Political Effectiveness*, p. 39.

17. Mukhopadhyay, *Gender, Citizenship and Governance*, 21 and Goetz, *Women's Political Effectiveness*, p. 41.

18. Shaheed Farida, *Imagined Citizenship: Women, State and Politics in Pakistan* (Lahore: Shirkat Gah, 2002); Waylen Georgina, *Analysing Gender in the Politics of the Third World—Gender in Third World Politics, Issues in Third World Politics Series* (Buckingham: Open University Press, 1996), pp. 5-23.

19. Tripp Aili Mari, *Women & Politics in Uganda—The Challenge of Associational Autonomy*, (Wisconsin: James Currey Publishers, 2000), p. 220.
20. Rai, *Gender and Democratization*, 242.
21. Constable Pamela, 'Pakistan's Predicament', Journal of Democracy 12/1/2001, 15-29: 16.
22. Shaheed, *Imagined Citizenship*, pp. 12-13.
23. Constable, *Pakistan's Predicament*, p. 15.
24. Graff Irene, *Invisible Women, Invisible Rights* 'Women's Rights to Election Participation with a Case Study of the 2001 Local Elections in Pakistan,' (Institute for offentlig retts skriftserie Nr. 6/2003, Oslo: Universitetet I Oslo, 2003); Pattan Development Organization, 'Transition to Democracy—Hopes and Expectations. Key Findings of Post-Election Survey Research' (Islamabad: Pattan Development Organization, 2003).
25. Constitution of the Islamic Republic of Pakistan: Articles 25, 27, 34, URL: www.pakistani.org/pakistan/constitution/.
26. Graff, *Invisible Women, Invisible Rights*.
27. Aurat Publication and Information Service Foundation, 'Developments on Women's Rights Issues During the Military Government's Third Year', Legislative Watch No 20 and 21, July and August 2003.
28. Graff, *Invisible Women, Invisible Rights*.
29. Aurat Publication and Information Service Foundation, 'Developments on Women's Rights Issues'.
30. Source: PILDAT, Pakistan Institute of Legislative Development and Transparency, 'Background Paper on Women Representation in Pakistan's Parliament,' 2004, p. 16.
31. Graff, *Invisible Women, Invisible Rights*.
32. Shah Aqil, 'Democracy on Hold in Pakistan' Journal of Democracy. 13, 1/2002, 67-75: 67.
33. The National Reconstruction Bureau/NRB, URL: www.nrb.gov.pk.
34. Mirza Naeem, *Women's Participation in Local Government Elections 2000-2001*, (Lahore: Aurat Publication and Information Service Foundation, 2002).
35. Naz Rukhshanda, *A Gender Review of The Legal Framework for Local Government in NWFP* (Peshawar: Aurat Publication and Information Service Foundation, 2004).
36. Mirza, *Women's Participation in Local Government Elections*.
37. Out of 74 women, 60 women were elected on the reserved seats for Muslim women and one woman on the reserved seats for Minorities, 13 women were elected directly. This actually increased the number of women in Parliament from 15 to 17 per cent, From: Bilal, *Women Parliamentarians*, p. 4.
38. Bilal, *Women Parliamentarians*, p. 4.
39. Pattan, *Transition to Democracy*, p. 11.
40. Graff, *Invisible Women, Invisible Rights*.
41. Mirza, *Women's Participation in Local Government Elections*.
42. Mirza, *Women's Participation in Local Government Elections*.
43. Pattan Development Organization, 'Voices of Women Councillors' (Islamabad: Pattan Development Organization, 2004).

44. Graff Irene, 'They Give Us Respect but no Rights—Women's Participation in Local Government in Pakistan, a Case Study of Four Union Councils in the North West Frontier Province,' (Institute of Law, Faculty of Law, Oslo: University of Oslo, 2004), p. 54.
45. Naz, *A Gender Review*.
46. Graff, *Respect but no Rights*.
47. Naz, *A Gender Review*.
48. Naz, *A Gender Review* and Graff, *Respect but no Rights*.
49. Interview with Samina Naz, Union Councillor Peshawar, (Aurat Foundation, Regional Office, Peshawar, 26.07.04).
50. Graff, *Respect but no Rights*; Pattan, *Voices of Women Councillors*; Mirza, *Women's Participation in Local Government Elections*.
51. Graff, *Respect but no Rights*; Pattan, *Voices of Women Councillors*.
52. Bari Farzana & Khattak Saba Gul, Power Configurations in Public and Private Arenas: The women's Movement's Response, In *Power and Civil Society in Pakistan*, ed. Anita M. Weiss & Gilani Zulfiqar S. (Karachi: Oxford University Press, 2001), page numbers not available.
53. Zia Shahla & Bari Farzana, *Baseline Report on Women's Participation in Political and Public Life in Pakistan*, International Women's Rights Action Watch—Asia Pacific, (Lahore: Aurat Publication and Information Service Foundation, 1999), p. 29.
54. Shaheed, *Imagined Citizenship*.
55. Yazdani Fauzia, *Women's Representation in Local Government in Pakistan: Impact Analysis and Future Policy Implications* (no place and publisher mentioned: 2004); Zia & Bari F., Baseline Report.
56. Yazdani, *Women's Representation in Local Government*, p. 23.
57. The Jamaat-i-Islami is the most dominant representative of a coalition of religious parties, the Muttahida Majlis-i-Amal (MMA). At time of writing this chapter the most central opposition on the federal level as well as in NWFP.
58. Interview with Samia Rahel Qazi, Jamaat-i-Islami (JI Office, Islamabad, 19.07.04).
59. Zia & Bari, *Baseline Report*, p. 31.
60. Yazdani, *Women's Representation in Local Government*; Shaheed, *Imagined Citizenship*.
61. Interview with Shahin Akter, District Councillor Peshawar (Aurat Foundation, Regional Office, Peshawar, 26.07.04).
62. Zia & Bari, *Baseline Report*.
63. Shaheed Farida, 'The Context of Women's Activism' In *Shaping Women's Lives—Laws, Practises and Strategies in Pakistan*, ed. Farida Shaheed, Sohail Warraich, Cassandra Balchin, and Gazdar Aisha, (Lahore: Shirkat Gah, 1998), 271-318: 299 and 301.
64. Interview with Maheen Saleem, Legislative Watch Team (Aurat Foundation, Federal Office, Islamabad, 07.07.04).
65. Shaheed, *Context of Women's Activism*, p. 304.
66. Shaheed, *Context of Women's Activism*, pp. 301-2.
67. Zia & Bari F., *Baseline Report*.

68. Interview with Noor Marjan, Jamaat-i-Islami, District Councillor Mardan, (Aurat Foundation, Regional Office, Peshawar, 27.07.04).
69. Interview with Tahera Abdullah, Founding Member of the Women Action Forum (WAF) and the Human Rights Commission of Pakistan (HRCP) (Yummi's Cafè, Islamabad, 06.07.04).
70. Bari Sarwar, 'LG By-election: Policy Issues' The News, (Islamabad Edition, 29 March, 2004), p. 6.
71. Shah Muhammad, *Sardari, Jirga & Local Government Systems in Balochistan* (Lahore: Edara-e-Tadrees Publishers, 1992), p. 26.
72. Government of NWFP, 'Planning and Development, Between Hope and Despair, Pakistan Participatory Poverty Assessment. NWFP Province Report,' (October 2003), p. 118.
73. Shaheed, *Context of Women's Activism.*
74. Shaheed Farida, Zia Asma and Soheil Warraich, eds. *Women in Politics: Participation and Representation in Pakistan*—with update 1993-97, Special Bulletin, 'Women Living under Muslim Law,' (Lahore: Shirkat Gah, 1998), p. 72; Aurat Publication and Information Service Foundation, *Gross Violations of Women's Electoral Rights in Swabi, Mardan and Dir, NWFP*, (Lahore: Aurat Publication and Information Service Foundation, 2001) Aurat Publication and Information Service Foundation, *Gross violations of Women's Electoral Rights.*
75. Aurat Publication and Information Service Foundation, *Gross Violations of Women's Electoral Rights.*
76. Tripp, *Women and Politics in Uganda*, p. 218.
77. Interview with Farooq Sultan Azam, Pakistan People's Party, District Councillor Mardan (Aurat Foundation, Regional Office, Peshawar, 29.07.04).

References

Aurat Publication and Information Service Foundation. 'Developments on Women's Rights Issues During the Military Government's Third Year.' Legislative Watch (No. 20 and 21/July and August 2003).
Aurat Publication and Information Service Foundation. *Gross Violations of Women's Electoral Rights in Swabi, Mardan and Dir, NWFP*. Lahore: Aurat Publication and Information Service Foundation, 2001.
Bari, Farzana and Khattak Saba Gul. 'Power Configurations in Public and Private Arenas: The Women's Movement's Response.' In *Power and Civil Society in Pakistan*, ed. Anita M. Weiss and Gilani Zulfiqar S., pages not available. Karachi: Oxford University Press, 2001.
Bari, Sarwar. 'LG By-election: Policy Issues.' The News, Islamabad Edition (29 March 2004): 6.
Bilal, Gulmina. *Women Parliamentarians: Swimming against the Tide*. Islamabad: Freedom Publishers, 2004.
Constable, Pamela. 'Pakistan's Predicament.' Journal of Democracy 12 (1/2001): 15-29.

Crook, Richard and James Manor. *Democracy and Decentralization in South Asia and West Africa—Participation, Accountability and Performance.* Cambridge: Cambridge University Press, 1998.

Goetz, Anne-Marie. 'Women's Political Effectiveness: A Conceptual Framework.' In *No Shortcuts to Power—African Women in Politics and Policy Making,* ed. Anne-Marie Goetz and Shirin Hassim, 29-81. London: Zed Books, 2003.

Goetz, Anne-Marie, and Shirin Hassim, eds. *No Shortcuts to Power—African Women in Politics and Policy Making.* London: Zed Books, 2003.

Government of NWFP—Planning & Development. *Between Hope & Despair, Pakistan Participatory Poverty Assessment. NWFP Province Report.* No place and publisher mentioned, October 2003.

Graff, Irene. 'They Give Us Respect but no Rights—Women's Participation in Local Government in Pakistan, a Case Study of Four Union Councils in the North West Frontier Province.' Institute of Women's Law. Faculty of Law. Oslo: University of Oslo, 2004.

Graff, Irene. 'Invisible Women, Invisible Rights—Women's Rights to Election Participation with a Case Study of the 2001 Local Elections in Pakistan.' Institutt for offentlig retts skriftserie nr. 6/2003, Oslo: Universitetet I Oslo, 2003.

Ikramullah Suhrawardy, Shaista. *From Purdah to Parliament.* Karachi: Oxford University Press, 2000.

Jeffrey, Patricia. 'Agency, Activism, and Agendas.' In *Appropriating Gender—Women's Activism and Politicized Religion in South Asia,* ed. Patricia Jefferey and Amrita Basu, 221-243. New York: Routledge, 1998.

Luckham Robin, Anne Marie Goetz, and Mary Kaldor. 'Democratic Institutions and Democratic Politics.' In *Can Democracy be designed?,* ed. Bastian Sunil and Robin Luckham, 14-60. New York: Zed Books, 2003.

Mirza, Naeem. *Women's Participation in Local Government Elections 2000—2001.* Lahore: Aurat Publication and Information Service Foundation, 2002.

Molyneux, Maxine. 'Mobilization without Emancipation? Women's Interests, the State and Revolution in Nicaragua.' *Feminist Studies 11* (12/1985): 227-254.

Molyneux Maxine and Razavi Shahra. 'Introduction.' In *Gender Justice, Development and Rights,* ed. Molyneux Maxine and Razavi Shahra, 1-43. Oxford Studies in Democratization. New York: Oxford University Press, 2002.

Mukhopadhyay, Matrayee. 'Introduction: Gender, Citizenship and Governance.' In *Gender Citizenship and Governance—A Global Source Book,* ed. Minke Valk, Sarah Cummings, and Henk van Dam, 13-29. Gender, Society and Development Series, KIT Royal Tropical Institute Amsterdam. London: Oxfam Educational, 2004.

National Reconstruction Bureau (NRB). 'Devolution of Power Plan' Online Available: http://www.nrb.gov.pk

Naz, Rukhshanda. *A Gender Review of The Legal Framework for Local Government in NWFP.* Peshawar: Aurat Publication and Information Service Foundation, 2004.

Norris, Pippa. *Electoral Engineering—Voting Rules and Political Behaviour.* Cambridge: Cambridge University Press, 2004.

Pattan Development Organization. 'Voices of Women Councillors.' Islamabad: Pattan Development Organization, 2004.

Pattan Development Organization. 'Transition to Democracy—Hopes and Expectations. Key Findings of Post-Election Survey Research: Election 2002.' Islamabad: Pattan Development Organization, 2003.

PILDAT—Pakistan Institute of Legislative Development and Transparency. 'Background Paper on Women Representation in Pakistan's Parliament.' No place and publisher mentioned, 2004.

Rai, Shirin M. 'Gender and Democratization: Ambiguity and Opportunity.' In *Democratization in the South—The Jagged Wave,* ed. Robin Luckham and Gordon White, 220-242. Manchester: Manchester University Press, 1996.

Robinson, Mark. 'Participation, Local Governance and Decentralized Service Delivery.' Paper prepared for a Ford Foundation Workshop in Santiago on New Approaches to Decentralized Service Delivery. Institute of Development Studies, March 2003.

Shah, Aqil. 'Democracy on Hold in Pakistan.' 'Journal of Democracy' 13 (1/2002), 67-75.

Shah, Muhammad. *Sardari, Jirga & Local Government Systems in Balochistan.* Lahore: Edara-e-Tadrees Publishers, 1992.

Shaheed, Farida. *Imagined Citizenship: Women, State and Politics in Pakistan.* Lahore: Shirkat Gah, 2002.

Shaheed, Farida. 'The Context of Women's Activism.' In *Shaping Women's Lives—Laws, Practices and Strategies in Pakistan,* ed. Farida Shaheed, Sohail Warraich, Cassandra Balchin, and Gazdar Aisha, 271-318. Lahore: Shirkat Gah, 1998.

Shaheed Farida, Zia Asma and Soheil Warraich, eds. *Women in Politics: Participation and Representation in Pakistan—with update 1993-1997.* Special Bulletin, 'Women Living under Muslim Law.' Lahore: Shirkat Gah, 1998.

Tripp, Aili Mari. *Women & Politics in Uganda—The Challenge of Associational Autonomy.* Wisconsin: James Currey Publishers, 2000.

Uzmi, Zartash and Nakhoda, Shehzaad. 'Constitution of the Islamic Republic of Pakistan.' Online Available: http://www.pakistani.org/pakistan/constitution/

Waylen, Georgina. 'Analysing Gender in the Politics of the Third World.' In *Gender in Third World Politics, Issues in Third World Politics Series,* pp. 5-23. Buckingham: Open University Press, 1996.

Waylen, Georgina. 'Women and Democratization—Conceptualizing Gender Relations in Transition Politics.' World Politics 46 (3/1994), pp. 327-54.

Wieringa, Saskia. 'Women's Interests and Empowerment: Gender Planning Reconsidered.' *Development and Change* (25/1994), pp. 829-48.

Yazdani, Fauzia, *Women's Representation in Local Government in Pakistan: Impact Analysis and Future Policy Implications.* No place and publisher mentioned, 2004.

Zia Shahla and Farzana Bari. *Baseline Report on Women's Participation in Political & Public Life in Pakistan.* International Women's Rights Action Watch—Asia Pacific. Lahore: Aurat Publication and Information Service Foundation, 1999.

10

Women's Representation in the Politics of Pakistan

Shahnaz Wazir Ali

Pakistan has achieved remarkable progress in women's participation in the formal political arena. The current proportion of women's representation also pushed Pakistan much higher in regional and international ranking of the GEM (gender empowerment measurement). It has moved up from 100th on the list of 102 countries in 1999, to 58th position in 2003 in the GEM index,[1] even higher than that of the UK and US.

It leads South Asia with the reservation of almost 33 per cent seats for women at all three tiers of local government (district, tehsil and union) in 2000, and about 17 per cent reservation of seats in the legislative bodies (the Senate, National and Provincial Assemblies) just prior to the general elections of 2002. Currently, there are 6 women ministers in the federal cabinet; 4 in Punjab; 2 in Sindh and 2 in the Balochistan cabinet. There is one advisor to PM with the status of a minister at the federal level, and one as advisor to the Chief Minister in Sindh. Most of the inductions in federal and provincial governments were made by the end of 2003 or during 2004. Except for Sindh, where a woman legislator holds the office of the deputy speaker of the Sindh Assembly, no woman holds a similar legislative office in any other legislature, nor does any woman in the country hold any political office above the post of minister.

Altogether, there are currently a total of 232 women in the legislative assemblies of Pakistan: 73 in the National Assembly, 18 in the Senate, and 141 in the four Provincial Assemblies. Of the 141 women in the Provincial Assemblies: 73 are in the Punjab Assembly, 33 in the Sindh Assembly, 23 in the NWFP Assembly, and 12 in the Balochistan Assembly.

This has been a substantial enhancement from the previous quota reserved for women at the local government,[2] provincial, and national level.[3] Of the 232 women, 205 are on seats reserved for women, 25 won elections on general seats (one later vacated her seat), two came on seats reserved for non-Muslims, and one on a seat reserved for technocrats. The overall proportion of women's representation currently in the national and provincial legislatures (232 out of a total of 1,170) is thus 19.8 per cent. During 1997–99, their overall representation was 11 out of a total of 787 [i.e.1.4 per cent].

In the 2002, elections altogether 188 women contested 163 seats as compared to 6,824 male candidates on overall 849 general seats. This meant that 57 women contested general seats in the National Assembly (NA) and 131 in the Provincial Assemblies (PAs). Since 13 women contested 2 seats each and 1 contested 3, there were overall 202 women candidates (3 per cent). Of these, 34 contested 31 seats from Punjab; 21 contested 14 seats from Sindh; 3 contested 3 seats from NWFP; and one contested one seat from Balochistan. No woman contested on general seats from Islamabad or FATA.

Of the total 202 women candidates, 101 contested the election on party tickets, both for the NA and the PAs, and an equal number of 101 were independent candidates. Of all the tickets awarded by political parties for the NA and the PAs, 18 were given by PML-Q. Party tickets were awarded to 38 women and 22 women contested as independent candidates. Among political parties, PPPP gave tickets to 10 women; PML-Q to 8; PML-N to 4; MQM to 4; PAT to 2; PTI to 2; and National Alliance, PMLZ, PML-J, TI, TPP, ANP, NPPWG and PWP to one each.

National Assembly: There were 279 women candidates against 60 reserved seats. MMA nominated 57 (34 from Punjab; 11 from Sindh; 8 from NWFP; 4 from Balochistan). PML-Q nominated 46 (26 from Punjab; 9 from Sindh; 8 from NWFP; 3 from Balochistan).

With more than 55,000 women contesting elections for local government in 2005, 28,550 women were inducted in the local government as a result of elections held in August 2005. The share of women in membership of major political parties is, however, not available.

The method of filling in women's seats, as well as non-Muslim seats, in the NA and the PAs is through a party list system of proportional representation, whereby the reserved seats allocated to a province are divided between parties in proportion to the total general seats won by them from that province in the concerned election. Indirect elections to women's reserved seats through a system of proportional representation, which is completely different from the mainstream direct election system, is criticized by many activist women and committed party workers. The indirect method of election deprives women of the opportunity of dealing directly with the electorate. This lack of electoral experience at the constituency level may, as in the past, impede their entry into mainstream politics.

Women on reserved seats, unlike those on general seats, have no geographical constituencies. Without representing a specific section of the electorate, or being able to effectively deliver at a constituency-level, their chances of winning a general seat at a later stage become limited. A number of women who came in on reserved seats were new to the political system and barely possessed knowledge of issues, legislation or policies. However, several who are party activists with a middle class background have a strong track record in politics as well as in activism on women's rights. A number of women, particularly in the ruling party, are merely close relatives of key party leaders, with no or minimal track record of party work or personal political background.

The reserved seats are allocated to each province as a whole; and the areas the women come from depends entirely on the nominations made and seats won by the different parties. The nomination system allows complete control over selection to the party leadership, opening the door to nepotism and creating a strong public perception of selections being made on the basis of relationship or influence, rather than merit. It also leads to disillusionment among women workers, who feel they have been ignored despite their background of party work and loyalty.

The nomination system also means that the women remain dependent on and accountable to their male-dominated parties, rather than the electorate. Without the support of a constituency base, their strength and influence within the party remains limited. The current system, whereby reserved seats are proportionately distributed among political parties, denies independent women candidates the opportunity to contest them.

Like several male parliamentarians who are close relatives of former or present politicians and parliamentarians, the majority of women who are elected on general seats belong to traditional political families who have been active in politics for years due to their strong economic or political background. They secured or were given tickets to retain their constituencies within the family, mostly in cases where no suitable male members were available among closest family circles, due to election rules and restrictions, particularly the graduation bar. However, there are a few exceptions too, and some active and senior party leaders were also able to win on party tickets.

Despite the number, the type of women that have come into National Assembly and Provincial Assembly on reserved seats tend to be proxy representatives and are invariably relatives of politicians. They don't come with experience—either institutional or professional. They are generally limited in their ability to participate and are usually not politically alive.

There are three broad categories of women's cadres in parties. First, there are ordinary women party workers, who are loyal to parties due to their strong political or ideological bonds with the parties or personal liking for the leadership. Second, there are those prominent women politicians and leaders, who have inherited political power and constituency from their families and have continued to play their role as key players in politics, both at the party and constituency level. Almost all of them come from upper class and feudal backgrounds. Their main preferences, however, emanate from the priorities of power with political expediency as a major factor behind their decision-making. Third, there are women members who are relatives of prominent or active male members of parties, mostly with an affluent background. Most of these women are not directly involved in politics, even with the activities of their parties. Ironically, they reap most of the fortunes of party politics and get maximum share in top party positions, and secure tickets as well as high positions in the government, if the party comes to power.

Women's share in political and legislative positions has always been marginal in Pakistan, with the situation further deteriorating after the provision of reserved seats expired in 1990. Most executive political positions (prime minister, chief ministers, ministers, speakers/deputy speakers of the assemblies, chairmen/deputy chairmen of the Senate, parliamentary secretaries) can only be held by elected members of the legislature. However, any eligible person can be appointed for several political positions, e.g. provincial governors, advisors and special assistants, by the concerned authority. The post of president can also be held by any eligible person through an election procedure laid down in the Constitution. The pace and progress to induct women into ministerial positions has been very slow.

Shaukat Aziz's government announced a 59-member federal cabinet, the largest in Pakistan's history, which included six women (one as federal minister and five as ministers of state). This increased the share of women in the federal cabinet to 10.1 per cent from the previous 3.7 per cent. However, most of the women were given posts of junior ministers. Zubeida Jalal was made Minister of Social Welfare and Special Education, after splitting it from the Ministry of Women's Development. The present cabinet includes 33 federal ministers (31 men and 2 women); and 26 ministers of State (21 men and 5 women).

Despite the advances made, women continue to face challenges that hinder the full realization of their potential as active interlocutors of policy-making and implementation processes. By and large, women's wings lack any significant decision-making power, tend to tow the party line with barely any autonomy, and play a minimal role in defining or influencing party agendas.

An overwhelming majority of women legislators (216 out of 232) are new entrants in formal political and legislative institutions and have no previous parliamentary experience. Only sixteen women legislators have some parliamentary experience, and that too of a limited nature. Most of them, however, have some kind of connection with politics through their families or relatives in political families. Almost half of them have sufficient political experience through affiliation with parties and women's wings, and nearly one fourth of them have some background of activism on women's rights issues mostly undertaken in collaboration with civil society organizations, with some pursuing women's causes independently as professionals.

Since most of them have not had professional institutional experience, therefore their knowledge is limited. These women do not know the complexities of the legislative system or the compulsions of power relations within their political parties and governance structures. They are not familiar with policies, strategies, financing, ground-based issues, administrative issues and high priority sectors like education and health. Political parties use them primarily to mobilize women voters during elections and provide polling agents in women's booths, or to demonstrate on behalf of the party when directed by the leadership. The latter usually takes place when the political party leadership is in crisis, or when support of party demands and positions is required. A majority of women legislators lack knowledge of political systems, legislative procedures, how to intervene in the budget-making process, constitutional rights and national laws concerning women, international covenants and GOP's international obligations on women's rights and human rights (CEDAW, CRC), the Beijing follow-up process, the NPA and women's legal rights issues.

On a more routine level, the women party cadre of major political parties is used for 'show of strength' in public activities, such as welcoming leaders at the airports and participating in public meetings. However, they are performing under difficult circumstances which include the authority structures of their respective parties, resistance from within parties and legislatures (mostly coming from feudal and gender-biased lobbies), party control over development funds of women legislators, unfriendly behaviour of male colleagues and lack of encouragement by party leadership.

There is an absence of a regular and structured interaction between the women's cadre and women legislators within parties. Similarly, there is a total lack of interaction among women public representatives belonging to different tiers of governance. Whatever sporadic interaction developed through occasional meetings and women's conventions usually results in rhetoric only and disarray, as no follow-up mechanisms exist to consolidate the initiatives undertaken. The phenomenon also hampers the evolution and development of a clear future course of action and consensus-building on crucial women's rights issues among women cadre within parties.

There are no capacity-building programmes or initiatives within parties to train and educate legislators, especially the new entrants. The committee system is exceedingly weak. The library also needs to be equipped with additional resource material. Sector specific specialists need to be inducted. Background notes and papers on current issues need to be circulated more often in light of which the agendas for the national and provincial assemblies be drafted so that informed decisions could be reached.

The change in attitude from the patriarchal sense of patronage to a more 'genuine feeling of partnership' towards women will be a slow and long process, depending on several factors, including women's own initiatives to strengthen their ranks and the gender-sensitization of parties. The process of change in attitudes and behaviours towards women and accepting women in their new leadership roles still has a long way to go.

NOTES

1. Political and Legislative Participation of Women in Pakistan, UNDP, 2005.
2. In the 1998-99 urban and district council elections in the Punjab, 12.7 per cent seats were reserved for women; and 25.8 per cent overall in Balochistan. In NWFP and Sindh (where elections were not held), the proportion reserved for women was 2.9 per cent and 23 per cent respectively.
3. The previous Constitutional provision for about 10 per cent reserved seats for women in the National Assembly and 5 per cent in the four Provincial Assemblies (none in the Senate) had expired after the 1988 general elections, thus there were no women on reserved seats in these assemblies till the enhanced reservation provision incorporated in 2002.

11

Decentralization and Women's Participation in Local Governance

Riffat Munnawar

Introduction

In most countries, decentralization has been instrumental in creating new political structures such as local government. Out of seventy-five developing countries with populations of five million and more, sixty-three have initiated transfer of power to local units of government.[1] What will be discussed here is how decentralization coupled with quota reservation influences the participation of women at the three tiers of local government in Pakistan.

There are numerous definitions of decentralization of governance. According to the Overseas Development Institute (ODI), decentralization is a form of governance that transfers authority and responsibility from central to intermediate and local governments.[2] In other words, it is devolution of powers to local authorities that are independent of higher authorities and may be able to utilize the authority and resources according to the needs of local communities.[3] Development literature uses decentralization as a tool to improve administrative and institutional performance through efficient and transparent decision-making.[4] Decentralization may be divided into three areas: political, administrative and fiscal. Administrative and fiscal decentralization refers to the reorganization of the central government by delegation of decision-making authority to local units or semi-autonomous authorities, whereas devolution means relinquishing political power to lower levels of government.

Political decentralization is one in which powers and responsibilities are devolved to elected local governments, a kind of democratic decentralization.[5] Democratic decentralization, as a form of governance, encourages the participation of subordinated groups, including women. It is responsive to the needs and interests of these groups. This leads to a question: why should women be included in decision making? International and bilateral development agencies agree that unless women are involved in decision/

policy-making at all levels of governance, improvement in their socio-political statuses will remain low. The international declaration on women in local government states:

> Systematic integration of women augments the democratic basis, the efficiency and the quality of the activities of Local Government. If Local Government is to meet the needs of both women and men, it must build on the experiences of both women and men, through an equal representation at all levels and in all fields of decision making, covering the wide range of responsibilities of local government. In order to create sustainable, equal and democratic local governments, where women and men have equal access to decision making, equal access to services and equal treatment in these services, the gender perspective must be mainstreamed into all areas of policy making and management in local government.[6]

Decentralization may provide more space and opportunities for women to represent their needs and interests than in the central government.

> The basic premise of decentralization that government is brought closer to people and therefore is more responsive to real peoples' needs and interests is undermined without strategies to mobilize voice of subordinate groups in society, and forging of institutionalized spaces for participation and accountability.[7]

Governance is an interactive process of governing which focuses on the interaction and interdependencies among various stakeholders at different levels. It provides space for women as one of the stakeholders in determining the local development agenda and managing resources to implement development projects.[8] It implies bottoms-up decision making involving all the concerned members at every level of government and non-government organizations. Good governance is linked with good policy, human rights, democratization, decentralization, and institution building, including state and private sector development. Furthermore good governance is transparent, responsible and effective in exercising of power and resources by the government with the participation of civil society.[9]

The International Union of Local Authorities (IULA) worldwide declaration on women in local government had emphasized the fact that justice, efficiency, diversity and change in the political system can only be achieved through the participation of women in politics.[10]

Decentralization is not a new phenomenon in Pakistan. It existed in the sub-continent before the independence of Pakistan. Non-representative regimes initiated local government to legitimize their control over the states. In the pre-independence period, it was the British imperial state that promulgated local government reforms. In the post-independent period, it has been institutionalized by subsequent military regimes in Pakistan.[11]

History of Local Government System in Pakistan

Before the advent of the British rule in India, a traditional rural local government system known as the village *Panchayats* (literally, a council of five persons) existed and performed administrative, judicial and local development functions.The *Panchayat* was not a representative of the whole village; rather it represented the upper castes and large farmers. The system of the village headmen existed in the Mughal reign and at the time of British government. The headman supposedly was the representative of the central government. In the rural Punjab, these *Panchayats* were responsible to assess and collect the Emperor's share of the harvest and deposit with the revenue functionaries. They also discharged judicial functions by resolving village feuds, arranged village festivals and imposed a code of conduct on local societies.

It is important to note that women rarely became members of these community leadership structures. Under the British Raj, the local Union committees were assigned to oversee the construction of roads, bridges, drains and dispensaries. In 1892, a form of indirect democracy was introduced into local government traditions. Members of the Union Councils were given the right to elect some members of the provincial legislatures, who in turn, elected central legislative members. This pattern was adopted by General Ayub Khan in the 1960s.[12] The colonial structure was based on an executive system of district administration, independent of political institutions. The district officer was head of the police, magistracy and revenue administration coordinating all other services. He was considered to be the Chief Executive of the local body who could take over (in emergent situations) all the functions of the local body.

After independence in 1947, the local government system deteriorated[13] (Islam 2000). While Pakistan adopted a federal constitutional structure, the executive powers remained in the hands of the national bureaucracy till the late 1950s. During 1958-69, the military government introduced the system of elected local governance. The realization that people should manage their own affairs gave rise to the Basic Democracies system resulting in a new system of local government across the country. The Basic Democracies system was seen as a substitute for universal suffrage and it served as an electoral college to elect the President and the legislative assemblies. Through this system 120,000 'Basic Democrats' were elected to serve in multi-tiered institutions of local government. The members selected their own head and he automatically became a member of the *Tehsil* council. The same principle was followed by the district and divisional councils and the provincial and national assemblies. However, with the fall of the Ayub Khan regime with which it was closely associated, Basic Democracies fell into disfavour.

If the first military government of Ayub Khan was the pioneer in devising an extensive system of local governments, it was the second martial law regime of General Zia that implemented the principle of elected local governments. Elections for local councillors were held on a non-party basis in 1979, 1983, 1987,[14] and in 1991. Now, the third military government introduced a new set-up of local government which has turned the historic power imbalance and created a fundamental institutional shift through its devolution policy. In the absence of elected assemblies, local governments were the only popularly elected bodies and thus played important political and developmental roles in the history of Pakistan. Before the new devolution plan 2000, all provinces had reserved seats for women, minorities and peasants. Elections were held under these provisions in 1979, 1983, 1987 and 1992.

The Local Government Plan—2000

The present government of General Pervez Musharraf promulgated Local Government Ordinance 2000 to develop a new integrated system with effect from 14 August 2001. This Ordinance was to function in the provincial framework and was to adhere to federal and provincial laws. The administration was committed to establishing democracy at the three levels of governance. A bottoms-up approach was adopted in implementing the pertinent reforms. According to the National Reconstruction Bureau, Government of Pakistan:

> The proposed Local Government Plan integrates the rural with the urban local governments on the one hand and the bureaucracy with the local governments on the other, into one coherent structure in which the district administration and the local police are answerable to the elected chief executive of the district. Citizen monitoring by elected representatives, the civil society's involvement with development, and a system of effective check and balances, completes the hard core of the political structure and system of the Local Government.[15]

These councils will serve as the schools of democracy. Local councils are considered as the primary institutions to ensure participation of local populations, under their own supervision, to regulate all aspects of their social life. According to Section 49 of the law, the union council is responsible for the construction and maintenance of roads, passages and streets, provision of street lights, tree plantation, maintenance of shamlats, sanitation, cleaning, public health, marriages, death registration, reconciliatory role in marital affairs, divorce and mediation in matters of alimony, arrangements of festivals, participation in civil defence work, cooperation with police, help in reconstruction in case of calamity, and water supply schemes. Moreover, the education department has also been placed under the supervision of local government (for details on the functions of District Councils, City Councils, and *Panchayats*, see Islam 1999).

The Structure of Local Government System 2000 (LGS) and 2005

Theoretically, the system is based on five fundamental principles: devolution of political power, decentralization of administrative authority, decentralization of management functions, diffusion of the power authority nexus, and distribution of resources to the district level. For efficient provision of services and development, the administration and the police would work under the elected head of the district. In the past, police and administration were not answerable to the elected representatives.

The LGS 2000 provided a three-tier Local Government structure with the District at the top, the *Tehsil*/Town at the middle level, and Union Council being at the lowest level. The District Government consists of the *Zila Nazim* and District Administration. The District Administration consists of district offices including sub-offices at the *tehsil* level that are answerable to the District *Nazims* assisted by the District Coordination Officers. The District Coordination Officer (DCO) is appointed by the Provincial Government and is the coordinating head of the District Administration. The *Zila Nazim* is accountable to the people through the elected members of the *Zila* Council. A *Zila* Council consists of all Union *Nazims* in the District, which in turn consists of the members elected on the reserved seats. These seats were reserved for women, peasants, workers, and minority communities. The *Zila* Council has its secretariat under the *Naib Zila Nazim* and has a separate budget. An attempt was made to introduce checks and balances into the system. The new system also addressed the specific needs and problems of large cities efficiently.

The District Government is responsible to the people and the Provincial Government for improvement of governance and delivery of services. *Tehsil*/ Town administration is the middle tier. *Tehsil* municipal administration is headed by the *Tehsil Nazim* and it consists of a *Tehsil Nazim*, *Tehsil* municipal Officer, *Tehsil* officers, Chief Officers and other officials of the local council service. The *Tehsil* municipal administration is entrusted with the functions of administration, finances, and management of the offices of local government and rural development, and numerous other subjects at the regional, divisional, district, *Tehsil* and lower levels.

The Union Council is the lowest tier. The Union administration is a corporate body covering the rural as well as urban areas across the whole district. It consists of Union *Nazim*, *Naib Union Nazim* and three Union secretaries and other auxiliary staff. The Union *Nazim* is the head of the

Union Administration and the *Naib Union Nazim* who acts as deputy to the Union *Nazim* during his temporary absence. The Union secretaries coordinate and facilitate in community development, functioning of the Union Committees and delivery of municipal services under the supervision of Union *Nazims*.[16] The distribution of seats at the three levels of governance is as follows:

District Council

All *Nazims* of Union Council become members of District Council

- 1 *Nazim* and 1 *Naib Nazim*
- 33 per cent seats reserved for women
- 5 per cent seats reserved for peasants and workers
- 5 per cent seats reserved for minorities

Tehsil/Town Council

All *Naib Nazim* of Union Councils become members of

- *Tehsil* council
- 1 *Nazim* and 1 *Naib Nazim*
- 33 per cent seats reserved for women
- 5 per cent seats reserved for peasants and workers
- 5 per cent seats reserved for minorities

Union Council Level

There are 21 seats/members in the Union Council

- 8 General Muslim seats (for men and women)
- 4 women reserved Muslim seats
- 4 workers and peasant-reserved seats (for men and women)
- 2 workers and peasant-reserved seats for women
- 1 reserved seat for minorities
- 1 *Nazim* (Council Head) and 1 *Naib Nazim* (Deputy Head)

In the year 2005, members at the Union council level were reduced to thirteen from twenty-one whereas there were no changes in the number of members at the Town and District levels. The distributions of members at the Union council level of the local government in year 2005 was such that each Union council had thirteen members which included six general seats (four for men and two for the women), four seats for the workers/peasants out of which two were allocated for men and two for women. One seat was reserved for the minorities. There was one seat for the Union *Nazim* (administrator) and one for the *Naib Nazim* (deputy administrator).[17]

Comparative Analysis of Women's Participation in 2000 and 2005 Local Government Elections

It was expected that reservation of quota would facilitate more women to participate in the second term of local government. This expectation was fulfilled in the local government election 2005. The total number of nominations received for women's reserved seats, according to the Election Commission of Pakistan, was around 56,753 (which is double the number of seats available). In the 2000–2001 local government elections, 11 per cent seats remained vacant for women's reserved seats. This proportion decreased in 2005 where only 3 per cent of the seats remained vacant. Another encouraging aspect was that there was a significant decrease (42 per cent) in the proportion of rejected and withdrawn applications.

Many women took the bold decision to contest elections for the seats of *Nazim* and *Naib Nazim* at all levels of local government. In the 2001 local government elections, fourteen women all over Pakistan contested for the position of Union Council Administrators against men, of whom eleven were elected to lead their Union Councils. Out of these eleven women, nine were from Punjab and two from Sindh. Two women were elected as Union Deputy Administrators from Punjab. One woman was elected Sub-district Council Deputy Administrator from Sindh. Four women contested for the District Administrators post, out of whom two were elected, one each from Khairpur and Nawabshah (Sindh). In total, sixteen women held the position of Administrator/Deputy Administrator at different levels of local government.

In the 2005 local government elections, in Punjab alone forty-four women contested for the seats of *Nazim* and thirteen women contested for the seats of *Naib Nazim*. This increased participation of women at these positions clearly indicates that women themselves as well as the community, consider women to be capable of holding these positions. On a positive note, one could also draw the conclusion that the Pakistani patriarchal society/structure is in a transformational stage in which new leadership in the shape of women is emerging at the grassroots level.

A brief view of the second generation women who came forward to serve in the local government is presented. The data is based on an extensive coverage of election campaigns of thirty female candidates, and in-depth interviews were conducted with a cross–section of women and participant observation of the election process was done to have an inside view of the political struggle these women had to make to enter the political arena.

Profile of Women Candidates

The social background of the candidates shows that 64 per cent of the women respondents were reasonably well educated, meaning that their educational qualification was equal and above high school level. Almost 60 per cent of these women (18 out of 30) belonged to age 45 and above, only nine of them were between age group 35-44 and three were in the age group 25-34. A relatively large proportion of women were in the age group of 45. This may be due to the fact that women in this age group have fewer family responsibilities as there are other female members to look after household activities. The presence of other female members could be supported by the fact that a substantial number (27 out of 30) of respondents lived in a joint family system. It was encouraging to note that majority (80 per cent) of these women candidates were contesting elections for the second tenure. This may be taken as a sign of their satisfaction with the local government system, and secondly, these experienced women may become more effective councillors as compared to the new entrants in the political system.

Besides this, a significant proportion (10 out of 30) of these women had other family members who were also contesting local government elections. Despite the fact that the local government election was supposed to be non-party based, yet majority of these women were nominated by their respective political parties. These women had long associations with their respective parties as political workers and were known to their communities. As mentioned above, these women were contesting election for the second tenure so their previous performances as local councilors might have played a crucial role in entering the political arena again.

The selection of candidates is not always based on an objective assessment of the candidate's capability and acceptability among local people. Often political leaders played a crucial role in the selection process. It was observed that, in some cases, more than two women were contesting the elections from the same political party platform. Different groups in the same political party were supporting different women candidates.

Election Issues and Campaigns

The focus of the electoral campaign in the 2005 local government election was on the availability of clean drinking water, electricity and gas supply; improved sanitation system; and better education and health facilities. Besides the provision of general basic facilities, women's issues such as women's rights, discrimination and violence against women were on the agenda. The coverage of the campaigns of some of these candidates highlighted the fact that local government elections were gaining the same importance as those of the general elections. The political party leaders were seen presiding at election meetings of the candidates and canvassing for them. Furthermore, the expenses of the election campaigns were borne by the affiliated political party. The women candidates who were contesting election independently lacked this social and economic capital but yet were able to win these elections.

Despite the restriction ordered by the Election Commission on the election expenditure, contestants from various parties breached the rule. Huge amounts of money was spent on the campaigns. It was a competitive display of money and power between political rivals. In some cases the candidates spent their own resources, received help from family and friends.

Conclusion

The reservation of quotas has institutionalized and legitimized women's representation in the local government system. Women are now coming forward in large numbers in local electoral politics. It seems that there is a shift towards the acceptance of women in public spheres. The image of the traditional Pakistani woman is changing and a more conducive environment for women is being created. The society at large is accepting that local government should be inclusive of women and they do play a prominent role in local government.

As it has been observed that there was complete involvement of the political parties in these local government elections, it is suggested that elections should be party-based. Each political party should fix a quota for women. This would lead to the development of a sense of worth and enhance self esteem among women. Effective female local leaders would be role models for other women. It is further suggested that quotas for women should also be fixed for administrative positions such as, *Nazims* and *Naib Nazims*.

However, more conducive environment is needed for women in public life. It was reported that some women candidates were harassed. Violent politics is another important aspect that needs to be given a thought. It has been observed that whenever violence and crime dominates politics, women as a group become automatically marginalized.

Annexure
Percentage of filed, rejected/withdrawal and contesting candidates
during 1st term and 2nd term

	Punjab		
	1st Election	Current Election	Incr/Dec
Muslim General			
a. Available Seats	27584	13846	
b. Nomination Filed	94943	71519	
	344%	517%	**173%**
c. Rejected/Withdrawn	17626	10309	**-42%**
d. Contesting Candidates	77317	61210	
	280%	442%	**162%**
Muslim General (W)			
a. Available Seats	13812	6928	
b. Nomination Filed	27691	18326	
	200%	265%	**65%**
c. Rejected/Withdrawn	4262	1567	**-63%**
d. Contesting Candidates	23429	16759	
	170%	242%	**72%**
Peasant & Worker			
a. Available Seats	13812	6928	
b. Nomination Filed	43078	33466	
	312%	483%	**171%**
c. Rejected/Withdrawn	6126	3817	**-38%**
d. Contesting Candidates	36952	29649	
	268%	428%	**160%**
Peasant & Worker (W)			
a. Available Seats	6906	6928	
b. Nomination Filed	12535	14113	
	182%	204%	**22%**
c. Rejected/Withdrawn	3455	2511	**-27%**
d. Contesting Candidates	9080	11602	
	131%	167%	**36%**
Minorities			
a. Available Seats	3493	3474	
b. Nomination Filed	5657	5519	
	162%	159%	**-3%**
c. Rejected/Withdrawn	1510	1475	**-2%**
d. Contesting Candidates	4147	4044	
	119%	116%	**-3%**
Nazims/Naib Nazims			
a. Available Seats	6906	6928	
b. Nomination Filed	13823	12790	
	200%	185%	**-15%**

c. Rejected/Withdrawn	3116	2663	**-15%**
d. Contesting Candidates	10707	10127	
	155%	146%	**-9%**
Grand Total			
a. Available Seats	72513	45032	
b. Nomination Filed	197727	155733	
	273%	346%	**73%**
c. Rejected/Withdrawn	36095	22342	**-38%**
d. Contesting Candidates	161632	133391	
	223%	296%	**73%**

NOTES

1. United Nations Development Programme (UNDP). *Women's Political Participation and Good Governance: 21st Century Challenges*, New York: Oxford University Press, 2000.
2. Overseas Development Institute. 'Decentralization and Governance' 2002. www.odi.org.uk/keysheets/
3. Beal Jo. 'Urban Governance: Why Gender Matters?' Gender in Development Monograph, Series #1. New York: UNDP, 1996.
4. Issac, T.M. Thomas. 'Campaign for Democratic Decentralization in Kerala: An assessment from the perspective of Empowered Deliberative Democracy,' Centre for Development Studies and Keral State Planning Board, 2000.
5. Robinson, M. 'Participation, Local Governance and Decentralized Service Delivery', Paper presented at the workshop on 'New Approaches to Decentralized Service Delivery,' Santiago de Chile, 16-20 March, 2003.
6. Evertzen, A. 'Gender and Local Governance.' SNV-Netherlands Development Organization, 2001. Accessed December 2003.http://www.bestpractices.org.
7. Mukhopadhyay. M. 'Decentralization and Gender equity in South Asiaan Issues paper,' 2005.
8. Evertzen, A. 'Gender and Local Governance.' SNV-Netherlands Development Organization, 2001, accessed December 2003, http://www.bestpractices.org.
9. Grindle, Merilee S. 'Good Enough Governance: Poverty Reduction and Reform in Developing Countries,' Department for International Development of the United Kingdom, 2005.
10. United Nations Development Programme *Political and Legislative Participation of Women in Pakistan*, New York: Oxford University Press, 2005.
11. Chema, Ali, Ijaz Khawaja, Asim and Qadir Adnan. 'Decentralization in Pakistan: Context, Content and Causes, in Mookherjee, D. and P. Bardhan,' Decentralization in 'Developing Countries: A Comparative Perspective,' 2004, accessed January 2005, http://www.arts.cornell.edu/e…

    Reyes, Socorro. 'Quotas for women for Legislative seats at the Local level in Pakistan,' Stockholm, 2002. International IDEA, accessed January 2005 http://www.idea.int

.......Lundberg, Paul. A Comparison of Decentralization in Pakistan and Nepal, PARAGON Regional Governance Programme for Asia, paper presented at the 2nd International Conference on Decentralization, Manila 25-27 July, accessed January 2005, http://www.decentralization.ws/countrypapers.asp

12. General Ayub Khan was the first martial law administrator,who ruled Pakistan from 1958 to 1969.

13. Islam, Zahid. *An Introduction To Local Government System in Punjab*, Aurat Publication and Information Services Foundation, Lahore, 1999.

14. Yazdani, Fauzia, 'Women Empowerment through Decentralization in Pakistan: Barriers & Beyond,' *Women & Empowerment experience by Some Asian countries*, ed by D.P. Singh, Manjit Singh, 2005.

15. National Reconstruction Bureau: 'Local Government Plan 2000.' Islamabad: Government of Pakistan.

16. Anwar, Farhan. *A Citizen's Guide to the District Government System*, Islamabad: Friedrich Naumann Foundation, 2002.

17. National Reconstruction Bureau Government of Pakistan, 2004.

12

Sharing Personal Experiences: Women in Pakistani Politics

Aazar Ayaz and Andrea Fleschenberg

Introduction

Social change generally occurs at a slow, incremental pace and unfortunately not, as desired by most activists, in 'historical jumps'. But there are signs that change is taking place: never before in the history of Pakistan (or of other countries in Asia, sub-Saharan Africa and Latin America with similar provisions) have women entered politics in such high numbers, creating a critical mass by their sheer presence.

In the 1950s, Pakistan was, to our knowledge, the first country to introduce quota regulations in the form of reserved seats (3-10 per cent) which lapsed after some years before being reintroduced by successive governments several times during the country's brief history. At the beginning of the twenty-first century, the military-led government under General Pervez Musharraf introduced unprecedented quota provisions of 17 per cent for reserved seats in both houses, the National Assembly and the Senate. Those seats are proportionally allocated to the political parties according to their electoral result and the party's list presented to election authorities prior to election date. Nonetheless, the country's strong women's movement requested a 30 per cent quota in accordance with a national consultation by the Ministry of Women and Development in May 2001 and the National Campaign for Restoration of Women's Reserved Seats in 1998.[2] But most important is the political space opening up for women.

Table 1: Gender Ratio in the National Assembly and Senate[3]

Election Year	Parliament		Senate	
	No. of Women	% of Women	No. of Women	% of Women
1977[Q]	10	4.7	n. a.	n. a.
1985[Q]	23	9.7	0	0
1988[Q]	24	10.1	1	1.1
1990	2*	0.9	1	1.1
1993	4*	1.8	1	1.1
1997	7	3.2	2	2.3
2002[Q]	73	21.3	17*	17

[Q]Quota regulation applied in form of constitutionally guaranteed reserved seats.
* Data of 2006.

In a gender-segregated society such as Pakistan, women now have a representative they can talk to and address their concerns, allowing female citizens social interaction with politicians often for the first time. For many women parliamentarians this is a first, too. Their experiences are mixed, especially for those on reserved seats. As one woman politician from the North West Frontier Province explained on conditions of anonymity:

> People still do not accept us—as we are selected and not elected, we face the problem that we are not seen as competitors. We live in a society where we are not used to speaking and dealing with men. The male MPs do not take us seriously, but it is difficult for women to exercise leadership as they are shy and men are strong.

The lack of support is encountered in all walks of parliamentary life: in the assembly sessions; in the interaction with the Speaker over allocation of speaking time and presentation of bills; in their own parties, where male colleagues are rarely supportive of women MPs and their agendas; and in media reports, as well as in the missing coordination among women parliamentarians themselves. On general seats, male family members are needed as mediators and socially acceptable faces to interact with members of the woman's constituency, particular in remote, inaccessible or tradition-bound rural areas of NWFP or Balochistan. Furthermore, gender-specific household responsibilities, family issues related to children, marriage and religion are also identified as challenges for the exercise of their mandate. 'We are here because our husbands are supporting us'—these are frequently repeated. The road leading towards independent politicians and political leaders in their own right is still a far cry for them.

'What have you done for women?' is a question mostly posed to women parliamentarians and local councillors from male colleagues and journalists. This relates to an important issue: are they primarily women's representatives? Or are they representatives of the whole constituency? This becomes further complicated for women on reserved seats. How successful can women politicians be under the current setup and the constraints coupled with the lack of resources and a restrictive environment?

Compared to other countries, almost all women parliamentarians interviewed emphasized their self-understanding as primarily women's representatives, especially those on reserved seats. Female members of parliament themselves remain an issue, a contested symbol and bargaining chip between the government and Islamic parties. They do not have their own vote bank and, hence, have low bargaining power within their parties to pursue their agenda. Consequently, they often tow the party (leader's) line and are not constituency—but residence-oriented in their policy projects. 'We have to discuss their issues and not ours. Politics is male-dominated and we fight to discuss our issues, in particular, health, education and honour killings', outlined a Provincial Assembly member from NWFP. The development of social infrastructure, awareness-raising of women's rights as well as the need for implementing laws such as the right to inheritance and marriage rights, are on top of their agenda. Disappointed with the legislative (non)achievements of supposed progressive women politicians, Saima Munir, from Aurat Foundation in Peshawar, explains the difficulties which doubly bind women parliamentarian and their advancement into politics:

> We face a dilemma: What we want from women in politics is women who take up women's issues and represent women. We have to decide what we want—change the status of women in the country or change the composition of the assemblies. We also want men to take up our issues.

While women parliamentarians themselves admit that they 'have done as much as they were allowed to do', to them, 'one term is not enough—at least a generation is required to change in mindset, to alter the socio-political climate for women, to build their capacities—and establish a voter bank, to run on general seats, and with a progressive, pro-women agenda. Sajid Qaisrani from Aurat Foundation, Islamabad acknowledges this difficult challenge, but also highlights success stories, small or big, of current women legislators and councillors, especially on the local level across Pakistan.

> At all legislative levels, women parliamentarians fared well, especially compared to their male colleagues although the general impression was that they have not performed—partly due to overstated expectations, the electoral procedures and lots of women being political newcomers. (...) They raised their voice against women

discrimination and women at the grassroots level have done a lot of development projects which helped women too. The problem is that those activities are not properly documented and disseminated to the public. Women are less open to corruption as they are not part of the system and issues dealt with, such as sanitation and water, relate to women. They worked harder than their male counterparts and the qualitative outcome of their policy projects has been better, less expensive, and was supervised by women councillors themselves.

Whether or not women can make a difference is not dependent on their personal background, their party affiliation or their supportive system, but largely on the perceived autonomy and legitimacy of the quota mandate itself. A first, clear electoral systemic trend has emerged in the last 20 years, i.e., when quota mandate has a direct relation with general elections. These are more sustainable and lead to political integration of women. Unless concrete steps towards integration are planned, quotas can mutate into mere paper tigers, which is counteractive to their initial objective, i.e. to serve as a temporary measure to change institutions' and actors' constellations towards a gender-inclusive democracy.

'After four years we can see a change—women who entered as rubber stamps began participating and built up capacities. We can't say we have empowered women, but it is a process and we want to institutionalize women empowerment,' highlights Rehana Hashmi of Women Political School in Islamabad. Coming from different political parties and social backgrounds, Pakistani women legislators (and their experiences portrayed through five of their representatives in this section) certainly differ on issues and agenda-setting strategies, but generally agree on what problems women parliamentarians face. Let's listen to their voices…

The following statements are transcribed manuscripts or speeches of the respective women politicians during the WPA conference in 2005 held in Islamabad. Please see the Appendix at the end of the chapter for the unedited, original version of the transcripts that has been included to preserve the authenticity of these female voices.

1. Tehmina Daultana, Member of the National Assembly, Pakistan

Tehmina Daultana is an educationist by profession. She graduated with an MA in History from University of Punjab in 1973. Her areas of legislative interest are in foreign affairs, education, and women development. She is a member of the Standing Committee on Government Assurance, Women Development Social Welfare and Special Education.

I think the best thing as per the topic of the conference is to just tell you of how I was able to get a little space in the present political system. I belong to an old political family but in it men, both old and young, hold sway and do not give any leeway to the women of the family. I realized that if I went and did the traditional thing and asked for permission to come into the field of politics, I would not be allowed to do so. Therefore, I joined a political party that our family supports—the PML-N. At the time I joined, Mian Nawaz Sharif was the President of the party. The only space I could get then was in the women's wing and this I accepted as I really needed a toehold into the party. I remember when I entered the political office on the first day, I found some women sitting there. They looked at me from head to toe rather critically, and asked me in an all knowing tone, 'Are you a begum? Why have you come here?' 'Well,' I said, 'I am no begum, I am basically an educationist and I have my own school. I want to join the political party, I want to sit with you, talk with you and work with you.' They laughed and said, 'You can't do it'. There was a very nice lady there by the name of Najma Hameed, and she admonished the others: 'Come on, give her some space, let her sit,' and I remember, she smiled at me. It was that little smile which made me sit down, otherwise I would have walked out. Thus, I began to work with the political party.

My goal was not just to sit around and be a silent spectator in the political party; I wanted to contest the elections for the National Assembly.[4] The first time I asked for an MNA seat was in 1990, and since I had very good relations with Mian Nawaz Sharif's family, I went to him directly and asked him, 'Why don't you trust a woman?' He smiled and said, 'Yes, we will.' I remember when the board met to allot seats, one of my cousins got a ticket for the provincial assembly, and another gentleman by the name of Akbar Bhatti got the National Assembly ticket, which was the one that I desired. I just stood up and said, 'You men will get the tickets because you are men. There might be women better than you but they will not get the tickets. But I will keep on fighting until I get it.' I remember the smiles on their faces and this is something that I cannot forget. Anyhow, I didn't do the usual thing in that I didn't change my party just because they did not give me the ticket. I stuck around as I intended to make a place for myself in the party and beat them at their game.

In 1993, I got the NA ticket but first I had to make sure that the men in my family were willing to support me. It was difficult, but I was able to do it. Then I had to convince my constituency in Southern Punjab which is very backward. Women of our family had never shown their faces in public in our constituency, but I decided that I could not fight elections without showing my face, and so I went ahead in a *chadder* (shawl). My family was aghast and told me that there was no way I could get more than a few votes and that this would be shameful for the family. I told them, 'Listen, I have made up my mind to fight, I am going to fight even if I am likely to lose.' To this, they did not have an answer.

The religious parties in my constituency posed the next threat to my candidature. Their contention was that, 'Ok, we will see what we can do for her, but it's better that she does not come to any of the conventions that we hold. Some male members can come but a woman must not.' I went and met their wives and said to them, 'I am a better candidate than any, please give me a chance, your men are not giving me a chance.' So this is how I made my way. One woman called in her husband and I said to him, 'Maulvi sahib, please give me a little space to stand on.' He didn't even look at me, he just looked at my feet and said, 'Ok madam, whatever you want to say tell my wife; don't come and talk to me.' But I said, 'No, I am here, I am going to talk to you and you are going to answer me.' So we sat down and I asked him, 'Maulvi sahib, in which way am I inferior to my male family members? Give me a chance and call me to any of your conventions.' I went to his convention and after that the other maulvis also gave in.

I was elected to the National Assembly and there were three other women members there. I would like to tell you here that people thought I would lose and it was conveyed to Mian Nawaz Sharif that if I lost, so would the MPA[5] of the district, and this would have a bad affect on other MNAs seats. There were three MNA seats and I was the only one who won and the three MPAs within my area won as well. Even my father and my uncle did not have the kind of lead that I had, i.e., I was 25.000 votes ahead of the other candidate. The candidates had a lot of money and Akbar Bhatti even had a newspaper supporting him. I was just a woman without much money but I had the determination to succeed.

When I took my place in the assembly it was time to prove that I was equal to the men there. I was the only woman in the Opposition. In the beginning, the men made me feel that I had to sit at the back. I said, 'No, I am not going to sit at the back, I am going to make my own space.' So while I was in the Opposition, people came to know that there was a lady whose name was Tehmina Daultana.

Neither for men, nor for women, is life easy. That's the way I look at it. If you have a goal, then plan accordingly, and work towards it.

This is my third election for the National Assembly. I contested from two seats. I did not win in one but did so from the other. However, at night they changed the results and the contestant from the PML (Q)[6] was declared the winner. Overall, I had about 100,000 votes from both the seats.

There's one thing that I would like to tell the women sitting here - There is enough space for you. There are enough areas where you can fight, and if you fight, you will win, but you will have to fight hard. Remember, if you feel that everything is going to be very easy, no, it will not be. And this is true for both, democracy and women—but in the end we will win, because we are right. We have to make space for each other.

Lastly, I would like to say best of luck to you ladies, keep up the fight. Inshallah, the last battle will be won by us.

2. Samia Raheel Qazi, Member of the National Assembly, Pakistan

Samia Raheel Qazi is currently President of JIP's Women Commission in Punjab and a member of the Standing Committee on Governance Assurance. Previously, she led the Foreign Affairs Women's Wing of JIP from 1995–2000. She is a member of Women Aid Trust (1996), International Union of Muslim Women (1996), Bazm-i-Iqbal (2001) and Al-Khidmat Foundation (1992). A lecturer by profession, Samia Raheel Qazi obtained her post-graduate degree in Islamic Studies from the University of Balochistan in 1991. Her areas of legislative interest are in education, foreign affairs and law.

Before sharing my experiences as a parliamentarian with you, I deem it pertinent to give you first an idea of the overall framework in which I view women's issues in political participation, economic empowerment, decision-making, and so forth.

To me, men and women are an integral part of each other and any attempt to portray them as competitors or oppressed and oppressor is bound to have catastrophic consequences for humanity in general and [the] final analysis of the situation. Their issues are intertwined with each other and the social equilibrium will be disturbed violently if either of them fails to perform his or her duties and is given the rights unilaterally. In other words, men and women being a part of society, have issues that are common to both, and one should not bisect them on the basis of gender. Similarly, [we] must also take into account that apart from our very survival, a happy, peaceful and smooth human life is directly contingent upon the establishment and strengthening of the institution of the family. Given the biological makeup, women play a key role both in establishing and sustaining it in the very first place. Therefore, the interests of this institution should always be kept in view while introducing any gender-specific policy at any level of state and society. All the state policies, including women-specific ones, must be family friendly. A stubborn division of issues on the basis of gender provides an opportunity to the ruling clique to exploit the situation accordingly. With vested interests in the viewpoint, they use them as a handy tool to usurp the attention of a big segment of society from the root cause of the problems. The tactics used by the Musharraf government in recent times also give credence to this assertion.

The issue of women's representation in the parliament also needs to be viewed in the same context. Giving a parliamentary role to women should not aim at implicitly or explicitly dividing society into two segments, namely men and women. I also believe that women's political representation, be that 33 per cent or 50 per cent or 100 per cent, is not going to make any real difference without revamping the whole system that allows a certain class of people to keep power under their control on one pretext or the other. With this rotten system intact, women's representation has effectively served for very little during the last few years except in creating a new elite class with vested interests in it. The socio-economic and political background of the majority of women parliamentarians gives credence to the assertion that the new clout has allowed the powerful class in society to further strengthen its control on the basis of power.

Therefore, women's political representation in parliament or other forums will remain a cosmetic move until attention is focused on the revamping of the whole rotten system. Furthermore, we have to avoid dividing issues on a gender basis, for this will have serious implications in the long run. And last but not the least, the state has to show an absolute commitment to safeguard and strengthen the institution of the family. Without ensuring these things, we would be doing no service to the nation and only creating new power clubs and groups who will be more interested in safeguarding their own interests than those of women or and any other segment of the society.

As for my experiences as a parliamentarian, I can just tell you that the present government has used the issue of women's representation as a pretext to extend its tenure and nothing else. The root causes of all the problems facing the nation still remain unaddressed, but the government seems determined to deflect the attention of the people away from them by using different petty tactics. This is the crux of all my experiences during all these years.

I would like to add that one really feels happy that there is women's representation, and awareness can be seen among women. Although MMA is thought to be an orthodox party, only in a truly Islamic spirit can any political system address gender equality. The Holy Prophet (PBUH) was the first person to present the theory of gender equality. He did not exclude anyone—nor has he preached that men can't perform domestic activities or a woman can't perform outdoor activities. So it is wrong to assume that Islam imposes any restrictions on women.

3. Kashmala Tariq, Member of the National Assembly, Pakistan

Kashmala Tariq is currently Executive Director of the Parliamentarians Commission for Human Rights and has served as President of the Peoples Student Federation (PSF) from 1993-95, Chief Organizer of PTI for UK (1998–2000), Secretary General of an Environmental NGO (Sath) from 1992-95, and as President of the Student Union at the London School of Economics (1998–99). Her areas of legislative interests are law, education and women development. She also holds a seat in the Standing Committee on Finance and Revenue, House and Library, and Law, Justice and Human Rights.

I would like to share my experiences and would like to add to what has been said here. I would like to talk about the challenges faced by women parliamentarians.

Being a woman parliamentarian and to be in politics is an enormous challenge, just as it is for women working in banks, hospitals, and in other walks of life. I think that it is altogether a very heavy task, a big challenge, and an uphill task, and it is like constantly swimming against the tide. This is even more so when you know what you are talking about, and have done your homework and if you intervene in any of the key issues.

One of the major problems we face here is that we are not brought into mainstream politics. Women who do not utter a word and who sit around idly saying yes to everything are preferred, and it's even better if they keep their eyes and ears closed and are deaf and dumb. We do not have democracy even within the parties.

I am not talking here in the capacity of a Muslim Leaguer or as an MNA. I am here as a human rights and a women rights activist, a feminist rather. Whatever I am sharing over here is not in the capacity of a parliamentarian. What I am saying over here is that we do not have democracy in the parties; our issues are not given weight, especially when there are reserved seats. Women who are given reserved seats, take it for granted that it is their absolute right. Now, over the period of last three years, we have really worked hard to prove ourselves—that we are better than men or we can work equivalent to men. There are very few women and they are bound to speak when they have to reply to a question posed by a woman or even by a man. So it is a constantly uphill task.

When we talk about the issues at the councillors or local bodies' level, I think that they don't get salaries. They do not get any remuneration with which they can pay their fare or look after their families. At least we are earning something and we give twenty-four hours to our profession now. We are public figures and we don't have time even for ourselves. I am a corporate lawyer by profession but I can't practice, because the commitment and challenge is so much that one day I am in Lahore, the other day I am in Islamabad and the third day I am abroad. So it is difficult for us to sit here. Similarly the same process would work for those councillors who are sitting at their end and taking care of their small *muhalla* or small town or whatever capacity they are in. They are very much ignored. They must be empowered and their empowerment comes through economic empowerment.

Today is the day of calling attention to domestic violence against women. In this issue, the bottom line is the economic empowerment of a woman. Most of us women are dependent on men and we look up to them, thinking that: 'Ok we are living in our husband's house and he is feeding us, he is the source of the income and he is supporting the family, so even if he is hitting us, abusing us, giving us mental torture and whatever else, it is all because of our weak economic position'.

This is why we should focus on women's empowerment, not only politically, but also economically.

Samia[7] has said a number of times that the place of women is at home and not in the Assembly. Why do we become hypocrites here? If Samia wants to practice what she is saying and if she has conviction in that, then she should resign and go home! Let other women come in. I have nothing personal against anyone, but this is an issue, which is why I am bringing it up.

Since we are concentrating on women in politics, I want to add that I think strengthening the political parties is important, and equally important is strengthening the role of the party's women's wing. Why can't we have women participating in the mainstream?

I don't go to the women's wing in the Muslim League, as I feel that there is a lot of leg pulling and I feel that these women are participating just for the sake of being there. Why can't we have an open democratic system? Why can't it be open to everybody? I am sure that the same questions are raised in every party, the People's Party or the MMA. There is just one set group sitting there and the rest are just shunted out.

So people say that we want to work, but we don't want anyone to indulge in character assassination. The easiest way to destroy a woman is to create a scandal about her. We need laws on sexual harassment, we need gender equality laws and we need to remove all the gender imbalances.

I introduced a bill on *karo kari* in the Assembly, which was supported by the opposition. My own party rejected that bill. Again, I have presented a bill on *hudood* and have given that bill to the President, the Prime Minister, and to the head of my political party. This time, I hope that the amendments we have proposed pass through successfully. We are trying to create women empowerment so that we all stand together.

However, here the point is of having a women caucus above party level. We tried it once and the women backed out. It was tried by Nilofer Bakhtiar. So at the end of the day, we don't stand united. We should admit that and we need to focus on the fact that women should at least stand above the party line.

We want women's uplift and we want to empower them. Let's come up with a crisis centre, let's come up with shelters. I think we can provide more effective crisis centres and shelters where women can be taken care of and proper education and training in some skill given to them so that they are economically empowered and tomorrow they don't have to look back.

In conclusion, I say that everybody has contributed in their own way. But there is still a long way to go and the battle is hard and long. We all have to work on issues which are related to the betterment of women. As a woman, I represent 80 per cent of the women of the country in the Parliament. I think that we should be involved in major decision making about Pakistan, about our own country. I will here again request that on the women's issues, all women should stand together. We should realize what other women are going through and we should have democracy within the political parties, which is very important. New leadership should be created and that can only happen if we give women confidence, give them a chance, encourage them and take them along. And I also believe that there should be a platform to mobilize and bring women out of their homes and give them the confidence so that they can stand with their men as a source of their strength.

4. Fauzia Wahab, Member of the National Assembly, Pakistan

Fauzia Wahab currently serves as the Central Coordinator of PPP's Human Rights Cell and is a member of the Standing Committee on Scientific and Technological Research. Ms Wahab has remained information secretary of the Pakistan People's Party Women's Wing, Sindh, since 1995. She has served her party as a member of the Advisory Council from 1994–96 and Chairman of Information Committee at Karachi Metropolitan Corporation from 1994–95. She received her B.A. degree from the University of Karachi in 1978. Her areas of legislative interest are in foreign affairs, education, finance and women's development.

My political journey started when I was twelve years old. We were living in Germany. My father was in the Pakistani Embassy and I was in class five when an election took place in school and I was elected the class representative. This is how I came to know politics, democracy, election, lobbying and connection with people. On the basis of my performance, I was re-elected in class six again as class representative. During this period, although I was very young, I started reading the political news in newspapers of my own accord. I was inspired by the civil rights movement going on in Europe during 1968–69. I was very impressed by Che Guevara, I liked the way he looked in pictures and I liked the rebellious look on his face.

In 1971, we came back to Pakistan and in 1974, when I was studying in college, the students' union elections were to be held and somehow I found myself taking part. I did not intend to stand for a post as my father had given me specific instructions not to get involved in student politics, however, when fate intervenes, there is not much one can do. So within two days I announced my candidature and after two days I was elected as the president of the students union in 1974–75. In the union we met people, invited people, realized our social responsibilities, our political responsibilities, and I remember for the first time I started to hear Mr Bhutto's press conferences and observe how he conducted himself. Of course, I was attracted to his ideology since I was brought up in Germany and the class concept was not in my mind.

I started thinking in terms of an egalitarian society. I started questioning why there are differences between people. My mother came from India and the concept of 'achoot' was dominant in her like the way it was in that society. Whenever our sweeper turned on the tap, she used to tell him to wash it again. I never understood why it was so. I started questioning the social norms and I felt that the panacea of our problem lay in developing an egalitarian society where people are not distinguished on the basis of their caste, creed or class. [It was] in university that, for the first time, I came to know the meaning of right and left and, since I had this background, I automatically joined the left party. In 1978, I was elected the Faculty Representative. At that time there was already a seat for women and usually women would get elected as Joint Secretary of the University, but I contested on an open seat and got elected as Faculty Representative, and later on I was also made the Chairman of the Library Committee. There was another very interesting thing at that time from the Left party. I was the only one who could get elected into that cabinet. The rest were either the representatives of Islami Jamiat-e-Tulba or the Pakistan Liberal Students Party.

After 1978, I had to follow the social norms. I got married, brought up children, looked after my husband and my in-laws as a dutiful girl is supposed to do. But somehow my liking for politics never vanished. It was always there.

I remember that in 1988 when party-based elections were called, I volunteered myself for the Pakistan Peoples Party and worked for the local representatives for election. We lost the elections because the MQM was an ascendant party and they controlled the city. Anyhow, my role was very minute and insignificant but I did work a little bit. I organized teas and talk programmes between the political office-bearers and the women in our locality and I did a little bit of public service in my area. Also, if there was any problem, I would sit by their side and whatever my own domestic problems, I was always with the women in my area.

In 1994, when the Peoples Party came to the power, it was the second time that Mohtarma Benazir Bhutto was the Prime Minister. She formed an advisory council in the municipality of Karachi and they were looking for a woman to preside in the Society zone and somehow, somebody remembered that there was one woman who came in 1988 and she volunteered to work for the party. So they looked for me. I remember that I was working as Assistant Manager in a leasing company when they approached me and they asked me if I was ready to join the advisory council. Although I had put politics behind me, that passion came back again and I immediately accepted the offer. After that there was no looking back, because two months later I was nominated as the Information Secretary, Pakistan Peoples

Party, Province Sindh, and then in 1997 my party asked me to contest elections from NA 193, Karachi.

In 1997, I contested the National Assembly elections and for the first time I was pushed into the harsh political realities of Karachi city and I realized that women have no importance and no political significance. Nobody was ready to hear me out; nobody was ready to listen to me. They were reluctant and wondered who this woman was, why she had been nominated, and thought that it must be a losing seat and there was no other applicant so I had been given the ticket for this seat. They looked at me in a skeptical way and of course they thought that a woman has no business in National Assembly politics and I landed up with just 1900 votes out of 300,000. It hurts to talk about those events—I used to go to peoples' doors and they would not open them. They thought it would be a waste of time talking to a woman; what vision would she have? What could she do? Could she solve their problems in the police stations? Could she give them relief from the land grabbers? Could she deal with the non-social elements of our area? That was their parameter for judging a person. They didn't ask me what vision I had for the country, what solutions I could offer. They were just talking in terms of what kind of relief I could provide in three matters: the police station, the land grabbers or the extortionists in our area.

In 1998, the chairperson, Mohtarma Benazir Bhutto, realizing my potential as a writer, nominated me as the head of the Human Rights Cell. I worked from that platform and in 2002 my name was nominated again and on the party list, I was number three from the Sindh province. After the elections, I made it to the National Assembly and now I am here, sitting in front of you.

I think the most important thing, if you want to enhance women's role in politics, is that you have to provide more space to the political parties. A woman cannot work in a vacuum. She has to have a platform. Unfortunately, in our society, political parties have never been given any importance. I think it is the process of political training that I underwent from 1994–2005 that has enabled me to talk to you, to understand the political dynamics in our country. Without that exposure at the political party level, I don't think that I would have been in a position to talk about the problems that we women in politics face. So the first and foremost thing to do is to strengthen the role of political parties and, after that, bring in more women into the political parties.

Unfortunately, we find socially active women in the rural areas of our country, but when it comes to the urban areas, we find women hesitating to come forward in politics. We feel that women have reservations. They want to be in the assemblies, they want to be in the union council, they want to be in the assemblies, but they don't want to go through the training programme or the process of joining a political party. Without that process, I don't think that a woman can achieve maturity or an in-depth understanding of politics. So again, I stress the need for enhancing the role of political parties. Secondly, I don't think that training of women legislators will make any difference. I feel that women should be encouraged to join political or social associations.

I remember, that for the local bodies elections, I asked a number of women to contest councillors' seats because it was not very expensive to do so. Here I would also like to comment on this aspect of expenses. Whenever I ask this question or put this suggestion to a woman, instead of her answering the question, the husband jumps in and says, 'Oh no, she cannot do it. She cannot manage it. She is not capable of politics so leave her out. She is only good at going to the tracks or looking after the house. She has domestic responsibilities and politics is not her cup of tea.'

Another problem that women in general face is the aspect of money that is involved in politics. If you are contesting at the local council level, start with the union council, the nazim seat. You need at least hundred to hundred and fifty thousand rupees. For a local councillor, one needs to have a minimum of ten to fifteen thousand rupees. For a provincial seat, the candidate has to have five to six million in his hand. For the national assembly seat, you need to have ten to twenty million to win a seat. Therefore, since women are not monetarily independent or strong enough, they are frequently unable to come into the electoral arena.

Why have I mentioned the aspect of money? I just want to give you a little breakdown. For a local councillor, the number of voters are usually between 25,000 to 35,000. So you have to reach at least six to ten thousand people. You need to convince them; you have to make the people know you are there. So how will you do that? You will need to have the posters, you have to have banners and then you have to provide them the cards so that they can vote—and all this costs you money. A banner will cost you 200 rupees and a local councillor must put up at least 50 to 60 banners. She has to distribute ten to fifty thousand posters. The expenses are similar in the national assembly elections. Besides banners and posters, you need seven to eight hundred thousand rupees cash in your hand on the day of elections. There are almost 200 to 240 polling stations and in each polling

station, if you are not a member of a political party, you must have at
least two polling agents. Polling agents cost you 200 and 250. Each
polling station has eight to twelve hundred voters. So you also have
to provide transportation for the voters so that they can go and cast
their votes. You have to have money for a camp office outside the
polling station. A camp will cost you Rs1000 to 1500 and you have to
have people to sit there and work at facilitating voters. Lastly, you
have to provide meals to the polling agents. So this is what you
require and, without this amount, you lose; you end up with 2,000
votes, like me.

5. Begum Jan

Dr Begum Jan, born in 1957, hails from the restive South Waziristan Agency,
Federally Administered Tribal Area (FATA), and did her M.D from the Medical
Faculty of Jalalabad Medical College, Afghanistan in 1989. She has founded the
Tribal Women Welfare Association in 1995 and was a member of the National
Commission on the Status of Women from FATA for the second consecutive time
in 2004. She is widely travelled and for her meritorious services in social work
sector, she has been awarded the Tamgha-e-Imtiaz by President General Pervez
Musharraf in 2004.

In 1996, during the era of Benazir Bhutto when people in tribal areas
were not given the right to vote—neither men nor women; at that time
I said in a seminar that neither the insane nor children are given the
right to vote. At that time we were a population of 7 million, which is
quite a large number. Somehow we got the right to vote. But there
were different issues that emerged—like tribal women not
understanding anything regarding votes. In 1997, when the votes were
being polled in Jamrod Khyber Agency, the BBC representative, Mr
Rahimullah Youzafzai, said to me, 'You tribal women don't understand
about votes,' and I responded, 'Don't speak like this, our women have
talent.' Anyway, I took along the representatives of CNN to Mula Gori
where there was an 80-year-old-woman. She was approached to
influence her vote, but she said, 'No, I will poll my vote in favour of
the umbrella and not the pigeon.' *Time* magazine covered this whole
story.

President Musharraf has tried hard to create political awareness in
the tribal areas, as has the ex-governor Iftikhar Hussain. But the root
of the problem, as I have noted, is our elders and bureaucratic political
agents. I raised the question to ex-senator Wasim Sajjad: 'You have
been in the Senate for quite some time, but has our tribal senator ever

talked about our women?' He replied that they had never talked about this issue. Then we thought that our tribal people were religious and when our Islamic government and our Islamic women came into the assembly the road would be clear for us and things would be in our favour. But the road is still not clear for us.

Women from FATA[8] are not given any seat in either the national or the provincial assembly. The votes polled in FATA were 63.5 per cent by men and 36.5 per cent by women. When 36.5 per cent votes were being polled by women, why should they not be given the right to participate in the assembly?

I have requested international donors to cooperate with the Tribal Women Welfare Association. I have asked our elders and MNAs several times to raise this issue in the assembly but they have not done so yet. As far as local government elections in the tribal belt are concerned, though they did take place, but with regard to women councillors, it was decided that they would be selected by the political agent. Neither the political agents nor elders want women to come forward.

It is also wrongly said that tribal women are uneducated. These women are very brave, and they have much talent. There are doctors, lawyers and postgraduates among them and it is wrong to think that they don't have awareness. Even our elderly women are aware. Our MNAs are not triple MAs. They don't want to let the tribal women come forward. Our elders want that their tribal women should just bring water, wood, and look after the children and work in the fields. But now times have changed and the government will have to help us. If the women of Gilgit and AJK are given the right to assemblies, why not those from the tribal areas? Are they not human?

As far as education among the women of the tribal areas is concerned, although the government allocates funds, they are misused by the elders. The same goes for health. Lady doctors and teachers are restricted in going about their duties and they are told that, 'You will get your half of the salary but you had better stay at home.' The women say, 'Ok, if we are getting our half of the salary and are threatened, then it is best to stay at home'.

I am also very angry with NADRA. As in Khyber and Mehmand agencies, one ID card for a woman was being prepared for Rs300. Tribal Women's Welfare Association was heading a campaign in FATA and the women asked us: what is the use of the ID cards to us? We told them that they will have an identity and their vote will be polled. When we asked the NADRA representatives as to why they were taking money from women, they said that this is because tribals have not paid the electricity bills. I asked why they were taking this from women and not from men and this issue was brought to the notice of Governor Iftikhar. It was then finalized that Rs 35 would be charged to prepare ID cards.

I tell the donor agencies that political awareness is very crucial in the tribal areas for all men, women, and children. Why are there suicide bombings? Because women send their children to madrassas since they have financial problems. Educated people are not concerned and so they don't pay attention to this issue. Our new generation will obviously be prepared for suicide bombings since they have financial problems and are very poor. I am requesting the donor agencies to persuade our MNAs and Senators to raise their voices for tribal women. I hope that I will soon get a response from donor agencies and from the women who are present here.

Appendix A

The following statements are transcribed manuscripts or speeches of the respective female politicians during the WPA conference in 2005 in Islamabad.

1. Tehmina Daultana, Member of the National Assembly, Pakistan

Tehmina Daultana is an educationist by profession. She graduated with an MA in History from University of the Punjab in 1973. Her areas of legislative interest are in foreign affairs, education and women development. She is a member of the Standing Committee on Government Assurance, Women Development Social Welfare and Special Education.

I think the best thing according to the mode of conference over here is to just tell you that how I was able to get a little space in this political system. I came from an old political family but in that old political family, old and young men are sitting and not giving way to any women. So I realized that if I go by the traditional way and ask them, that I like to come into politics, I won't be there. So I joined a political party of our family. That was PML-N, and at that time Mian Nawaz Sharif was the President. So I went and joined. The only space I could get was in the women's wing and I said alright, I need a little space just enough to stand on and that's all. But I remembered the first day, when I entered the political office, there were women sitting out there. I was dressed up in my usual clothes and they had a good look at me. They looked at me right from the foot till my head and there was a critical look in their eyes and (...) they looked as if they knew everything and they said 'who are you? a begum? Why have you come here?'. 'Well,' I said, 'I am no begum, I am basically an educationist and I have my own school. I want to join the political party, I want to sit with you, talk with you, work with you.' They had a laugh and said 'you can't do it'. There was a lady, whose name is Najma Hameed, a very nice lady, and she said, 'Come on, give her space, let her sit', and I remember, she smiled at me. It was that little smile which made me sit down because I intended just to walk out (...).

So I worked with the political party. My target was not just to sit with the political party; my target was to fight MNA elections[4]. First time I asked for a MNA seat was in 1990. I had very good relations with Mian Nawaz Sharif's family so I asked and said that 'why don't you trust a woman'. He smiled and said yes we will and I remember when the board was sitting to allot seats, one of my cousins was there, who later on got the ticket but provincial ticket and there was another gentleman whose name was Akbar Bhatti who got the national ticket, the one I desired. And I just stood up and said that 'you men will get the tickets because you are men and there might be women better than you but they will not get the tickets but I will keep on fighting for it until I get it'. I remember the smile on their faces, something that I cannot forget but anyhow, I didn't do the usual that if I do not get the ticket here I will leave my party, go to another party; I stuck. And I intended to stay, make my place and beat them.

In 1993, I got the MNA ticket and [I had to]… make sure that the men in my family were willing to support me. So I had to get hold of the will and said that 'you all want the ticket, it's better to give it to me than you fighting with each other it—and then all of you support me'. How I convinced them? It was difficult but I was able to do it. So first was getting the ticket, second was going to my constituency and fighting it.

Well, (…) I reached the constituency in Southern Punjab which is very backward. We are never used to show our face in our constituency so I said that I cannot fight elections without showing my face so I took a *chadder* (shawl) and said 'I am going to show my face'. So my family said 'what are you going to do? (…) You better sit Tehmina; we don't think that you can make it. You will have very few votes and it will be very shameful for the family'. I said 'listen, I have made my mind to fight, I am going to fight and I am fighting to lose'. And there they did not have an answer. Anyhow, I was able to manage that situation, [but] then I had problems with religious parties in my constituency. They said that 'ok we will see that what we can do for her but it's better that she does not come to any of the conventions that we hold. Some male members can come but a woman can't come'. I went and met their wives and said that 'I am a better candidate than any, please give me a chance, your men are not giving me a chance'. So I made my way through this way. Woman called the husband and I said '*maulvi sahib*, please give me a little space to stand on'. He didn't even look at me, he just looked at my feet and said 'ok madam what you want to talk, talk to my wife and don't come and talk to me'. But I said 'no, I am here, I am going to talk to you and you are going to answer me'. So we sat down and I [asked] 'maulvi sahib in which way am I less than any male family member? Give me a chance and call me to any of your conventions.' I went to his convention and then the other *maulvis* also gave me the space.

I went into the assembly, we were only four women. I would like to tell you that people thought that I will lose and that was conveyed to Mian Nawaz Sharif: 'she will lose in the district and her MPA[5] will lose, she will have bad affect on other MNAs seats'. There were the three MNAs seats and I was the only one who won and my three MPAs, they won. Even my father and my uncle had not the lead which I had which was 25.000 [ahead of] the other candidate. I would like to tell you that the other candidate had a lot of money, Akbar Bhatti, who has a newspaper behind him. I was a simple woman, not with so much money but a wish to make it.

Anyhow, I went in the assembly. The second part was now to make space for myself with other men. I was the only woman in the opposition. In the beginning the men made me feel [to] sit [in the] back. I said 'no, I am not going to sit [in the] back, I am going to make my own space'. So in the opposition, I made my own space and after sometime people came to know that there was a lady whose name was Tehmina Daultana so that life is not easy, neither for men nor for women. (…) That's the way I look at it: if you make a target, a plan according to your target, work towards the target.

This is my third MNA election. This time I fought from two seats. From one seat, I did not win but from [the] other seat I won. At night, they changed the results and the other fellow was made to win because he was from PML-Q[6], he was made to win. Overall I had about 100,000 votes from both of my seats. (...)

And one thing is for sure that I would like to tell the women sitting here that there is enough space for you. There are enough areas where you can fight, you can fight, you will win, but you will have to fight hard enough. Remember, if you feel that everything is going to be very easy, no, it isn't. Neither for democracy nor for women— but in the end we will win, because we are on the right. We have to make space for us. In the end, I would like to say best of luck to you ladies, keep up the fight. Inshallah, the last battle will be yours.

2. Samia Raheel Qazi, Member of the National Assembly, Pakistan

> Samia Raheel Qazi is currently President of JIP's Women Commission in Punjab and is a member of the Standing Committee on Governance Assurance. Previously, she led the Foreign Affairs Women's Wing of JIP from 1995-2000. She is a member of Women Aid Trust (1996), International Union of Muslim Women (1996), Bazm-i-Iqbal (2001) and Al-Khidmat Foundation (1992). A lecturer by profession, Samia Raheel Qazi obtained her post-graduate degree in Islamic Studies from the University of Balochistan in 1991. Her areas of legislative interest are in education, foreign affairs and law.

(...) Before sharing my experiences as a parliamentarian with you, I deem it pertinent to give you first an idea of the overall framework in which I view women issues such as political participation, economic empowerment, decision making and so forth.

To me, men and women are an integral part of each other and any attempt to portray them as competitors or oppressed or an oppressor is bound to have catastrophic consequences for humanity and [the] final analysis of the situation. Their issues are intertwined with each other and the social equilibrium is to be disturbed violently if any of them fails to perform his or her rights or duties dually. In other words, being a part of the society their issues are very much common and one should not bisect them on the basis of gender. Similarly [we] must also take note that apart from very survival, a happy peaceful and smooth human life is directly contingent upon th[e] establishment and strengthening of the institution of [the] family. Given the biological makeup, women play a key role both in establishing and sustaining it in the very first place. Therefore, the interests of this institution should always be kept in viewpoint while introducing any gender-specific policy at any level of state and society. All the state policies including women specific [ones] must be family friendly. [The] stubborn division of the issues on the basis of gender provides an opportunity to the ruling clique to exploit the situation accordingly. With vested interests in the viewpoint, they use them as a handy tool to *woodwind* the attention of a big segment of the society from the root cause of the problems. The tactics used by the Musharraf government in recent times also give *creodonts* to this assertion.

Thus the issue of women's representation in the parliament also needs to be viewed in the same context. [Granting a] parliamentary role [for] women, it should not be aimed at implicit[ly] or explicit[ly] dividing the society into two segments, namely men and women. I also believe that women['s] political representation, be that 33% or 50 % or 100 %, is not going to make any real difference without revamping the whole system allowing a certain class of people to keep the power under their control on one pretext or the other. With this rotten system intact, women representation has practically served very little during [the] last few years except creating a new elite class with vested interests in it. The socio-economic and political background of the majority of women parliamentarians give creodonts to this assertion that the new clout has allowed the powerful class of the society to further strengthen its control on the basis of power. Therefore, women political representation in parliament or other forums is to remain a cosmetic move unless attention is focused on the revamping of the whole rotten system. Furthermore, we have to avoid dividing issues on gender basis; it is to have serious implications in the long run. And last but not the least, the state has to show an absolute commitment to safeguard and strengthen the institution of [the] family. Without ensuring these things, we would be doing no service to the nation but creating new power clubs and groups who shall be more interested in safeguarding their own interests than [those of] women and any other segment of the society.

Coming to my experiences as a parliamentarian, I can just tell you the incumbency has used the issue of women representation as a pretext to extend its tenure, nothing else. The root causes of all the problems facing the nation still remain unaddressed, but the government seems determined to reflect the attention of the people from them by using different pity tactics. This is the crux of my all experiences during these whole years. I would like to add that one really feels happy that there is women representation and awareness can be seen among women. Although MMA is thought an orthodox party, [...] only in truly Islamic spirit any political system can address gender equality. The Holy Prophet (PBUH) was the first person who presented the theory of gender equality. He hasn't excluded anyone—that men can't perform domestic activities or a woman can't perform outdoor activities. So it is wrong to assume that Islam imposes any restrictions on women.

3. Kashmala Tariq, Member of the National Assembly, Pakistan

Kashmala Tariq is currently Executive Director of the Parliamentarians Commission for Human Rights and has served as President of the Peoples Student Federation (PSF) form 1993-95, Chief Organizer of PTI for UK (1998-2000), Secretary General of an Environmental NGO (Sath) from 1992-95 and as President of the Student Union at the London School of Economics (1998-99). Her areas of legislative interests are law, education and women development. She also holds a seat in the Standing Committee on Finance and Revenue, House and Library and Law, Justice and Human Rights.

I would like to share my experience and would like to add what I have been hearing over here. I would like to answer [to] what are the challenges [...] faced by women parliamentarians.

I would like to say that, being a woman parliamentarian, it is an enormous challenge to be here in politics like women working in banks, women working in hospitals and women working in other walks of life. I think that it is altogether a very heavy duty task, a big challenge and an uphill task and like constantly swimming against the tide. Especially if you are a worker, especially if you know what you are talking about, especially if you have done your homework and if you intervene any of the key issues. So one of the major problems that we face over here is that we are not brought into the mainstream politics. They prefer women who do not even utter a word and who are sitting there in an idle capacity and saying yes to everything. And they keep their eyes and ears close and are deaf and dumb. We do not have democracy even within each party.

I am not talking here in the capacity of Muslim League or [as] MNA. I am here as a human rights and women rights activist, a feminist rather. Whatever I am sharing over here is not in the capacity of a parliamentarian. What I am saying over here is that we do not have democracy in the parties; our things are not given weight and especially when we talk about the reserve[d] seats.

Women, who are given reserved seats, are taken [it] for granted and that is absolutely right. Now, over the period of last three years, we have really worked hard to prove ourselves that we are better than men or we can work equivalent to men. Whereas those men, they do not perform as such (…). [Women] are very few and they are bound to speak when [they] have to reply to any question posed by a woman or a man and whatsoever. So it is a constantly uphill task what we are doing.

When we talk about the issues at the councillors or local bodies' level, I think that they don't get salaries. They do not get any remuneration by which they can pay their fares, by which they can look after their families. At least we are earning something and it is our profession now. We are giving 24 hours to our profession, we are public figures. We don't have even time for ourselves. I am a corporate lawyer by profession but I can't do it because the commitment and challenge is so much that one day I am in Lahore, the other day I am in Islamabad and the third day I am abroad. So it is difficult for us to sit here. Similarly the same process would work for those councillors who are sitting at their end and taking care of their small *muhalla* or small town or whatever capacity they are having. They are very much ignored. They must be empowered and the empowerment comes though the economic empowerment.

Today is [the] day against domestic violence against women. …[At] the end of the day, the bottom line is the economic empowerment of a woman because we all are mostly dependent on men and we look up at them and say that ok we are sitting in our husband's house and he is feeding us, he is the source of income and he is supporting the family so even if he is hitting you, he is abusing you, he is giving you mental torture and whatever, it is all because of your weak economic position. So we should focus on women's empowerment, not only politically but also economically.

Samia[7] has said a number of times that the place of women is at home and not in [the] assembly. (…) Why [do] we become hypocrites here? If she wants to follow what she is saying and if she has conviction in that, then resign and go home. Let the other women who can perform. I am not getting personal to anyone but it is an issue; that is why I am bringing it up. It happens in the political parties that we promote our relatives.

Another thing since we are concentrating on women in politics: I think that strengthening the political parties is important and (…) the role of [the] women wing. Why can't we have a mainstream women participation (…)? I don't go to the women's wing in [the] Muslim League as I feel that there is a lot of leg pulling and I feel that these women are participating just for the sake of being there. Why can't [we] have an open democratic system? Why can't it be open to everybody? I am sure that the same would be happening to every party, the People's Party or the MMA. There is just one set group sitting there and the rest are just shunted out.

So people say that we want to work, we don't want that somebody do our character assassination. The most easiest thing to pull down a woman is to scandalize her or to do her character assassination. We need laws on sexual harassment, we need gender equality laws. We need to remove all the gender imbalances.

I introduced a bill on *karo kari* in the assembly, supported by the opposition. My own party rejected that bill (…) in front of everybody. Again I have presented a bill on *hudood* and I have given that bill to the President, to the Prime Minister and to the head of [my] political party. This time, I hope that the amendments, that we have proposed, go through successfully and we are looking for a change for women empowerment so that we all stand together.

But here the point is of having a women caucus above party level. We tried it once and the women backed out. It was tried by Nilofer Bakhtiar. So at the end of the day, we don't stand united. We should admit that and we need to have a focus that women should at least stand above party line. (…)

We want to take up women, we want to empower them. Let's come up with a crisis centre, let's come up with shelters. I think we can provide them with more effective crisis centres and shelters where women can be taken care of and proper education and training of some skill should be given to them so that they are economically empowered and tomorrow they have not to go back.

So [at the] end of the day I say that everybody has contributed in their way. It is a long way to go, it is a long battle. We all have to work on issues which are related to the betterment of women, because being a woman, I represent the 80% of women in the country in the Parliament. But not only that, I think that we should be involved in major decision making which is of course about Pakistan, about our own country. I will here again request that on the women issues all the women should stand together. We should realize for what the other women are going through and we should have democracy within the political parties, which is very important. New leadership should be created and that can only be created if we give them the confidence, give them a chance, encourage them and take them along. And I believe that there should be a platform. (…) We need to mobilize and bring women out of the houses and give them the confidence that they can stand with their men as the source of their strength.

4. Fauzia Wahab, Member of the National Assembly, Pakistan

Fauzia Wahab currently serves as the Central Coordinator of PPPP's Human Rights Cell and is a member of the Standing Committee on Scientific and Technological

Research. Ms. Wahab has remained information secretary of the Pakistan People's Party Women's Wing, Sindh, since 1995. She has served her party in functions such as member of Advisory Council from 1994-96 and Chairman of Information Committee at Karachi Metropolitan Corporation from 1994-95. She received her B.A. degree from the University of Karachi in 1978. Her areas of legislative interest are in foreign affairs, education, finance and women development.

My political journey started when I was twelve years old. We were living at that time in Germany. My father was in the Pakistani Embassy and I was in class five when an election took place and I was elected the class representative. This is how I came to know what politics is, what democracy is, what election is, what lobbying is and what is connection with people. And on the basis of my performance, I was re-elected in class 6 again as class representative. During this period, I unintentionally started looking or reading the political news in the newspapers although I was very young at that age. I was inspired by the civil rights movement going on in Europe during 1968-69. I was very much impressed by Che Guevara, I liked the way he looked like in pictures and I liked the rebellious look on his face.

And then, in 1971 we came back to Pakistan and in 1974 I was studying in college when the students' union elections were called and somehow I found myself in the election arena, although I was not intending for it because my father had given me specific instruction not to get myself involved in student politics. But you know, when fate decides something, you just cannot stop it. And within two days I announced my candidature and after two days I was elected as the president of [the] students union in 1974-75. [In the] students union (...) we met people, we invited people, we realized our social responsibility, our political responsibility and I remember for the first time started hearing Mr. Bhutto's press conferences and was observing that how he use to conduct himself and then, of course, I was attracted to the ideology since I was brought up in Germany, so the class concept was not in my mind.

I started thinking in terms of [an] egalitarian society. I started questioning that why are there differences? I remember that my mother came from India and the concept of "achoot" was dominant on her like the way it was on the whole society. Whenever our sweeper opened the tab, she used to say him to wash this again. I never understood (...) why it is so. I started questioning the social norms and I felt that the panacea of our problem lies in developing an egalitarian society. A society where people are not distinguished on the basis of their cast, creed or class and this is how my thinking developed and then I reached university. And for the first time I came to know the meaning of (...) right and left and, since I had this background, (...) I automatically joined the left party ... and in 1978 I got elected as the faculty representative. At that time there was already a seat for women and usually women used to get elected as the joint secretary of any university but I contested on open seat and got elected as faculty representative and later on I was also made the Chairman of the Library Committee. There was another very interesting thing at that time from my party, the left party. I was the only who could get elected into that cabinet. The rest were either the representative of Islami Jamiat-e-Tulba or the Pakistan Liberal Students Party. After 1978, I had to follow the social norms, got married, brought up children, looked after my husband, looked after my in-laws—as a dutiful girl is supposed to do. But somehow my liking for politics never vanished, it was always there.

I remember that in 1988 when ... party-based elections were called, I volunteered myself for the Pakistan People's Party and worked for the local representatives for election. We lost the elections because the MQM ...ascended and they were controlling the city. Anyhow, I was there but my role was very minuet, insignificant but I did a little bit of working. I organized and mobilized tea and talk programmes of our political office bearers with our local women in our locality and I did a little bit of public service in my area. And if there was any problem, I used to [sit] at their side, whatever my own domestic problems were but I was always with my local women in my area.

In 1994 when the People's Party came to the power, it was the second time that Mohtarama Benazir Bhutto was the Prime Minister, she formed an advisory council in the municipality of Karachi and they were looking for a woman [to preside] in the society zone and somehow, somebody remembered that there was one woman who came in 1988 and she volunteered for us. Lets find out so they looked for me. I remember that I was working as Assistant Manager in a leasing company when they approached me and they asked me [if] I was ready to join the advisory council. [Al]though I put politics behind my back and I had shut off my eyes from politics, but somehow that passion come again and I immediately accepted that offer and after that there was no looking back because after two months I was nominated as the Information Secretary, Pakistan People's Party, Province Sindh and then in 1997 my party asked me to contest elections from NA 193, Karachi.

In 1997, I contested the National Assembly elections and for the first time I was pushed into the harsh political realities of Karachi city and I realized that women have no importance, they have no political significance. Nobody was ready to hear me out, nobody was ready to listen to me. They were reluctant: who is this woman, why has she been nominated, this must be a losing seat and there was no other applicant so this woman has been given the ticket for this seat. They looked at me in a sceptical way and of course they thought that a woman has nothing to do at National Assembly politics and I landed up with just 1900 votes out of 300,000. It hurts to talk about those events—when I used to go at peoples' doors and [they] would not open their doors and they thought it would be waste of time of talking to a woman. What vision does she have? What can she do? Can she solve our problem in the police stations? Can she give us any relief from the land grabbers? Can she deal with the non-social elements of our area? That was their parameter for judging a person. They didn't ask me what vision I have for the country, what I thought what can be given as a solution. They were just talking in terms that what kind of relief you can provide in these three matters: the police station, the land grabbers or the *extronisia* in our area.

Anyhow, 1997 was over and in 1998 the chairperson, Mohtarma Benazir Bhutto, realizing my potential as a writer, nominated me as the head of the Human Rights cell. I worked on that platform and in 2002 my name was nominated again. On the party list, I was on number three from the Sindh Province. And after the elections, I am [now] in the National Assembly, sitting in front of you.

I think the most important thing, if you want to enhance the women's role in politics, is [that] you have [to] provide more space to the political parties. A woman cannot work in [a] vacuum. She has to have a platform. Unfortunately, in our society political parties have never been given any importance. I think it is the process of political training that I underwent from 1994-2005 that has enabled me to talk to you, to understand the political dynamics in our country. Without that exposure at the political party level, I don't think that I would have been in that position to talk about the problems that we women in politics face. So the first and foremost thing is to strengthen the role of political parties and, after that, bringing in more women in political parties.

Unfortunately, we find socially active women in the rural areas of our country but when it comes to the urban areas, we find women hesitating in coming forward into politics. We feel that women have reservations. They want to be in the assemblies, they want to be in the union council, they want to be in the assemblies but they don't want to go through the training programme or the process of political party and, without that process, I don't think that a woman can achieve the maturity or in-depth of politics. So again, I stress the need of enhancing the role of political parties. Secondly, I don't think that training of women legislatures will make any difference. I feel that women should be encouraged to join the political or social associations. (...)

I remember, [that] for the local bodies elections, I ask [a] number of women to contest councillors seats because its not very expensive. I also come to this aspect of expenses. Whenever I ask this question or put this suggestion to the lady—instead of her answering the question -, the husband would jump in and he would say 'oh no, she cannot do it. She cannot manage it. She is not capable to do politics or leave her. She is good in going to the track or looking for the house. She has got the domestic responsibilities but politics is not her cup of tea.'

And another problem that women in general face is the aspect of money that is involved in politics. If you are contesting at the local council level, start with the union council, the *nazim* seat. You need at least from hundred to hundred and fifty thousand rupees. For a local councillor, she needs to have minimum ten to fifteen thousand rupees. For a provincial seat, the candidate has to have five to six million in his hand. For the national assembly seat, you need to have ten to twenty million to win a seat. So therefore, since women are not monetarily independent or strong enough, [at many times they] are unable to jump into the electoral arena.

Why have I mentioned the aspect of money? I just want to give you a little break down. For a local councillor, the number of votes are usually between 25,000-35,000. So you have to reach at least six to ten thousand people. You need [to] convince; you have to make the people know you are there. So how will you do that? You will need to have the posters, you have to have banners and then you have to provide them the cards so that they can vote and all this costs you money. A banner cost you 200 rupees and for a local councillor she has to put up at least 50-60 banners. She has to distribute ten to fifty thousand posters. Similarly are the expenses in the national assembly elections. Besides banners and posters you have to have seven to eight hundred thousand rupees cash in your hand on the day of elections. There are almost 200-240 polling stations and each polling station, if you are not a member of political party, you have to have at least two polling agents. Polling agents cost you 200 and 250. Each polling station has eight to twelve hundred voters. So you have to provide transportation for the voters so that they can go and cast their votes. You have to have money for a camp office outside the polling station. A camp cost you 1000-1500 and you have to have people who are sitting and [doing] the work there. And, last one, you have to provide the meals to the polling agents. (...) So this is what you require and, without that amount, you are the loser; you end up with 2,000 votes as I ended.

5. Begum Jan

> Dr Begum Jan, born in 1957, hails from the restive South Waziristan Agency, Federally Administered Tribal Area (FATA) and did her M.D from the Medical Faculty of Jalalabad Medical College, Afghanistan in 1989. She has founded the Tribal Women Welfare Association in 1995 and was a member of the National Commission on the Status of Women from FATA for the second consecutive time in 2004. She is widely travelled and for her meritorious services in social work sector, she has been awarded the Tamgha-e-Imtiaz by President General Pervez Musharraf in 2004.

In 1996 during the era of Benazir Bhutto when people in tribal areas were not given the right to vote, neither men nor women, at that time I said vocally in a seminar that neither insane nor children are given the right to vote. At that time we were [a population of] 7 million, which is quite a big number. (...) Anyway, somehow we got the right to vote. But there were different issues that were emerging—like tribal women don't understand anything regarding vote and so on. In 1997 when the votes were being polled in Jamrod Khyber Agency, the representative of BBC, Mr. Rahimullah Youzafzai, said to me that 'you tribal women don't understand about votes' and I responded to him 'don't speak like this, our women have talent'. Anyway, I took along the representatives of CNN to Mula Gori and there was a woman of 80 years. She was tried to be influenced in using her vote, but she said 'no; I will poll my vote in favour of *umbrella* and not *pigeon*'. Times magazine covered the whole story about this issue.

President Musharraf has tried hard that there should be political awareness in the tribal areas. In this regard ex-Governor Iftikhar Hussain has also tried. But the real roots of the problem, which I have noted, are our elders and bureaucratic political agents. I have raised the question to ex-senator Wasim Sajjad: 'You have been in the Senate for quite sometime, but did ever our tribal senator talked about our women?' He replied that they have never talked about this. Then we thought that our tribal [people] are religious and when our Islamic government and our Islamic women came into assembly, we thought that now the road is clear for us and the things will go in our favour. But still the road is not clear for us.

Women from FATA[8] are not given any seat in either national or provincial assembly. The votes that were being polled in FATA were 63.5% [by men] and female were 36.5%. When there are 36.5% votes being polled by women, then why should [they] not be they given the right in the assembly? I am requesting to international donors so that they cooperate with the *Tribal Women Welfare Association*.

I have asked several times to our elders and MNAs to raise this issue in the assembly but they have yet not done so. As far as local government elections in the tribal belt are concerned, though they took place somehow. But regarding women councillors, it was decided that she will be selected by the political agent. Political agents and elders, they don't want women to come forward. It is also wrong when it is said the tribal women are uneducated. These women are very brave, they have much talent. They are doctors, lawyers [and] post graduates are among them and it is wrong [to think] that they don't have awareness. Even our aged women are aware. Our MNAs are not triple MA or are they? They don't want to let the tribal women to come forward. Our elders want that their tribal women should just bring water, wood and look after the children and work in the fields. No, now the time has changed. But the Government will have to help us. As the women of Gilgit and AJK are given the right to assemblies (...) why not from tribal areas? Are they not human?

As far as education of the women of the tribal areas are concerned: Although [the] Government allocates funds, but they are misused by the elders. The same goes for health. Lady doctors and teachers are restricted to go on their duties and they are told that 'you will get your half of the salary but you better stay at home'. They say 'ok, if we are getting our half of the salary and have no threat then why not better stay at home'.

I am also very much annoyed with NADRA. As in Khyber and Mehmand agencies one ID card for woman was being prepared for 300 rupees. Tribal Women's Welfare Association was heading a campaign in FATA. The women were saying that what is the use of the ID cards to us? We told them that you will have the identity and your vote will be polled. When asked from the NADRA representatives that why are you taking money from women? They replied that because tribals have not paid for the electricity bills. I asked that why are [you] taking this from women, why don't you take it from men? On this issue, I have really opposed them and when this issue reached to Governor Iftikhar, it was finalized to prepare ID cards for 35 rupees.

I request the donor agencies that political awareness is very crucial in tribal areas, either for men, women or children. Why is there suicide bombing? Women send their children to *madrassas* because they do have financial problems. Educated people don't look back. Our new generation will either be prepared for suicide bombs as they have financial problems and are very poor. I am requesting the donor agencies to do something for the brainwash of our MNAs and Senators so that they raise their voice for tribal women. I hope that I will soon get the response from the donor agencies and from the women who are sitting over here.

NOTES

1. This introduction is largely based on a newspaper column published by Andrea Fleschenberg shortly after WPA 2005: 'Do women matter?,' *The Nation* 11.01.2006, Online. Available: http://nation.com.pk/daily/jan-2006/11/columns5.php [20 October 2006].
2. http://www.quotaproject.org/displayCountry.cfm?CountryCode=PK [20 October 2006].
3. The data included in this table starts with 1971 after the secession of East-Pakistan (Bangladesh). In elections held during the late 1980s to late 1990s the success of women candidates from the Pakistan People's Party (PPP), headed by Benazir Bhutto, have been outstanding on general seats: PPP women candidates won 3 out of 4 seats in the 1988 elections; in 1990 both female legislators came from the PPP, in 1993 three out of 4 and in 1997 three out of six. (Sources: Farida Shaheed, *Imagined Citizenship: Women, State & Politics in Pakistan* (Lahore: Shirkat Gah Resource Centre, 2002), 89; Shahla Zia and Farzana Bari, 'Baseline Report on Women's Participation in political & public life' (Islamabad: Aurat Foundation, 1999), 50; http://www.ipu.org/wmn-e/classif.htm, retrieved 20 October 2006).
4. Elections for a parliamentary mandate in the National Assembly of Pakistan.
5. Member of the Provincial Assembly.
6. PML-Q is currently the ruling party, supported by President Pervez Musharraf.
7. Samia Raheel Qazi.
8. Federal Administered Tribal Areas.

References

Fleschenberg, Andrea. 'Do women matter?,' The Nation (11.01.2006). Online. Available: http://nation.com.pk/daily/jan-2006/11/columns 5.php. 20 October 2006.

Shaheed, Farida. *Imagined Citizenship: Women, State & Politics in Pakistan*. Lahore: Shirkat Gah Resource Centre, 2002.

Zia, Shahla and Farzana Bari. 'Baseline Report on Women's Participation in political & public life.' Islamabad: Aurat Foundation, 1999.

Contributors

Aazar Ayaz is the Executive Director of *The Researchers*, a research based development organization based in Islamabad, Pakistan. He is associated with many community report and support programmes in governance, human rights and gender. His major research areas are women's political empowerment and decentralization in Pakistan.

Drude Dahlerup is a professor of Political Science, University of Stockholm, Sweden. She has published extensively about women in politics, the history of the women's movements and feminist theory, e.g. *The Redstockings. The Development, New Thinking and Impact of the Danish Redstocking Movement 1970-1985, vol I-II. Gyldendal* 1998 (in Danish). She was editor of *The New Women's Movement. Feminism and Political Power in Europe and the USA.* Sage 1986. Her latest book *Women, Quotas and Politics,* ed., Routledge 2006 is the first global study of the use of quotas, based on research in all major regions in the world. See the website www.quotaproject.org (together with International IDEA).

Claudia Derichs is Professor of Political Science at the University of Hildesheim, Germany. She received her PhD from the Free University (FU) of Berlin, and was associated with the University of Duisburg-Essen's Institute of East Asian Studies and the Institute of Political Science at various positions. Her research interests include nation and state building, Islam and political reform in Southeast Asia and the Middle East and comparative gender studies of East, South and South East Asia. Most recent publication: co-editor of *Wahlsysteme und Wahltypen. Politische Systeme und regionale Kontexte im Vergleich* [Electoral systems and election types. Political systems and regional contexts in comparison], Wiesbaden 2006.

Andrea Fleschenberg is Research fellow at the University of Hildesheim, Germany. She was previously Lecturer of Comparative Politics (with special emphasis on women in politics, transition studies, Asian studies) at the Universities of Cologne and Duisburg-Essen, Germany. She was Visiting Professor at the Universitat Jaume I, Castellon, Spain, in 2006 and Visiting Professor at the University of the Punjab, Lahore, Pakistan, in 2007. She is a board member of the German Asia Foundation. Her research areas are transitional justice with special emphasis on Europe and Southeast Asia;

gender and politics (with special emphasis on women and leadership in South and Southeast Asia, gender and development, women and political participation, and gender and democratization).

Dagmar Hellmann-Rajanayagam is currently working as Lecturer in Tamil Literature LMU Munich and as Reader at the University of Passau, Germany. Previously, she had been teaching in various institutes and has visited many countries like Asia, Malaysia, Madras/India, Sri-Lanka, and Singapore, and worked as a Research Assistant at South Asia Institute, Department of History, University of Heidelberg, Germany. She is also working as a consultant for German courts on refugee questions and as a coordinator and country chapter author for SIPRI-UKM project on arms procurement decision making processes.

Kazuki Iwanaga is currently working as Associate Professor and Senior Lecturer in Political Science and heads the Department of Political Science at Halmstad University, Sweden. His teaching and research interests are, among others, Japanese Politics, women and political communication, and women in Thai politics. Recent publications: *Women in Thai Politics* (2005), Working Paper, Center for East and Southeast Asian Studies, Lund University; *The Politics of Gender in Asia* (co-editor, forthcoming), Copenhagen: NIAS Press; *Women's Political Participation and Representation in Asia: Obstacles and Challenges* (editor forthcoming), Copenhagen: NIAS Press.

Patricia Loreskär is a Research Assistant at the Department of Political Science at Halmstad University and teaches International Relations.

Marion Regina Müller is currently working as project coordinator with the German Heinrich-Böll-Foundation in Kabul, Afghanistan. Previously she worked for the GTZ with Aurat Foundation in Peshawar, Pakistan. As a facilitator and advisor for NGOs and bilateral organizations, she has an intensive working experience in Bangladesh and Pakistan in the fields of women's rights, gender-based violence, gender relations, women's political participation, participatory planning/evaluation methods, civil society mobilization, and the designing and implementation of trainings and awareness-raising campaigns.

Jackie F. Steele is a doctoral candidate at the School of Political Studies, University of Ottawa, Canada. Her interests include feminist theories of citizenship, republicanism, philosophy of language, political representation, electoral systems design, Canadian constitutionalism, women's rights in Japan, Canada and Québec. Ms Steele was a Visiting Researcher at the Gender, Law and Policy Centre (*Sendai*). She has published on the Liberal Women's Caucus, the parity proposal in Nunavut, and the impact of patronymy upon women's political subjectivity.

Manon Tremblay is Professor of Political Science and heads the Research Center on Women and Politics at the University of Ottawa, Canada. She is currently working as the French co-editor of the Canadian Journal of Political Science. She has written extensively on women and politics in several countries. Her articles have appeared in the Australian Journal of Political Science, Canadian Journal of Political Science, International Review of Women and Leadership, International Political Science Review, Journal of Legislative Studies, Political Science (New Zealand), and Party Politics. Publication: *Sharing Power: Women, Parliament, Democracy* (co-editor, 2005), *Women and Electoral Politics in Canada* (Oxford University), *Women and Political Representation in Canada* (University of Ottawa).

Lourdes Veneracion-Rallonza, currently holds the chairpersonship of the International Studies Program at Miriam College, Philippines, and the position of International Programs Director. She is also a faculty associate for the area of women, politics and governance at the Women and Gender Institute. She has also chosen to be one of the chapter writers for *The Women's Political Participation and Representation in Asia: Obstacles and Challenges* book to be published by Nordic Institute of Asian Studies (NIAS) and edited by Dr Kazuki Iwanaga.

Dr Khalida Ghaus, is currently heading SPDC a research institute and was also the Chairperson of Karachi University's Department of International Relations and head of Centre of Excellence for Women Studies. She has extensively worked on Pakistan's foreign policy, gender and development. She has been working as a gender specialist for several years for the federal and provincial governments, and has successfully completed several research projects for international NGOs. She has two dozen published articles to her credit.

Shahnaz Wazir Ali, is the Executive Director of The Pakistan Centre for Philanthropy. Prior to this, she served as the Senior Education Specialist at the World Bank, and as the Education Specialist in SP Multi-Donor technical support unit administered by the World Bank. She also served as Member of the National Assembly and Minister of State for Education in the Federal Government and subsequently, in the second term, as Special Assistant to the Prime Minister on Social Sectors.

Riffat Munawar has a background in Sociology and has been teaching in the Punjab University since 1990. She holds MA degrees from both Punjab University and University of Wollongong, Australia. She has recently completed her PhD thesis on 'Women's Political Participation and Empowerment' at the Punjab University. Her areas of interest are gender relations, women's empowerment and multicultural societies. She has a number of publications in the forth-mentioned areas.

Index